THE EASTERN SHORE OF VIRGINIA

By the Same Author

THE EPISCOPAL CHURCH IN ACCOMACK COUNTY
GEORGE YEARDLEY
THE GIRL IN THE RURAL FAMILY
THE PARKSLEY THREE ARTS CLUB

The Eastern Shore of Virginia 1603-1964

Nora Miller Turman, M.A., C.G.

Illustrated with
Sixteen pen-and-ink sketches
Six floor plans
Seven maps

HERITAGE BOOKS
2007

HERITAGE BOOKS
AN IMPRINT OF HERITAGE BOOKS, INC.

Books, CDs, and more—Worldwide

For our listing of thousands of titles see our website
at
www.HeritageBooks.com

A Facsimile Reprint
Published 2007 by
HERITAGE BOOKS, INC.
Publishing Division
65 East Main Street
Westminster, Maryland 21157-5026

Copyright © 1964 Nora Miller Turman

Originally published by
The Eastern Shore News, Inc.
Onancock, Virginia
Library of Congress catalog card number 64-17509

— Publisher's Notice —
In reprints such as this, it is often not possible to remove blemishes from the original. We feel the contents of this book warrant its reissue despite these blemishes and hope you will agree and read it with pleasure.

International Standard Book Number: 978-1-55613-147-X

Preface

This book gives an account of the outstanding events in the order in which they took place on the Eastern Shore of Virginia, from the first English landing on record to the opening of the Chesapeake Bay Bridge-Tunnel. It is by no means a complete history, for the records of any century contain enough information for a volume larger than this. Only a few of the important people could be used in the narrative, and it is hoped that readers whose favorite ancestors were not included will be tolerant. Since the writer has no ancestors on the Shore, there was nothing personal about the selection.

The Eastern Shore of Virginia forms the southern part of the crescent-shaped Delmarva Peninsula which lies between the Atlantic Ocean and Delaware Bay on the east, and Chesapeake Bay on the south and west. The ocean islands help form the crescent which has a very irregular under curve next to Chesapeake Bay. The coast lines are broken by numerous tidal streams and necks of land in assorted sizes and shapes. The Delmarva Peninsula takes its name from Delaware, Maryland, and Virginia, the states among which it is divided.

Virginia's part was divided into two counties in 1663. Northampton County, which begins at Fishermans Island, has a land area of 226 square miles and a population of 75.1 per square mile. Its population in the 1960 census was 16,966. Accomack County begins at Machipongo and Occohannock creeks and extends to the Maryland line. It has a land area of 470 square miles and a population of 65.2 per square mile. Its population in 1960 was 30,635.

The land of the Shore gives the appearance of being almost level but there is enough variation for it to be divided into three surface areas. The central part, which was bounded by the original bayside and seaside roads, has an elevation of 25 to 45 feet above sea level. The areas next to Chesapeake Bay and the ocean vary from 25 feet to sea level or below. The salt marshes, or sea meadows, belong to the land at low tide and to the sea at high tide. However, there are some small tracts of land near both the bay and the ocean with elevations above 25 feet. The soil is fertile and the land requires no terraces. A few sand dunes may be seen next to the bay but any resemblance to them inland indicates a nearby irrigation pond.

There are more than a hundred named towns, villages and hamlets in Accomack and Northampton counties. Sixty-six of these have post offices. Only three of the towns are large enough to have mail delivery. Well-kept farm houses between the settlements make it hard to tell where one village ends and another begins.

The distance from the north terminus of the Bridge-Tunnel to the Maryland line is 72 miles. Every exit or crossroad leads to something of historic or recreational interest. Some are to hunting and fishing sites which give the Shore the unofficial title of "Sportsman's Paradise." Others are to historic shrines or monuments and one leads to Chincoteague Ocean Beach.

This narrative of the Eastern Shore of Virginia begins in the year 1603 and ends with the opening of the 17.6 mile Chesapeake Bay Bridge-Tunnel to the mainland. The book was written for the general reader but the chapter notes may help it find an audience among historians.

CONTENTS

CHAPTER		Page
I	1603-1625	1
II	1625-1634	13
III	1634-1642	27
IV	1642-1652	43
V	1652-1663	53
VI	1663-1674	64
VII	1674-1700	76
VIII	1700-1714	92
IX	1714-1752	104
X	1752-1790	118
XI	1790-1800	138
XII	1800-1840	156
XIII	1840-1870	173
XIV	1870-1900	191
XV	1900-1920	209
XVI	1920-1940	223
XVII	1940-1960	240
XVIII	1960-1964	253
Appendix		268

ILLUSTRATIONS

	Page
DEVICES FOR PUNISHMENT	37
DORMER WINDOW HOUSE Hills Farm	89
HILLS FARM Floor Plan	90
HUNGARS CHURCH	112
BIG HOUSE, LITTLE HOUSE and KITCHEN Drummonds Mill Farm	119
DRUMMONDS MILL FARM Floor Plan	120
TWO ROOM and LOFT HOUSE Debtors Prison	134
DEBTORS PRISON Floor Plan	135
GAMBREL ROOF HOUSE End View	140
END VIEW Floor Plan	141
ONE ROOM and LOFT HOUSE Seymour Kitchen	146
SIAMESE TWIN HOUSE Little Room, Colonnade and Kitchen of Seymour House	147
BIG HOUSE, LITTLE HOUSE, COLONNADE and KITCHEN Seymour House	148
SEYMOUR HOUSE Floor Plan	149
ICE HOUSE	170
ASSATEAGUE LIGHTHOUSE	184
BIG HOUSE, COLONNADE and KITCHEN The Rectory	187
THE RECTORY Floor Plan	188
OLD POINT COMFORT Pennsylvania Railroad Steamer	201
VIRGINIA LEE Pennsylvania Railroad Steamer	231
KERR PLACE Eastern Shore of Virginia Historical Society Building	258
POCAHONTAS Flagship of the last Ferry Fleet	264

MAPS

ACCOMACK PLANTATION 1627   15

ACCOMACK AND NORTHAMPTON COUNTIES 1700   93

THE EASTERN SHORE OF VIRGINIA 1800   157

MAGISTERIAL DISTRICTS AND BOUNDARY
    CREEKS 1870   192

RAILROADS AND MAIN STATIONS 1900   210

CREEKS AND NECKS 1920   224

THE DELMARVA PENINSULA 1964   267

NOTE

The following explanations are offered relative to information contained in this printing of **The Eastern Shore of Virginia 1603-1964.**

Page	Line	
1	3	Reference is made to modern reckoning of longitude.
28	20	The wife of William Cotten was a sister-in-law of William Stone.
43	3	The date should be July 28, 1643.
43	10	The date should be March 1643 N. S.
110	25	The General Assembly of 1732 provided for local sponsorship for licensing attorneys rather than providing for the direct licensing of attorneys.
197	16	It was George R. Mapp who became the third superintendent and not John R. Mapp.
272	40	William T. Fitchett was Circuit Court Judge from March 1882 to March 1884 between two terms of Benjamin T. Gunter.
274	38	The reference to the Clerk of Court should be Robert H. Oldham rather than Robert H. Oldham, Jr.
274	49	In the list of Superintendent of Schools for Northampton County, the name should be D. W. Peterson rather than W. D. Peters.
280	1	John Andrews Upshur was graduated from the United States Naval Academy in the class of 1921.
280	44	Henry Alexander Wise was the son of Edward S. Wise rather than Edgar S. Wise as stated.

Chapter I

1603-1625

At dawn on July 29, 1603, a fifty-ton ship was riding anchor at 37 degrees 7 minutes and 3 seconds north latitude and 75 degrees 54 minutes and 3 seconds west longitude. This was at the entrance to Chesapeake Bay and the young captain was gazing at tree-covered land at the north side. Soundings showed it was not safe to go nearer so arms and ammunition for eight men and boys were being put into one of the landing boats. The captain was prepared to carry out one of the orders of his famous uncle in England.

The captain was Bartholomew Gilbert, and his uncle who owned the ship was Sir Walter Raleigh. Captain Gilbert had been with exploring parties in the northern part of the North American continent then called Virginia, but this was his first voyage with full responsibility. Plans were well under way when Queen Elizabeth I died on March 24 and her cousin James of Scotland became King James I of England the following day, which was New Year's Day of 1603. Sir Walter knew the elderly Queen's days were numbered and he was eager to prove to the successor that he had not abandoned his patent in the New World. Although he had sold part of it to a group of merchants, he still hoped to find survivors of the Roanoke Island Colony and reinforce their settlement. Captain Gilbert was ready to carry out the last of his orders. This was to land and see if any trace could be found of Sir Walter Raleigh's colony that had vanished from Roanoke Island almost fifteen years before.

The ship had come to Virginia by the southern route and docked at enough islands where "lignum vitae" grew to fill every foot of cargo space. Lignum Vitae is a hardwood timber which brought a high price when running works for clocks and other machinery were made of wood. It was also in demand for ten-pin balls. A fifty-ton shipload of this product, found only on American islands, would pay the expenses of the voyage and leave some profit for the owner and members of the crew. Captain Gilbert was well pleased with his assignment up to this point.

He left the ship in a landing boat carrying five men and two boys and enough arms and ammunition for all. Although the level tree-covered land looked near under the cloudless sky, almost a mile of rowing was required to reach the shore.

The captain and five heavily-armed men went ashore while the boys were left to guard the boat. Hostile Indians must have been watching the ship for some time as warriors were near the landing site with arrows in place and bows bent. Members of the landing party were killed in sight of the boat. Captain Gilbert and another member of his party were dead before noon. Master Thomas Canner and one companion returned to the landing boat in time to help the boys overpower a band of Indians who were trying to take it.

Presumably other Europeans had been here and the Indians regarded all pale-faced men as enemies. Earlier explorers might have been Spanish, English, French or Dutch. The Spanish had a temporary settlement near Jamestown between 1570 and 1572. The southern shore of the entrance to Chesapeake Bay is on Captain John White's map of 1585, and the north side is indicated as the bank of a river. Explorers from the other countries are known to have made landings farther north.

Thomas Canner wrote the account of this landing on July 29, 1603, during the voyage back to England, or immediately after the ship reached its home port in the early autumn. His writing is the first account of a European landing in the geographical area of the Eastern Shore of Virginia. Thus, the Shore's written history begins in 1603.

On June 2, 1608, Captain John Smith left Jamestown

CHAPTER I — 1603-1625

with a party of fourteen men to explore and map the Chesapeake Bay. They were aboard the supply ship *Phoenix* which was towing the three-ton shallop that had been assembled and launched at Cape Henry by the first expeditionary force to Jamestown in April 1607. This open boat with sails and oars was to be their home for most of the summer. The greatest ambition of the party was to find a passage to the Pacific Ocean, or "South Sea" as they called it.

The exploring party left the *Phoenix* near Cape Henry and crossed to the southern tip of the Eastern Shore peninsula over water slightly to the south of the bridge and tunnel system. These men proceeded with caution and they had a good reason to be both cautious and frightened when they came in sight of land.

Two grim and stout savages with long poles like javelins stood as sentries. The poles had sharp points with hooks fashioned from bone at one end. When they asked who the white men were and why they came, Captain Smith must have given them a satisfactory answer in their own language. These Indians were a part of the Powhatan confederacy and spoke the same language as those in the vicinity of Jamestown. Likely through trading expeditions with the Indians on the mainland these Indians had heard about the settlement at Jamestown and some of the wonderful goods the English used in trading for corn and furs. Anyway, the men were directed to the Indian King's house at Accomack where they were cordially received. Before departing, the visitors learned that the "javelins" the Indians were holding when they landed were implements for spearing fish.

The Englishmen found fish plentiful and the fishmonger in the party had no difficulty in providing a daily supply to be cooked over the fire built in a box of sand on the boat. With the supplies brought from Jamestown and some edible wild berries, these explorers fared well while they took soundings of some creeks and made short trips on land to record their findings on the map. Although the task was not finished until late in the summer, the area that was to become the Eastern Shore of Virginia was covered in two weeks.

The map and later references to it in writings of others in England indicate that Captain Smith included the Eastern Shore mainland as well as the islands near the mouth of Chesapeake Bay in the Smith Islands group. He drew two Indian King houses and called them Accomack. When the group of islands including Watts and Tangier were discovered they were recorded as Russell Isles in honor of Walter Russell, "doctor of physicke," in the exploring party. Before the mapping of the Chesapeake Bay area was completed, each member of the party had been honored with the name of some place on the record. Keale Hill, possibly the present site of Onancock, was named for Richard Keale, and Watkins Point which is on the Virginia-Maryland line was named for another member of the party.

Although some writers have said Captain Smith sent a copy of his map of the Chesapeake Bay area to England in the fall of 1608, the copy has never been found. He likely revised it before his final departure from Jamestown in October 1609. The earliest surviving copy was published in 1612. A part of the description of Virginia published with the map is local and some general statements help characterize the Eastern Shore of Virginia:

> "There is but one entrance by sea into this country and that is at the mouth of a very great Bay . . . The Cape on the south side is called Cape Henrie in honor of our most noble prince . . . The north Cape is called Cape Charles in honor of the most worthy Duke of York. Within is a country that may have the prerogative over the most pleasant places of Europe, Asia, Africa and America . . . Heaven and earth never agreed better to frame a place for man's habitation."

Among the streams mentioned in the description of Virginia at this time were Occohannock and Accomack rivers.

The Virginia government sent fishing parties to the area around Cape Charles at regular intervals. Their mission was not only to catch and salt fish but also to see that no foreign nation established an outpost here to use in the event England became engaged in a shooting war. There was still as much danger that Spain might try to wipe out the entire settlement as there had been since the arrival of the expeditionary force in 1607. Captain Samuel Argall, who succeeded Captain Christopher Newport as admiral of Virginia in 1611, made a survey of the east side of the bay and its potential harbors in the spring of 1613. Thomas Savage was the interpreter. Sir Thomas Dale, marshal of Virginia from 1611 to 1614, made one voyage to the Eastern Shore.

In June 1614, a few weeks after Sir Thomas Dale became lieutenant-governor, he sent a detachment of seventeen men under Lieutenant William Craddock to the Shore to buy some land from the Indians on which to establish an outpost. This land was bought for the Virginia Company and later records indicate that it was on the south side of Accomack River. Documents show that the land purchased was above the islands at the mouth of the bay and some years later the Virginia Company made use of this tract without further negotiations with the Indians.

Salt works were set up on the largest island where the sea water was the most salty. The men could maintain a watch for enemy ships which might enter the bay. At least one experienced salt maker had been sent from the ancient trade guild in England to direct this phase of the work. Sea water was boiled in large kettles over wood fires and stirred with shovels to keep the salt from forming solid lumps. As water evaporated more was added until a kettle was at least half full of crystallized salt. From 250 to 300 gallons of sea water were required to make a bushel of salt which weighs seventy pounds. The salt was then dried and put into hogsheads and brought to the mainland in the small boat which could anchor near the shore of the island. At intervals a ship from Jamestown brought supplies for the men and took the salt and salted fish back to Jamestown. From there it was sent to other settlements at Henricus and Bermuda City and possibly Kecoughtan, now the city of Hampton.

By the spring of 1617 the outpost had been abandoned and the men were back in the James River area. Just how much land they cleared and how much food they grew at the outpost is not recorded, but it was customary for men at any outpost to grow vegetables. These men probably tried this soil for tobacco growing. Thomas Savage returned as interpreter for a merchant in the autumn of 1617 and traded with the Indians for corn.

Sir George Yeardley arrived in Jamestown in April 1619 with a commission to divide the land according to regulations worked out by the Virginia Company and to set up a civilian form of government. He was instructed to reserve large tracts of public land to pay expenses of the government according to the prevailing custom in England. No patents were issued for land on the east side of Chesapeake Bay and no people were sent over here before the General Assembly was organized in July 1619, but Governor Yeardley was aware of the favorable conditions for a settlement and the necessity of developing the north side of the entrance to Chesapeake Bay under the government at Jamestown.

In the fall of 1620 Governor Yeardley sent a group of men in charge of Captain John Wilcox to the Eastern Shore and English people have been here ever since. The exact number has not been found but deductions from the amount of land they cleared indicate about seventy-five. They were under contract to work on public land in the borough of Elizabeth City, one of the four governmental divisions that had been organized. No public land had been laid out in the area that is now Hampton when these tenants arrived.

The contracts under which these men and others who came to work on public land were different from those of the apprentices of the early years and indentured servants who began coming in 1619. Each man was provided with transportation from England, "victuals," wearing apparel, weapons for defense, tools and implements, seed, cattle and living quarters for the first year. He got half of the tobacco, corn and other commodities he grew and half of the increase of the cattle in his charge. The other half of the products went to the Virginia Company. After the first year each man provided his own food and clothes. The contract lasted for seven years. A thrifty man could accumulate enough worldly goods to go in business for himself in this time.

Thomas Savage again came as the interpreter and stayed to establish a family whose descendants have helped give the Eastern Shore a prominent part in founding and defending our state and nation.

In the spring of 1621 a group of men arrived at Jamestown to tend land to support the office of Secretary. At the advice of Governor Yeardley, Master John Pory, who served in that office from the spring of 1619 to November 1621, placed these tenants on the Eastern Shore. A 500-acre tract on the north side of Kings Creek was designated as the Secretary's land. Contracts were the same as for the men on Company land.

Although only men and boys made up these two settlements on public lands, organized community life was part of the routine from the beginning. The first religious services were conducted by a reader and the Reverend Francis Bolton began serving the Shore as a circuit-riding minister from Elizabeth City in the autumn of 1621. A quotation from a letter dated July 25, 1621, from the Virginia Company to Governor Yeardley shows that men on public land had first consideration from a minister employed by the Company:

> ..... We have sent you two sufficient ministers: Mr. Haut Wyatt, who is to be minister to the Governor's tenants, and Mr. Francis Bolton whom we have consigned to Elizabeth City.

Church services in such settlements were held in a building used for cooking and eating and recreational purposes.

The presence of a number of prominent people near Cape Charles, and their participation in church and government some years before they patented land, may be explained by a patent issued in England on June 11, 1621. This patent was for a 5000-acre tract to Sir Richard Bulkley. It was on Elizabeth Island next to Cape Codd, presumably Cape Charles. Governor Yeardley was notified that such a patent had been issued, and that the people were to be subject to the government at Jamestown. The first settlers likely arrived in the fall of 1621 with breeding stock to start the cattle industry there, as well as to grow tobacco.

After the Indian Massacre on March 22, 1622, the people in the most dangerous parts of the Upper James River area were evacuated and resettled. Among these were Lady Elizabeth Dale's tenants consisting of men and boys in Charles City Borough. Along with her cattle they were relocated near Old Plantation Creek. Although they had been in Virginia since 1619 no land was patented by her. An unknown number of other people came to the Shore from the James River area this year and the next.

The first women came to live on the Shore in 1622 and at least two of these could have been among the adventurous maidens who came to Jamestown to find husbands. Margaret Epps, wife of Captain William Epps, the first commander of Accomack Plantation, and Hannah Savage, wife of Ensign Thomas Savage came to Jamestown in 1622. Captain Epps had been in Virginia since 1619 and Ensign Savage had been here since 1608.

In this year of 1622 Sir George Yeardley and Thomas Savage completed negotiations with the Indian King for two necks of land for which patents were eventually secured. The Savage tract was on the north side of Accomack River opposite the Company land. The Yeardley tract was between Mattawoman Creek, now called the Gulf, and the main prong of Hungars Creek, which is the present Mattawoman Creek. However, neither tract was occupied at this time.

Ensign Savage built a house east of the Company land and lived there for the next several years. He grew tobacco and probably started a herd of cattle but he was not permitted to engage in fur trade with the Indians in competition with the government.

Captain Epps presumably lived on the Secretary's land until he got a certificate for a patent on the south side of Kings Creek opposite this tract.

In 1623 a 3000-acre tract of public land was laid out at

CHAPTER I — 1603-1625

the east end of Elizabeth City Borough, now Fort Monroe, and some of the men from the Eastern Shore were moved there after the crops were harvested. On November 21 of this year the Governor and Council at Jamestown issued the first order for the people of Accomack Plantation to pay a designated part of the minister's salary. Up to this time he was paid by the Virginia Company and from the proceeds of land set aside for a glebe, or minister's home, at Elizabeth City. The order directed Captain Epps, commander, to see that 10 pounds of marketable tobacco and 1 bushel of corn for every planter or tradesman above the age of sixteen years, alive at the time of the harvest of the crop, be paid to the minister. This was the regulation fee which had been fixed by the Virginia government. Presumably Mr. Bolton continued to live in Elizabeth City and serve the people of the Shore as a circuit-rider by boat.

In February 1624 Accomack Plantation was represented at a stormy session of the General Assembly. Captain John Wilcox, overseer of the Company land, and Henry Watkins, overseer for Lady Dale, were the Burgesses. King James I had annulled the charter of the Virginia Company and only a decree of the highest court in England was needed to make the annulment final. The fate of the representative government which had functioned for almost five years was unknown. The King had never favored it and some members of the Virginia Company who sought Royal favors had criticized it. This Assembly was also concerned about the ownership of land in fee simple when the charter was annulled. Some existing laws were strengthened and additional ones were passed to make this government more closely conform to the English Parliament after which it was patterned. A new law of this year gives some idea of the date of the first church built on the Shore:

> "There shall be in every plantation a house or room which the people use for the worship of God, and not to be for any temporal use whatsoever. And there shall be a place empaled to be used only for the burial of the dead."

Another law emphasized an earlier one that all land was to be bounded by the surveyor as soon as his services were available. The owner was to pay him 10 pounds of tobacco for each 100 acres bounded and recorded.

The surveyor was Captain William Claiborne who came to Virginia in 1621. His first assignment was to lay out the public lands and then work for individuals for the above designated fee. The Governor and Council issued certificates for designated tracts but the patents were not confirmed until the surveyor recorded the boundaries. Although the Virginia land books show private tracts recorded in 1623, there is no record of a private survey on the east side of the bay until 1627.

After the General Assembly of 1624 adjourned, Burgesses Wilcox and Watkins returned to Accomack Plantation to explain the laws to the people. The census at this time showed that the population was 79 men, women and children. The charter of the Virginia Company was annulled on June 24, 1624, and Virginia became England's first Crown Colony.

A church was built on the Secretary's land. It must have been started as soon as the cultivation of the crops was finished. Later records show it was on the north side of Kings Creek and, in keeping with the custom of England, there was burial space for officials in the chancel.

After the harvest was finished in the fall of 1624, the rest of the Company tenants were transferred to Elizabeth City. No list of names of those sent to the Shore in 1620 has survived but no doubt some of the people came back to stay as soon as their seven-year contracts were fulfilled. The Company land and buildings were offered for lease.

The census of 1625 showed a population of 51. There were 44 males and 7 females. The decline in population was due to the removal of the Company employees to the mainland. This census also showed 19 houses, 16 storehouses, 1 fort, 5 boats, 3 swords, 54 guns of various kinds, 150 pounds of powder and 601 pounds of lead and shot.

These early houses presumably were built of unseasoned lumber with the vertical weatherboarding extending from the ground to the roof. Chimneys for such houses were made of damp clay around frames of wood. Such houses as these were used for tenants and small farmers even into the next century. They were fire hazards since a law was eventually enacted forbidding the building or use of a frame and clay chimney near a public tobacco warehouse.

A list of the people in the census of 1625 is of interest since some of the names are still found on the Shore. They have been arranged alphabetically by surnames rather than as they appear on the census record.

William Andrews, age 25, in the *Treasurer*, 1617
John Askume, age 22, in the *Charles*, 1624
John Baker, age 20, in the *Ann*, 1623
Robert Ball, age 27, in the *London Merchant*, 1619
Thomas Belson, age 12
William Bibble, age 22, in the *Swan*, 1620
James Blackborne, age 20, in the *Sampson*, 1619
Frances Blore, age 25, in the *London Merchant*, 1620
John Blore, age 27, in the *Star*, 1610
William Burdett, age 25, in the *Susan*, 1615
Henrie Charlton, age 19, in the *George*, 1623
Thomas Cornish, age 25, in the *Dutie*, 1620
Daniel Cugley, age 28, in the *London Merchant*, 1620
William Davis, age 33, in the *William and Thomas*, 1618
Edward Drewe, age 22, in the *Sampson*, 1618
Margaret Epps, in the *George*, 1622
William Epps, in the *William and Thomas*
Robert Fennell, age 20, in the *Charles*, 1624
Thomas Gaskoyne, age 24, in the *Bona Nova*, 1619
Nicholas Granger, age 15, in the *George*, 1618
Thomas Graves, in the *Mary and Margaret*, 1608
Solomon Green, age 27, in the *Diana*, 1618
Charles Harmar, age 24, in the *Furtherance*, 1622
Margaret Hodgskins, born in *Virginia*
Nicholas Hodgskins, age 27, in the *Edwin*, 1616
Temperance Hodgskins, in the *Jonathan*, 1620

John Howe, age 25, in the *Margaret and John*, 1621
Benjamin Knight, age 28, in the *Bona Nova*, 1620
James Knott, age 23, in the *George*, 1617
William Munnes, age 25, in the *Sampson*, 1619
John Parramore, age 17, in the *Bona Venture*, 1622
Peter Porter, age 19, in the *Tiger*, 1621
Thomas Powell, in the *Sampson*, 1618
Nicholas Raynberd, age 22, in the *Swan*, 1624
Edward Rogers, age 26, in the *Ann*, 1623
Hannah Savage, in the *Sea Flower*, 1622
Thomas Savage, in the *John and Francis*, 1608
Apphia Scott, in the *Gist*, 1618
Percis Scott, born in *Virginia*
Walter Scott, in the *Herculese*, 1618
William Smith, age 26, in the *Sampson*, 1618
Thomas Sparkes, age 24, in the *Swan*, 1616
Nicholas Sumerfield, age 15, in the *Sampson*, 1619
Thomas Warden, age 24, in the *Ann*, 1623
John Washborne, age 30, in the *Jonathan*, 1620
Perregrin Watkins, age 24, in the *George*, 1621
John Wilcox, in the *Bona Nova*, 1620
Briggett Wilkins, age 20, in the *Warwick*, 1621
John Wilkins, age 26, in the *Mary Gould*, 1618
Henry Wilson, age 24, in the *Sampson*, 1619

Chapter II

1625-1634

The first week in July 1626, Captain Epps received an important and pleasing communication from Jamestown. Sir George Yeardley had returned with a commission as Royal Governor for the rest of his life. The people of Accomack Plantation prayerfully hoped he would have many years of service. Sir George was a man of integrity and experience, while Captain John Harvey, his potential successor, was looked upon with disfavor. Captain William Claiborne would take charge of the Secretary's land although he was not expected to live on this side of the bay. Captain Claiborne had come to Virginia as surveyor in 1621, and was already a member of the Council. Since both the Governor and Secretary had business interests on the east side of the bay, the settlers were confident that Accomack Plantation would get its share of attention from the government at Jamestown.

Captain Epps, commander, had the authority to administer oaths and try cases in which compromise seemed possible. Differences which were not settled in this manner, and more serious ones, were tried before the Governor and Council at Jamestown or Elizabeth City. Church wardens were responsible for the moral conduct of the people and were required to report offenders to the court.

The year 1627 was one of progress and growing stability for Accomack Plantation, as the settled area of the Shore was called. Captain Claiborne surveyed and recorded the first land on the Shore in February when he came to look after the Secretary's land, and before the year ended several tracts were recorded in the land books at Jamestown.

On February 3 Captain William Epps had a patent for

450 acres recorded for the transportation of 9 people. This land was on the south side of Kings Creek opposite the Secretary's land. Three days later Clement Dilke had a lease recorded for 20 acres of Company land with a house on it. The lease was for 10 years; however, a few months later Dilke got a patent for 100 acres for the transportation of himself and his wife. One could patent 50 acres of land for each person whose transportation he paid from England to live on his land for a designated time, usually seven years.

Approximately 160 acres of improved Company land with buildings were accounted for in recorded leases after the employees who were settled here in 1620 had been transferred to Elizabeth City. However, this land was available for patent when the leases expired. Records of leases show that the Company land and Secretary's land met near the shore of the bay.

At this time there were three distinct settlements in Accomack Plantation. They were at Accomack from the river by this name to the settled land south of Kings Creek, at Old Plantation Creek down on the shore of the bay, and at Magothy Bay next to Cape Charles. Some settlers wanted to move northward to the fertile land between the picturesque creeks which are arms of Chesapeake Bay on the west and the Atlantic Ocean on the east. If Thomas Savage had not already cleared and cultivated some of his land north of Accomack River, he was eager to do so. When the 1625 census was taken, he was living next to the Company land and had two servants. The men could have crossed the river to work and return at night. No doubt he was one of the petitioners for authority to move northward. He owned land but no acreage or boundaries had been recorded. The action of the court on such a petition presented October 13, 1627, is:

> The court, being informed that diverse planters at Accomack, Old Plantation Creek and Magothy Bay on the eastern shore of the bay, desire to seat themselves in such places as may be inconvenient and dangerous, has resolved not to permit their transplanting, but to

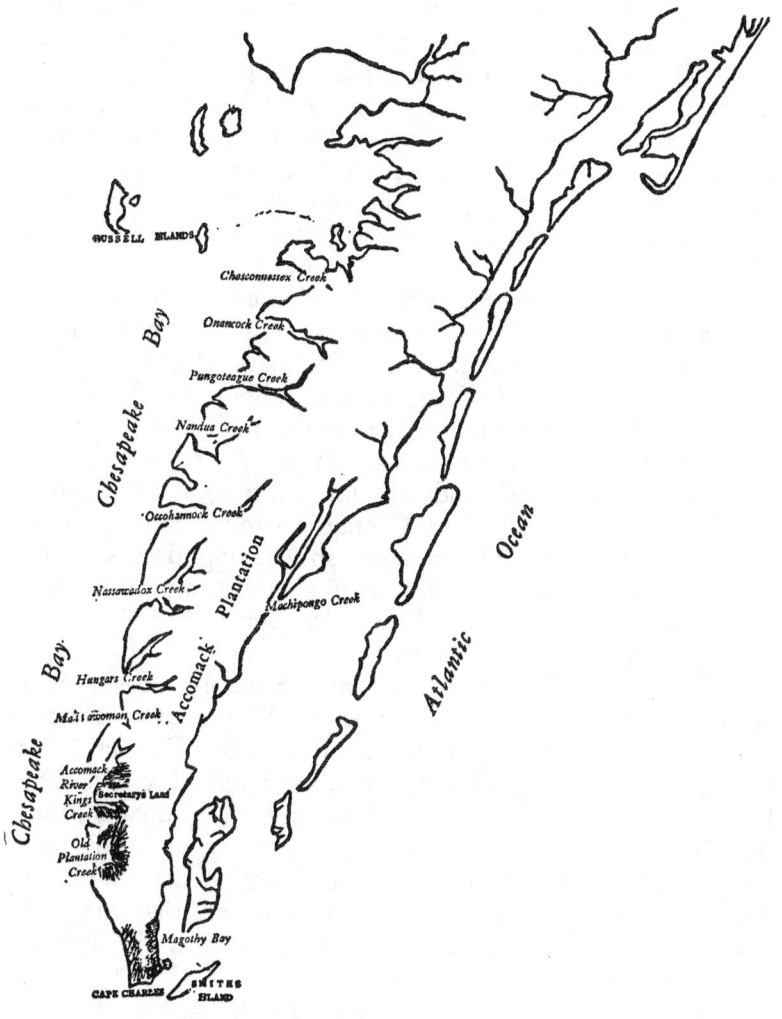

ACCOMACK PLANTATION 1627

keep them seated closely together and encourage the full planting of the forest rather than any other place.

Following this verdict Thomas Savage decided to get a patent for the small tract of land on which he lived next to the Company land. He used a plan which neither affected his dividend, the land of an undetermined acreage due him for services rendered, nor the servants whose transportation he had paid. He had his wife secure the patent which is recorded:

> Hannah Savage, wife of Thomas Savage of Accomack, 50 acres on the eastern shore within the precincts of the Plantation of Accomack, December 12, 1627, (page 57 in Virginia Land Book I). This is a neck of land abutting north on the main river, whereupon they are now seated, south on the mainland, east on the long creek and west on Curtaile Creek, dividing same from land of Captain Clement Dilke. This is for her personal dividend, she having defrayed the charges of her own transportation and came in the *Sea Flower* with Captain Ralph Hamor in 1622, as by good certificate appeareth.

Sir George Yeardley died a month before the surveyor made his December trip to Accomack Plantation. According to the terms in his commission from King Charles I the Council chose an acting Governor to serve until Captain John Harvey arrived. This interim Governor was Captain Francis West, a brother of Lord Delaware. Sir George's will left the 3700 acres of land on the Shore to his eldest son Argoll, then nine years of age. This meant that the land would remain unsettled until the heir reached the age of twenty-one years.

The latter part of this year of 1627, Captain Thomas Graves succeeded Captain Epps as commander of Accomack Plantation. He had been in Virginia since 1608, and had served as a Burgess when the General Assembly was organized in 1619. Since his name appeared in the census of 1625, he apparently had chosen the Eastern Shore as his home and was waiting to have his land surveyed and recorded. His authority in administering justice, like that of his successor, was limited to cases which showed promise of settlement by compromise.

The announcement of a marriage at Jamestown in 1628 was of interest to the people of Accomack Plantation. Acting Governor Francis West married Temperance Yeardley, thus becoming the step-father of Argoll Yeardley, the potential owner of a large neck of land to the north of this plantation. Governor West acquired two other step-children, Francis and Elizabeth Yeardley. Temperance West died before February 5, 1629. On this date Governor West "gave power and authority to Dr. John Pott and his brother John West." He took this step after declining a request of the court to give bond as administrator of the Yeardley children's estate. Before the court met on March 2, Captain West left for England where the estate would be settled.

The outcome of the settlement interested the people of the Shore and they did not have to wait too long for the verdict. Ralph Yeardley, brother of Sir George, qualified as temporary administrator when the report of his brother's death reached England. Temperance had not been there to qualify and she married without giving bond to protect the children's inheritance as specified in Sir George's will. Captain West sued the estate in court in England, but lost his case. Since Temperance had not actually come into possession of her inheritance, Captain West did not share in the estate. Ralph Yeardley became guardian of the children. This settlement meant that Argoll would have money to develop his land when he was of the age to possess it.

The year 1629 brought some changes in the geographical area of Virginia which extended from the Cape Fear River on the south to 40 degrees north latitude where New England began. After the charter of the Virginia Company was revoked in 1624, the King had the authority to reassign the land as he saw fit. By 1629 King Charles I found some of his father's associates ready to help him hasten the reassignment of this vast area. Sir Robert Heath, former attorney general of England, and associates were given a proprietary patent for all that part of Virginia between 31 and 36 degrees north latitude, or south of Albemarle Sound. The area was named Carolana, Latin for Charles. This was of no concern to the people of Accomack Plantation, but the next symptom of a proprietary grant alarmed them.

In October 1629 Lord Baltimore arrived at Jamestown with part of his family and associates from Newfoundland. He had been secretary of state under King James I and was made a nobleman while serving in this capacity. In 1621 he had obtained a proprietary patent for a tract of land in Newfoundland. According to the terms of the patent he was to exercise the authority of a king and be subject only to the King of England. He spent a large sum of money in trying to develop farming and a fishing industry there by 1628 when he decided to go there to live. After finding the "winter climate there to disagree with his constitution," Lord Baltimore decided to sail for Virginia before another winter set in. No doubt he and Sir Robert Heath worked together in planning for proprietary grants in Virginia.

Acting Governor Pott gave Lord Baltimore a cool reception but allowed him to purchase supplies for his boat and to leave some members of his family at Jamestown. Lord Baltimore explored the coastal area from Hampton Roads to Albemarle Sound and both sides of Chesapeake Bay to its head. And he likely made an overland trip across the four-mile isthmus to Delaware Bay before returning to Jamestown. Since the time had expired for a temporary stay in Virginia, Governor Pott offered to administer the Oath of Supremacy, which acknowledged the King of England as the head of church and state. Because of his religious belief, Lord Baltimore declined to take this oath. He left immediately for England which he must have planned to do anyway.

The Jamestown government sent Captain William Claiborne to England to report to Sir Francis Wyatt, the Earl of Southampton and others, who were potential guardians of Virginia with her private enterprise system of economy and representative government, about Lord Baltimore's suspicious stay in Virginia.

In February of 1630 Accomack Plantation chose four Burgesses to the session of the General Assembly which Governor John Harvey had instructed to meet in March. Although King Charles I had declined to authorize him to do this, Governor Harvey knew better than to attempt to govern the colony without this legislative body which had been organized eleven years earlier. From the autumn of 1624 the General Assembly had no official status in England and the laws it made were signed only by the Governor and his Council. Captain Thomas Graves, Edmund Scarburgh I, Obedience Robins and Henry Bagwell represented Accomack Plantation at this first session of the General Assembly called by Governor Harvey.

Captain Graves, commander, had patented 200 acres of land south of Captain Epps' patent, and slightly to the south of the present town of Cape Charles. Henry Bagwell had patented no land but was probably living on his future patent at Old Plantation Creek. Edmund Scarburgh, and Obedience Robins, chirurgeon, seem to have been associated with the Bulkley patent at Magothy Bay. Robins' mother was Mary Bulkley who could have been a daughter of Sir Richard, the patentee of 1621. After Sir Richard's death his second son, Thomas Bulkley, inherited the patent and may have sent Scarburgh, an attorney, to take charge of the enterprise which was short-lived. Four Burgesses for this and later sessions indicate four settlements on the Shore. This session of the Assembly did little that affected Accomack Plantation other than to review and emphasize the laws already in effect.

Reports from England revealed nothing about Lord Baltimore's plans for getting a part of Virginia other than that he was conferring with King Charles and those closely associated with the English government. His delay in taking action indicated that he had something very important in mind, and that he was moving with caution.

Accomack Plantation was represented in the General Assembly of March 1632 by Edmund Scarburgh and John Howe. The latter had leased 30 acres of Company land with buildings four years earlier. At this session of the Assembly monthly courts were authorized for Accomack Plantation and some other settlements where it was inconvenient for people to go to the general court for appeals and to be tried for serious offenses. Such an important step required confirmation by the English government so commissioners were not appointed until autumn.

Early in the summer a shocking report about Lord Baltimore's patent reached Virginia. He had asked for "all that tract of land in Virginia between James River and Carolana." King Charles signed his petition, but enough pressure was brought by friends of Virginia and those with business interests here to get the petition withdrawn before it reached the Privy Council for its seal. Lord Baltimore immediately submitted a petition for an alternate patent which he must have planned while cruising in Virginia waters in the fall of 1629.

The second petition asked for all the present Delmarva Peninsula from the entrance of Chesapeake Bay to 40 degrees north latitude near the present city of Philadelphia, and the land westward to the longitudinal line of the head water "of the first fountain of the most westerly stream flowing to Potomac River, then following the south bank to the mouth of this river." Some historians have said there was a second petition asking only for the peninsula between Chesapeake Bay and the Atlantic Ocean, but such a petition is unknown to present-day researchers. Lord Baltimore proposed the name Crescentia, the "land of Crescense," for this patent, but King Charles preferred Terra Maria in honor of his Queen. The English for this is Maryland. The King signed this charter early in April, and it passed the seal of the Privy Council before the news got out.

Again, friends of Virginia with her land in fee simple and representative government rallied to the cause. Upon the advice of the Attorney General of England final approval was delayed. A manuscript copy of this charter and printed documents show the charter as it must have been written but with the land and islands south of Watkins Point on the north bank of "the River of Wighco," now the Pocomoke, reserved for the Crown.

A glimpse at Lord Baltimore's patent in Newfoundland showed that he had half of the fishing rights in a river there, so he must have known by experience to ask for the entire Potomac River. Lord Baltimore died on April 15, 1632, and the Maryland patent was issued to his eldest son, Cecillius Calvert, who became the second Lord Baltimore. This patent passed the Great Seal of England on June 30, 1632. Saving the lower part of the peninsula left the land policy intact, and left Virginia in control of the entrance to Chesapeake Bay.

Governor Harvey and the Council held a monthly court at Accomack on July 5. No doubt these officials got the sentiment of the people regarding commissioners to be appointed if the English Government approved a monthly court for Accomack Plantation and some other areas far removed from the places of existing monthly courts.

The General Assembly met in September 1632. Burgesses from Accomack were Captain Thomas Graves, John Howe, Henry Bagwell and Charles Harmar. The latter was overseer for Lady Dale's land and had patented 100 acres of land at the mouth of Old Plantation Creek in 1628. The monthly court for Accomack was established. It was authorized to try cases in which the amount involved did not exceed 100 pounds of tobacco or 5 pounds English money. It was also empowered to try criminal cases not involving life or limb. Any verdict could be appealed to Jamestown provided the parties involved were willing and able to bear the expense.

This General Assembly provided for highways to be laid out at such places as the commissioners of the monthly courts regarded as necessary, or as the parishioners of each parish agreed upon.

Existing laws to safeguard the free enterprise economy on which Virginia was founded were strengthened. Persons leaving Virginia to live in New England, or elsewhere, were required to have a license or pass, signed by the Governor.

Shipmasters were not to transport people who had not given ten days notice of their intention to leave. The penalty for disobedience to this law made the shipmaster responsible for any debts owed by the person transported.

Some other laws enacted, or reenacted, this year dealt with duties of the ministers and church wardens. The minister was required to keep a book in which were written the day and year of every marriage, christening and burial. All of these rituals, as well as preaching and administering Holy Communion, were to take place in the church except when necessity required the service elsewhere. Marriage ceremonies could be performed only between the hours of 8:00 a.m. and 12:00 noon, after the banns were read in church on three Sundays or a license was issued by the Governor. Church wardens were elected each year during the Easter season. The minister and one church warden were required to attend the June quarter court at Jamestown and submit a list of all marriages, christenings and burials during the previous year. They were also required to give an account of all levies and expenditures of that year.

The commissioners for the monthly court of Accomack Plantation were appointed by the Governor. The law required a member of the Council to be a member of each court. Captain William Claiborne was appointed commander of this court. Other commissioners appointed in September 1632 were Captain Thomas Graves, Captain Edmund Scarburgh, Charles Harmar, Obedience Robins, John Howe and Roger Saunders. Saunders was the only member who had not served as a Burgess. He had leased 50 acres on the north side of Old Plantation Creek in 1628 and in June of 1632 he patented 300 acres in the same vicinity. The oath of a commissioner, like that of other public officials, was solemn and serious. Captain Claiborne and the four Burgesses took their oaths in Jamestown.

Henry Bagwell was the first clerk of the monthly court of Accomack Plantation. He had served as a Burgess in 1630. This is the oath administered to a clerk:

You shall swear that you will well and truly serve

CHAPTER II — 1625-1634

in the office of a clerk for the monthly court held at Accomack, within the government of Virginia. You shall attend the commander and court at every monthly court there held, unless any lawful cause or impediment prevents you, then and there to draw up all orders of court, and to do and perform all such acts and things as are incident to the said office. Rightly and justly according to the capacity of your understanding you shall do no wrong to any person for any gift or other behest or gain. And you shall do and execute all things belonging to the said office, or place, so long as you shall there continue, according unto the account of your knowledge, power and abilities. So help you God.

When the monthly court was organized in Accomack Plantation, slightly over 2000 acres of land had been bounded and recorded, but names which appear in the early court records and in the land books within the next five years show that many people were on improved land and waiting for it to be surveyed. The population was more than 300 in 1632. The people seem to have accepted the verdict of the Governor and Council in 1627 and refrained from starting new settlements.

Although the details of two sessions of the monthly court of Accomack Plantation are lacking, the names of the commissioners present at each have survived. Since the commissioners were appointed in September, it is assumed these sessions were for November and December 1632. After this time the records are continuous.

The earliest deed of a sale of property in these court records was made before the court was organized and is recorded as follows:

> These present shall witness that I, Captain Edmund Scarburgh for full satisfaction in hand received, do bargain and sell to John Wilkins, and by these present do assign and deliver to the said John Wilkins, his heirs and assignees, one brown cow with a white patch upon her hip and two white hind legs, she being about four years old, with her black cow calf a month old, and

one black cow with a broad head and a broken horn, she being about five years old. In witness of the same I, the said Captain Scarburgh have hereunto put my hand this last day of April 1632.
In the presence of William Berryman
Edmund Scarburgh

The court met at Accomack on January 7, 1633, and heard six cases. Among these was a law suit in which the defendant was ordered to pay an acknowledged debt within two weeks or be imprisoned until he made satisfaction for the whole debt.

At the next session of the Accomack Court petitions were presented by Robert Swanson and John Wilkins for fourteen days work which the Plantation owed to each for attendance on the Burgesses at Jamestown. The court ordered Captain Graves and Captain Scarburgh to see that Swanson and Wilkins were paid. Both Swanson and Wilkins became sizeable landowners.

The earliest sessions of Accomack Court were presumably held in a house on the Secretary's land near the church. There was no prison, so some responsible person was paid to keep in his custody a person sentenced to prison.

Roger Saunders died before August 29, 1633. As a member of court he was entitled to burial within the church. Captain Thomas Graves had gone to England and Captain William Claiborne could not attend regularly. Governor Harvey and the Council appointed four new commissioners.

At a court at Accomack on December 30, 1633, with Captain Claiborne present, the oath was administered to William Stone, William Burdett, William Andrews and John Wilkins. William Stone came to Virginia at an unknown date and married Verlinda Graves, daughter of Captain Thomas Graves. He was associated with his uncle, John Stone, the first person known to get permission to patent land beyond the bounds fixed in 1627. He had a certificate for the neck north of the Yeardley tract and had a sizeable cattle industry under way before his untimely death in 1634, when William Stone inherited his land and got a patent in his own name. William Burdett lived on Old Plantation Creek; Andrews also lived near Old Plantation Creek. John Wilkins, the last of the new commissioners, had been to Jamestown the previous year to attend the Burgesses from Accomack Plantation.

The first complete inventory of the estate of a deceased person was filed with the court on January 13, 1634. This was the estate of William Bats, a bachelor. He left his worldly goods to five men, one of whom he named as his executor. His estate consisted of 16 pounds 19 shillings sterling, 1833 pounds of tobacco, 7 barrels corn, staves for 100 hogsheads, 1 bed and bolster, 1 fowling piece (gun), 2 hogs and 2 suits of wearing apparel. If William Bats was one of the Company tenants who returned to the Shore after his contract was up, he is a good example of what a thrifty man could do on his own in Virginia.

Leonard Calvert, brother of Lord Baltimore, arrived at Point Comfort with two ships and settlers for the proprietary colony of Maryland the last of February 1634. Governor Harvey had previously received orders from King Charles I to give them aid and assistance in getting started. This included selling them breeding stock to start herds of cattle and sheep. Only Governor Harvey gave these settlers a friendly welcome. They went north of the Potomac River and founded the first settlement in Maryland at St. Marys.

On March 14, 1634, Virginia was divided into eight counties to be governed like counties in England. Among these was Accomack County, covering all the area of the Eastern Shore of Virginia. The settled area had spread northward after the petition for such expansion had been rejected by the Governor and Council in 1627. Captain John Stone received a patent south of the second prong of the original Hungars Creek. His nephew William Stone inherited the property. The population of the Eastern Shore was increasing steadily and most of the inland area referred to as "the forest" in 1627 had been patented by the time the county was formed.

Edmund Scarburgh I died in 1634. He lived at Magothy Bay, presumably on part of the large tract of land patented by Sir Richard Bulkley in 1621. Edmund Scarburgh had a large cattle industry. The fact that he had employed Thomas Savage to secure the services of some Indians to round up those cattle that were running wild in the woods shows that he had been in the business for several years. Hannah Scarburgh, widow, sold some cattle on January 9, 1635. Later in the year Edmund Scarburgh II, who had been in school in England, came to Virginia to take charge of the business. He patented the first land in the Scarburgh name.

Tobacco was used for money. Some entries in an inventory filed at the first session of the court of Accomack Plantation reveal its exchange value for certain commodities: A barrel of corn was worth 40 pounds of tobacco; a breeding sow was worth 60 pounds; a pound of beaver skin was worth 10 shillings; and an otter skin was worth 5 shillings. This inventory was taken from the debts of owners of a ship who were being sued. Incidentally, Thomas Savage was due wages as well as part of the commodities secured in trade on the expedition from which the ship had recently returned.

Chapter III

1634 - 1642

At a court held at Accomack on July 5, 1634, county government began. The commissioners were continued from the Plantation court. Those present at this meeting were Captain William Claiborne, Obedience Robins, John Howe, William Stone, William Burdett, William Andrews and John Wilkins. A quotation shows the first business of this session:

This day was read an order from the Governor and Council dated March 14, last past, requiring that sheriffs shall be appointed in the several parts of the colony. In conformity to which order at this time Mr. William Stone was chosen sheriff of Accomack, and thereupon the said William Stone was sworn to execute the said office.

The oath of a sheriff, like that of a clerk, gave some idea of his duties. He was to collect and turn over to the proper authorities all tobacco and money that belonged to the Crown and to do right as well to the poor as to the rich. He was to employ bailiffs and administer the oath to them and be responsible for serving all warrants. The sheriff was sworn to be in the county at all time unless he was licensed by the Governor and Council to be absent. Like the clerk, he was to take no gifts for promise of favors.

Captain William Claiborne had been appointed lieutenant for Accomack. He designated Obedience Robins as his deputy and expected a commission to be issued by the Governor and Council. However, Captain Thomas Graves, who seems to have been on a trip to England, returned and became deputy by the October term of court.

The population of the new County of Accomack, recorded in England the following year, was 396. This was presumably the report made in June 1634, at Jamestown, by the minister and a church warden.

The county court had the authority to issue certificates for land to be settled and improved. After a house was built and a garden and orchard were fenced and some land was cleared and planted, the Governor and Council exchanged the certificate for a patent. This was at the rate of fifty acres for each settler brought into the colony. Records show that some substantial houses had been built by this time and good furniture had been bought in England. However, much of the time of the court was taken up with small lawsuits, trying cases involving irritating behavior among neighbors and transferring property. Bills of sale were acknowledged in open court and ordered to be recorded.

Mr. William Cotton was the minister at least from 1635 until his death in 1640. The date of his arrival in Virginia has not been found. He had been here during the time of the court of Accomack Plantation, and at times had to bring suit for parts of his salary. His wife was a sister of William Stone and thus a niece of Captain John Stone.

At an undetermined date a tract of land, presumably 100 acres, was designated for a glebe, or minister's farm. Later records show that this was about a mile below the present town of Cape Charles, fronting on the bay. Although a survey was never recorded, it was identified by a local historian by the surveys of tracts that joined it. Mr. Cotton probably lived in a house on the Secretary's land until the glebe house was built.

The church on the north side of Kings Creek had been repaired the previous year. Both the roof and cracks between the weatherboarding were in need of repair after ten years of use. On May 19, 1634, the court sentenced a man to the task of "daubing" the church for striking another man. At the same court another man, presented to the court for swearing, was fined.

On September 14, 1635, William Cotton, minister, "presented an order of Court from Jamestown for building a parsonage house on the Glebe Land." This was to be done by the vestry which was a part of a county government. The court immediately appointed:

> William Cotton, minister, William Andrews, Captain Thomas Graves, Obedience Robins, John Howe, William Stone, William Burdett, John Wilkins, Alexander Mountney, Edward Drew, William Berryman and Stephen Charlton.

This first vestry of twelve men included seven commissioners. Only William Claiborne, a member of the Council, was not chosen as a vestryman. The men whose names appear officially for the first time had established themselves as businessmen.

The vestry met on September 29, 1635, and took action that provides the earliest description of a house on the Eastern Shore. It compares favorably with the houses whose brick foundations have been uncovered and preserved at Jamestown. The order of the vestry is:

> It is agreed by this vestry that a parsonage house shall be built upon the Glebe Land by Christmas next, and that said house shall be 40 feet long and 18 feet wide, and 9 feet to the wall plates, and that there shall be a chimney at each end of the house, and upon each side of the chimneys there shall be a room, the one for a study, the other for a buttery. Also there shall be a partition near the midst of the house with a door. And there shall be an entry and two doors, the one to go into the kitchen and the other into the chamber.
>
> Also it is agreed that the new church wardens shall hereby have power to agree with workmen for the building of the said house and to provide nails. At the next session of the vestry they are to bring (the) an account of all charges belonging to the building of the said house.

The specifications for this parsonage house bear a resemblance to a brick house that is still standing. It is the Sturgis house near Jamesville, thought to have been built within twenty years after the Parsonage House. The surviving house is 35½ feet long and 20½ feet wide, with a partition near the center. It has inside chimneys, which could have provided for little rooms on the sides, and an enclosed stairway on one side. Little niches for salt and spices are below the mantel in the kitchen. The inventory of a member of the court and vestry when the Parsonage House was authorized shows a house with rooms corresponding to the present Sturgis House. With these contemporary records we can visualize the parsonage house with a high-pitched roof and two doors facing the bay.

William Cotton left a will, but no inventory was filed. Other inventories of the time provide some basis for visualizing the furnishings. A table and frame was in the kitchen which served as a family room and likely a meeting place for the vestry. This piece of furniture had two trestles with drawers which were kept by the wall when the table was not in use. Likewise, the top stood by the wall. By this arrangement a large table could be used without cluttering up the room. Chairs had tall straight backs and may have been upholstered with leather. A small chest with a lock and key was usually in this room. Cooking utensils used at the fireplace were iron pots, brass kettles, stew pans, skillets with lids for baking, and open skillets. Linen napkins, table cloths, pewter bowls and other serving dishes, pewter spoons and pewter water containers were standard furnishings. William Cotton may have brought along some silver spoons, salt-cellars and a tankard.

Furnishings of the bedroom, or chamber, were bedsteads with curtains and valances, feather mattresses, blankets, quilts, linen sheets and towels, and a looking glass. A large chest with a lock and key held the linens and wearing apparel. Books, and records which the minister was required to keep, were in the study. A little room under the roof had an extra bed or two and a sea chest, with seldom-used items in it.

A fenced garden of at least one acre for vegetables, fruit trees and vines was a requirement for each household. Herbs for seasoning were introduced when the English first came

CHAPTER III — 1634-1642

and this glebe would have had a patch. Likewise, figs had been introduced at Jamestown near its beginning, and some trees would have been started in this glebe orchard as soon as the house was built.

At a meeting of the vestry the following spring certain regulations of special interest were passed. The clerk was to be paid a peck of corn and two pounds of tobacco for every tithable person, and it was to be collected along with the minister's pay. The minister was allowed 10 pounds of tobacco and 1 bushel of corn for every man and boy 16 years of age or older. The sexton was to receive 50 pounds of tobacco for every person buried within the church. The clerk was to have 10 pounds of tobacco for every grave made anywhere, and 15 pounds for those in the church. A new burying ground was authorized at the head of Old Plantation Creek and transportation was to be provided for the minister when he was called there to conduct funerals. The clerk was responsible for seeing that the graves were made there as well as at the church. A penalty was exacted for absence of a vestryman at a meeting, without due cause. The first offense carried a fine of 10 shillings, a second was 20 shillings and a third was prosecution for contempt before the Governor and Council at Jamestown.

At this meeting the vestry issued an order for the church wardens to purchase a pulpit cloth, a carpet (cover for the Communion Table), a beaker, a chalice and a chest. In early records the chalice seems to have been a cover for the beaker, or communion cup, and it was used for the bread as a paten is now used. The sacred vessels were kept in the chest.

Ensign Thomas Savage died before February 19, 1635. Since he was the first Englishman to come to stay and establish a family whose descendants still feature in state and national affairs, his biographical sketch is a part of this narrative:

> Thomas Savage came to Virginia with Captain Christopher Newport on his first return here after leaving the original settlers at Jamestown in 1607. When they landed Captain John Smith had just been released

by the Indian King, Powhatan, after Princess Pocahontas saved his life. The records tell us that Thomas was 13 years of age at this time. From this we find the date of his birth in 1595.

Being chosen as an apprentice by the Virginia Company shows that he was a lad of promise. Only three were in the expeditionary force and three others in what is known as the First Supply. Such boys got a sound basic education in a grammar school, conducted by the trade guilds in London. Likely Thomas was under close observation during the voyage to Virginia, and he must have scored high in politeness, neatness, memory, tact, respect for authority and other character traits which businessmen looked for in selecting apprentices. His apprenticeship period would last until he reached the legal age of tweny-one years.

In the spring of 1608 Captain Newport took him to Powhatan's home on the north side of the York River to live with the Indians and learn their language so he could serve as an interpreter. In exchange Powhatan let his son go to England. Although records indicate that Thomas stayed with the Indians for three years, he made regular trips to Jamestown and sometimes stayed for days or weeks. It was not easy for a boy to learn a new language and not waver in his ability to keep his English intact unless he kept in touch with those who spoke English. This first venture of training an interpreter was an honor to Thomas and a responsibility of the Jamestown officials.

His first voyage to the Eastern Shore was with Captain Argall in 1613, when he explored the potential harbors this side of the bay. When Sir Thomas Dale sent a detachment of men to establish an outpost and make salt here in 1614, Thomas Savage came as the interpreter. In 1618, he came on a trading expedition with Captain John Martin's ship. At this time he was employed by Captain Martin and lived at Brandon, on the James River. When the General Assembly adopted

CHAPTER III — 1634-1642

a policy for interpreters at its first session in 1619, Thomas returned to Jamestown to work for the government for wages.

In the spring of 1620 he came as interpreter for the detachment stationed south of Accomack River and he lived on the Eastern Shore the rest of his life. He must have made many voyages to the head of Chesapeake Bay with trading parties for the Company, the English government, and in time for individual ship owners. The accounts of a ship owner, who had become so deeply in debt that the local officials took it over the year before Thomas' death, showed that the interpreter was owed three pounds three shillings and three pence for two voyages. For one of these voyages he also was owed two bushels and two pecks of corn. However, Thomas became a land owner at an early date.

The Indian King gave him the neck of land north of the Accomack River in 1622, or earlier, but some years were to lapse before he actually possessed it. After he married he lived near the Company land. The census of 1625 listed his wife Hannah and two servants. Their son John was born later that year. The land books sent to England listed only three owners of private tracts of land east of the bay. One of these was "Ensign Thomas Savage, his divident." He was entitled to 100 acres for his personal adventure and an undetermined amount for meritorious service as interpreter. Another 100 acres was due him for the two servants and still another 50 acres for his wife. Like other people on land that was eventually to be surveyed and recorded, the location of his tract was not designated on any records. In 1627 his wife Hannah patented 50 acres where they were living. This was probably Thomas' home the rest of his life, but at least in 1630 he was developing what is now Savages Neck. He would hardly have left his wife and little son at "The Long Point" at the bottom of the neck while away on trading expeditions.

Thomas Savage lived in peace and accord with his neighbors. He did not appear in any suit in the court records of Accomack Plantation, or the short time he lived after the county was organized. He died before February 19, 1635, age 40 years.

On August 24 of this year the location of his land was described in the patent issued for his son John, then ten years of age:

Mrs. Hannah Savage, relict of Ensign Thomas Savage, late of Accomack, planter, a parcel of land lying in Accomack, bounded with the Creek of Accomack on the south, the great bay on the west, Wiscapanso (formerly Mattawoman) on the north and the main ocean on the east. Which land was granted unto her husband by the King of the Eastern Shore as by deed calling himself Esmy Shichans. Renewed in the name of John Savage.

On February 19 of this year one Richard Hudson brought suit against Hannah Savage for 600 pounds of tobacco owed him for his services. Since this amount was larger than the court was authorized to handle, the case was referred to the Governor and Council. The outcome is unknown.

When Accomack County elected Burgesses for the General Assembly in the spring of 1635, the leaders knew that a stormy session would be held. Governor Harvey was attempting to exert as much authority as Leonard Calvert had in Maryland and this was offensive to guardians of representative government. During the previous year he caused Secretary William Claiborne to be removed from office. Incidentally, provision was made at that time for leasing the Secretary's land. The Governor and Council were in disagreement and the General Assembly supported the Council.

On April 28, 1635, Governor Harvey was forced by the General Assembly to vacate his office. A set of grievances against him was prepared for officials in England and Captain John Harvey agreed to go to the homeland to defend himself. Captain John West was elected acting governor.

Although the names of the Burgesses were not found,

CHAPTER III — 1634-1642

the method of choosing them is on the record. The commander notified all free men to meet at the sheriff's house on a designated date to elect the Burgesses. Such an election was held a month before the session was to meet.

Captain Thomas Graves disappeared from the records before the court met on November 16, 1635. There is no indication that his family ever lived on the Eastern Shore although he had featured in public life here from 1627 when he became the second commander of Accomack Plantation. His family may have stayed in England most of the time. His son John Graves secured a patent for land in another county by right of descent on August 9, 1637. Captain Graves' daughters presumably were married before they came to Virginia. Ann married William Cotton, minister; Catherine married Captain William Roper; and Verlinda married Captain William Stone. Neither of his three sons ever appeared in the records of Accomack. Although Captain Graves patented 200 acres of land north of Old Plantation Creek in 1628, there is no indication that he lived on it. A house on the Secretary's land apparently was his home and a meeting place for the court.

When the Accomack County court met on May 1, 1637, there were two new commissioners. Captain John Howe, who had served as a Burgess in 1632 and 1633, was commander. The other new commissioner was Nathaniel Littleton who lived in the Magothy Bay area. He was a future leader in county and colony affairs. On July 3 of this year, Henry Bagwell was sworn in as sheriff and John Dawe succeeded him as clerk of court.

There are indications that the Maryland colony was trying to persuade residents of Accomack County to go there to live. On November 20, 1637, the court passed the following:

> It is thought fit and so ordered by this court that no freeman or hired servant, or any person or persons whatsoever, shall depart from this plantation of Accomack without a special license from Captain John Howe, commander. And if any person or persons shall so de-

part without such license, they that transport them, or in any way assist in their transportation, shall suffer such penalty and punishment as shall be thought fit.

Captain Howe died less than two months after this ordinance was passed. A court order on February 12, 1638, pertaining to his estate, shows that he was buried in the chancel of the church:

> "It is ordered by this court that Mr. William Cotton, minister, shall forthwith be paid out of the estate of Captain John Howe, deceased, by the overseers of the said estate, for his funeral service, and his grave in the chancel."

A state of unrest still existed at Jamestown. Captain John Harvey had returned to resume his office as Governor in the spring of 1636, but found the Council ready to oppose his dictatorial powers. Likewise, in England, relations between King Charles I and Parliament were such that some people feared a civil war between followers of the King and those who sided with Parliament. This condition might have caused Governor Harvey to appoint John Howe as commander and Nathaniel Littleton as his substitute when they were selected as commissioners. Later records show that Obedience Robins was not of the Crown Party. The General Assembly still had not been authorized, but it had not been forbidden. Its petitions and orders were signed by the Governor and Council.

Although the court was extremely busy in hearing civil cases involving less than 500 pounds of tobacco or five pounds sterling, it handled numerous cases with sentences given in the form of fines or physical punishment. Most of these were legal in England and in time were authorized by the General Assembly in Virginia. Descriptions of the instruments the court owned for physical punishment, along with pictures of such equipment preserved in museums in England, give some idea of methods used to maintain law and order in Accomack County in the 1630's.

The pillory was an instrument with a yoke which held a man's head in full view while he stood for a designated

DEVICES FOR PUNISHMENT
top to bottom, left to right
Stocks   Whipping Post
Pillory   Ducking Stool

number of hours. Stocks had holes through which a man's hands and feet were put and locked in place while he sat for the duration of the prescribed sentence on the edge of a board. Whips were a part of the court's equipment, and a man was paid to use them. The usual sentence was 30 lashes or more on the bare shoulders of the convicted person to be administered in the presence of the court.

The ducking stool was used for women. This instrument was somewhat like platform scales of our time, but with a long board with a chair at one end. This board was raised and lowered by a windlass and a rope. When a woman was sentenced to ducking, the instrument was rolled to the bank of the creek where the water was deep enough for the victim to be completely submerged each time the board was lowered. Other punishments also were meted out. At one time two women were sentenced to be towed across Kings Creek. On September 25, 1637, the court sentenced two women to "be ducked" for abusing a neighbor and his wife with vile and scandalous speeches. Scolding and backbiting were other crimes for which women were ducked. Sometimes they were given the alternate sentence of a fine. If they chose the ducking they were lowered and raised until they said they repented of the offense.

On February 19, 1635, a man was convicted of speaking disrespectfully of the minister. His sentence was to build a new pair of stocks and sit in them during three Sabbath days during divine services, then ask the forgiveness of the minister. On August 8, 1636, a conviction of a false accusation of a neighbor, regarding a hog that had died, carried a sentence of one hour in the stocks. The stocks were used frequently.

When a person was kept in prison to await trial, the sheriff received 50 pounds of tobacco per month for board. If the prisoner was convicted, he paid it. If he was acquitted, his prosecutor paid his board.

Although theft was rare, specific cases are of interest. There was more than one case of persons milking the cows of others and keeping the milk. On June 16, 1635, a servant man was convicted of milking a cow "by stealth" and sentenced to be whipped in view of the court.

At times the court handed out sentences for public work as punishment. For example, one man was sentenced to repair the church. Building a ferry boat for the use of those attending church was another sentence of this nature.

The court owned a set of branding irons similar to those used for marking cattle at a later date, with VG (Virginia Government) outlined in letters about three inches high. When people brought new containers of quart, gallon, peck and bushel contents to be tested by comparison with a standard set owned by the court, the iron was put in a bed of coals. As the court passed on a container by filling it with corn from the standard measure, a paid man put the VG seal on it with the red-hot iron. A fee in tobacco was charged for testing and sealing such containers. A barrel of corn contained forty gallons.

Cattle marks were cut into the ears of the animal by its owner. Early deeds of sale designated the animal by color, but earmarking was an old practice in England and was used on the Shore from the beginning. The first reference found to earmarking was in 1634. The first deed of sale with such markings included was made in the presence of the court on May 4, 1635, for the sale of "one black cow about four years old, cropped on the left ear and slit on the right." Other marks in use were: "cropped on both ears and slit in the right ear," "cropped on left ear, cropped on right ear," "cropped on left ear and a hole in right ear," and "a flower de Luce (fleur-de-lis) on the left ear." There must have been some method of registering cattle marks in this period since certain bills of sale merely stated "his mark" after the description of the cow. Listing cattle by name and age became a practice and was used in inventories. The same mark was used for other livestock.

The demand for breeding cattle, and some idea of the extent to which this industry had developed, is indicated in an order which Lady Elizabeth Dale sent her overseer in 1636. It was recorded on March 27, 1637:

I have given you two former warrants for the sale of 30 cattle. I now permit you to sell all above 100. I want you to reserve 100 of kine and young cattle together for my use although you should be offered a very great price for them. All above said 100 are to be sold to the best advantage and profit. (A cow was valued at about 600 pounds of tobacco.)

Although Lady Dale never came to Virginia, she conducted a profitable business in Accomack County where her tenants were placed after being evacuated from the borough of Charles City in 1622. Her land was not surveyed and recorded but its bounds were generally recognized by her neighbors and the court.

Trading with the Indians was a profitable business and trading cloth was among the items used in exchange for beaver, otter, and wildcat skins. Trade had been established between Virginia and New England in the early 1620's and by this time Accomack was sharing in it.

The inventory of the estate of Thomas Lee, filed January 7, 1639, indicated that Accomack County had a silversmith. Apparently he combined this trade with tailoring and lived in the home of David and Joan Windley near the original settlement on Accomack River. He left his estate after his debts were paid to Joan Windley, wife of David Windley. He had no furniture other than a bed and its fittings. His personal belongings included a remarkable amount of wearing apparel for the time, as well as a comb and brush.

His silver forge was appraised at 1 pound 8 shillings sterling, and silver spoons were worth 1 pound 16 shillings. Other items appraised in English money were a silver toothpick, a whistle, a silver bodkin, a pair of horns set in silver (probably used as a salt cellar) and one dram cup. His chest of tools which could have been for silversmithing, along with the forge, and tailoring equipment were appraised at 50 pounds of tobacco. Thread, needles, buttons and loops were valued at 75 pounds of tobacco. A bundle of silk, ribbon and points were other items of a tailor.

Sir Francis Wyatt returned to Virginia as Governor

and Captain General the last of February, 1639. His commission was issued by the English government on January 11. The people of Accomack County who had been in Virginia between the fall of 1621 and the spring of 1626 knew of his policy of fairness to all, and his strong support of representative government. His commission included the English government's authority to call the General Assembly. Although it had been meeting and functioning since 1619, all petitions and orders had been signed only by the Governor and Council since Virginia was converted into a Crown Colony in 1624.

At a court held on September 18, 1640, an order was read for a list of all patents and land boundaries to be sent to Jamestown. Argoll Yeardley, who had returned to Virginia more than a year earlier with his wife Frances, and was living south of James River, took steps to have his 3700-acre tract surveyed and made plans to have a house built. The court ordered the guardian of John Savage to have his tract of an unknown acreage surveyed.

On January 11, 1641, Argoll Yeardley attended his first session of Accomack County's court. He was not only commander but also a member of the Council, the first resident Council member the Eastern Shore had ever had.

John Savage's mother and guardian died before May 17, 1641, when two witnesses testified that "on her death bed she had asked that John Webster be made guardian of her son and orphan of Ensign Thomas Savage, her former husband." After Savage's death she had married Daniel Cugley, a neighbor. The court appointed John Webster as John's guardian and instructed him to see that the land was put to the use of John Savage. Four thousand acres of the land had apparently been surveyed and the guardian was billed for taxes at the rate of one shilling for each fifty acres.

The boundaries were designated as Cherrystone Creek, formerly Accomack River, and Savages Creek, originally Mattawoman Creek. This change of names of streams was becoming general in Virginia and sentiment was growing for the Indian name Accomack to be replaced by an English name for the county.

By the end of the year 1641 the settled area of Accomack County extended beyond Nassawadox Creek and the population was about 700.

Chapter IV

1642-1652

After the name of the Eastern Shore county was changed from Accomack to Northampton, the first court was held on July 28, 1642, with Argoll Yeardley as commander. The number of commissioners had been increased to ten and eight were present.

Sir William Berkeley was now Governor and Captain General of Virginia. The change of the county name had been authorized by an Act of the General Assembly in March along with new names for some other counties. When the General Assembly of March 1642 adjourned, five of the eight original counties in Virginia bore the names of English shires or counties. Northampton was named for a shire northwest of London, from which some of the leaders of the Eastern Shore had come. However, Governor Berkeley's responsibilities were far greater than sanctioning the change of county names.

Strengthening the defense system of the colony was of utmost importance. Civil war was expected to erupt in England at any time, between the party that had supported King Charles I while he pushed England more and more toward an absolute monarchy and those who resisted him. Members of both parties were leaders in Northampton County, but they could be depended upon to stand together for the defense of their homes, property and representative government. The immediate need for strengthening the defenses was against the Indians. Need for a defense against the Netherlands, a former friend of England, was indicated.

From the beginning every able-bodied man on the Eastern Shore, as well as the rest of Virginia, was a part of the militia. Regular drills and target practice were held under the commanders, or their deputies. After the formation of counties in 1634, the commissioners were military leaders under the presiding officer who had the title of commander.

Northampton County was divided into six military districts covering all the settled area. That area from the north side of Nassawadox Creek to the north side of Hungars was put in charge of William Andrews and Stephen Charlton. Captain William Stone was in charge of the area from Hungars to the north side of Mattawoman, formerly the main prong of Hungars. Argoll Yeardley, commander, was in charge of the area from Mattawoman to a designated house south of Savages Creek, formerly Mattawoman. This put Commander Yeardley in charge of both streams which bordered on his land.

Obedience Robins, who had acquired a sizeable acreage and developed his business and industrial pursuits on and near the original Company land, and Phillip Taylor were in charge of the district which started at Savages Neck and extended to Kings Creek. The district from Kings Creek to a point on Old Plantation Creek was under William Roper and Edward Douglas. The area on to Magothy Bay Point, now the entrance to the bridge-tunnel system, was under John Neal and Edmund Scarburgh. Anyone who failed to obey the security regulations of these officers was to be sent to Jamestown for sentencing.

On April 19, 1643, the court requisitioned all powder and shot. Owners were paid for it in tobacco from the annual assessment. John Nuttall was employed to distribute it among all free men. When a man was called for military duty he was ordered to bring his musket and ammunition, as well as food and drink for a week. At times men were ordered to be armed at all times, even in church. Although the Eastern Shore Indians did not take part in the Indian Massacre of 1644, security measures were as rigid as those on the mainland of Virginia.

The homes and means of earning a living on the Eastern Shore were worth defending. Owners were thinking of

CHAPTER IV — 1642-1652

their posterity as well as their own well-being. A man usually made his will before starting on a dangerous journey or during serious illness. Much can be learned about the property of the people through their wills and inventories of the estates of people who left no wills. Some of these show the number of rooms in a house and the furnishings in each, as well as the vocation of a man through the tools he possessed. One or more guns appeared in every inventory during this period.

The will and inventory of Phillip Chapman, made on November 21, 1644, just before his death shows that his house had three rooms and it must have resembled the parsonage house built in 1635. The furnishings were listed "in the room where he lieth, in the kitchen and in the little room." His wife had predeceased him and he gave specific instructions for caring for his orphan children and saving the property for them when they reached the legal age of 14 years for girls and 21 years for boys. He arranged for his hogs and personal property to be sold to pay any debts and funeral expenses, and for his cattle and land to be kept for his children. His executors were to be the guardians.

According to law a child was to be supported out of the income from an estate. In case there was not enough to support him, unless a relative took him, he was apprenticed to someone who would teach him a trade. Inherited property could not be sold for his rearing and education. It had to be held in trust until he reached the age to take charge of it. The usual charge for board for a minor was 600 pounds of tobacco a year. Clothes and medicine were extra. Charges found on the records for schooling indicate that 350 pounds of tobacco a year was the tutoring fee for a child. When the wife was left as executrix and guardian, usually no specific instructions were given.

The inventory of the estate of William Burdett, who had become a commissioner in 1633, is not only revealing, but forms the basis for some calculated guesses at answers to some questions which have been raised many times. Burdett lived on the land which became Arlington Plantation and the site of a temporary governor's house before the end of the century. Contents of the inventory indicate that he had a house large enough to keep the commissioners overnight in 1642 when sessions of the court were held at Fishing Point.

Burdett's inventory included nine feather beds with bolsters. The finest of these, along with a suite of green curtains and valance, was appraised at 1000 pounds of tobacco. There was a table and frame, which consisted of two low cabinets and a portable top which were placed against the wall between meals. The chairs, and tableware of pewter, were numerous enough to serve the commissioners and a jury.

This inventory included "a court cupboard with two old wrought cushions and an old green cupboard cloth." He also had seven chests and a trunk, indicating that he was an importer of perishable goods which required the protection of chests during the voyages. Luxury items included two silver salts, a silver wine cup, a warming pan, and one dozen plain silver spoons. Another entry in the inventory suggests equipment of a person taking paying guests. This was four "melted" candlesticks.

This estate was appraised at 63,115 pounds of tobacco. It included 59 head of cattle and 32 goats, as well as his lengthy list of household items. This inventory did not show all the contents of his house since Alicia, his wife, had been married before. He left one son, Thomas Burdett. Alicia was destined to have two more husbands. Her last marriage will help explain the change of the name of this place to Arlington.

While the settlement at Old Plantation Creek was developing as a business and church center, Obedience Robins was expanding his cattle and tobacco raising activities on the south side of the mouth of Cherrystone Creek, formerly Accomack River. In 1642, he and an associate, John Wilkins, employed an itinerant millwright to erect a windmill. Considering the cost, this must have been used for grinding grain on certain days and for sawing lumber the rest of the time. Mills which used wind for power had been found in

CHAPTER IV — 1642-1652

the Virginia colony from 1619. A small tower of brick and wood held the wheels and belts which operated the grinding stones or saws while the large circular frame equipped with canvas strips harnessed the wind to turn the wheels. The windmill built in 1642 cost 220 pounds sterling and 20 barrels of corn. Robins and Wilkins also furnished all the iron needed in its construction.

The owner of a mill was permitted to charge one sixth by weight of the grain brought to his mill as a fee for grinding. Indian corn and wheat were the principal grain crops at this time.

Early in the year 1643, Edmund Scarburgh II, the eldest son of one of the Burgesses of 1630 was elected to this office. The other Burgess from Northampton for this year was Phillip Taylor. Edmund II had patented 1050 acres of land since he came to Virginia in 1635, some months after his father's death. He was the first person to have a patent recorded in the Magothy Bay settlement. By 1640 Edmund was a licensed surveyor. His election as a Burgess was the beginning of a long and stormy career in public affairs.

At a session of the General Assembly in November 1645, a law was passed pertaining to the handling of estates of deceased persons:

> "All administrations shall be granted at the county courts where the person did reside. All probates of wills there made and the wills recorded together with the appraisements, inventories and accounts. Records are to be sent to Jamestown to be recorded under the seal of the colony."

John Savage took charge of his business affairs in 1646. Two years earlier his guardian was required to pay quitrents on 4000 acres of his land. This is the first time any designated acreage of the Savage land appeared on the records. It was less than half of John's eventual possession. He married Ann Elkington and they lived at his house at "The Long Point," at the bottom of the neck. His step-father Daniel Cugley died in 1647 and John became the guardian of his half-sister, Margaret Cugley. John Savage's estate must have yielded a sizeable profit while he was a minor since he began bringing in settlers to satisfy requirements for his eventual tract of 9000 acres. The records do not reveal just how much land his father received for meritorious service as interpreter for the colony, but he laid the foundation for his son to get a clear title to one of the largest tracts of land on the Shore in his lifetime.

Although the growing of a sufficient food supply for each family was a part of the economic system of the colony from the first private ownership of land, people got careless at intervals and laws had to be strengthened. The General Assembly of March 1647 enacted a law providing for careful supervision to see that every planter grew three acres of corn for each of his tithables. On June 16, 1647, the Northampton County Court ordered the constables in the different precincts to visit the land of all the planters to see that they had planted as much corn as directed by the Act of the Assembly. The penalty for being short of the required acreage of corn was the loss of all tobacco grown that year. The proceeds from the forfeited tobacco were turned over to the public account.

The General Assembly of 1647 also provided for the boundary line of the two parishes in Northampton to be moved to the northward. Settlements had moved up the Shore so rapidly since the division of the county in 1642 that inspecting the upper part for corn acreage would have been a greater task than that in the lower part. Although the constables were paid for their services, a man could spend only a limited time in public service without neglecting his own business.

Since the church was a vital part of county government, a glimpse at the buildings and the first parish division should make for a better understanding of events at this time.

The original church building on the north side of Kings Creek, erected in 1625, served the entire Eastern Shore until a chapel of ease was built at Fishing Point in 1638. The minister lived at the glebe between these two churches after

CHAPTER IV — 1642-1652

the house was built there in 1635. William Cotton, minister, died in 1640, but an immediate successor was appointed. In 1643 the General Assembly authorized the division of Northampton County into two parishes with Kings Creek as the dividing line. By the end of 1643 Northampton had two ministers. This indicates that the original church was to be abandoned and a new one built in the middle of the upper parish. The new church was built on the north fork of Hungars Creek in the area then called Nassawadox, now Bridgetown. The Act of the General Assembly in 1647 moved the dividing line to Savages Creek, and then on a straight line from its head to the seaboard side. For some unknown cause Northampton County had ceased to be notified to elect Burgesses for the General Assembly in 1647. Only the resident member of the Council was present when Governor Berkeley pled for loyalty to the Crown.

In January 1650 the people got a first-hand report of conditions in England after the beheading of King Charles I. Henry Norwood, a cousin of Governor Berkeley, spent a few days in Northampton after coming ashore in Lord Baltimore's colony, and making an overland journey through the Eastern Shore of Virginia. A summary of parts of the Norwood diary gives interesting details about Argoll Yeardley's family and a description of the Eastern Shore, as well as something of conditions in England early in Cromwell's administration.

Henry Norwood left England in September 1645 along with some officers of the disbanded royal army, other royalists and servants. The captain of *The Virginia Merchant* had been paid six pounds for the passage of each refugee, as those royalists may be called, and his servants to Jamestown. The number of passengers exceeded three hundred. Foul winds, stops in the Caribbean Islands for water and fresh food, and eventually, a terrific storm caused the ship to get far off its course. Early in January 1650, the ship made a temporary landing. Norwood and eighteen others decided to stay on an island rather than take a chance on reaching their destination on the battered ship. Norwood's servant remained aboard the ship to look after his master's goods after fixing a bundle of food, ammunition, and trinkets for Indian trading.

In time the people on the island were befriended by the Indians and the head man offered to take Norwood to the Kickotank king where he stayed until January 24 when an Englishman arrived from Northampton with an Indian guide. The Indian king had sent a messenger to Northampton with an account of the presence of the white people here.

Norwood learned that the ship had reached the James River and Governor Berkeley had conveyed a message to officials at Northampton regarding members of the party who were left on the Eastern Shore. Norwood learned that he was then about fifty English miles from Northampton, but that the walking distance would be twice that much since the trail went around the heads of numerous creeks and swamps on the Eastern Shore. He was given some encouragement about the journey when he was told that he would encounter no stones or shrubs with thorns. On the journey he found a cleared and marked path which was used by Indian traders.

Norwood came to the house of Stephen Charlton where he was graciously entertained, then he went on to the house of Argoll Yeardley where he expected to get passage to Jamestown. In the diary we find this entry:

"My next stage was to the house of Esquire Yeardley, a gentleman of good name, whose father had sometimes been Governor of Virginia. There I was received and treated as if I had been that man of honor the King of Kickotank had created me. (The Indian had asked Norwood to give him his old coat.) It fell out very lucky for me that Yeardley had not long before brought over a wife from Rotterdam, whom I had known almost from a child. Her father (Custis by name) kept a victualling house in that town, lived in good repute and was general host of our nation there. The esquire knowing I had the honor to be the Governor's kinsman, and

CHAPTER IV — 1642-1652

his wife knowing my conversation in Holland, I was treated more like a near relation than a man in misery and a stranger. I stayed there for ten days. I was welcomed and feasted not only by the esquire and his wife, but by many neighbors who were not too remote."

Argoll Yeardley had a spacious house on the northwest side of his neck of land facing Mattawoman Creek. It was suitable for entertaining the Governor as well as his kinsman Henry Norwood. Some of the furniture seems to have been in his father's house when he was Governor of Virginia. Argoll returned to Virginia as a married man. His wife Frances had died at an undetermined date prior to 1649 leaving three children. Ann Custis was the first member of that family to appear in the records. Her brother John Custis II came to Virginia at the same time she did and he and his wife were likely among those who met Henry Norwood before he "left in a sloop" from Argoll Yeardley's house for Jamestown.

Norwood reported that members of the Royal Party in large numbers were seeking refuge in other lands since the civil war, which ended with the beheading of King Charles I at Whitehall Palace on January 30, 1649. Cromwell and his parliament enacted laws which affected noblemen, clergymen who would not renounce the Anglican form of worship and follow one prescribed by Parliament, and others who would not bow to the military government. The sad prospect of affairs in the homeland caused many to choose America. His party decided on Virginia in preference to Barbados or the Leeward Island where many went as fast as they could get passage. Fortunately, English currency did not change with the government, so the people who had money were able to bring it with them.

By the year 1650 land was patented as far north as Craddock Creek and the population was above 1000 men, women and children. The Commonwealth government in England was too busy to concern itself too much about Virginia and Northampton County this year; however, new problems arose and old ones returned. Rumors of an Indian attack were spread and depositions taken before the court showed that precautions should be taken. People had become somewhat lax since the aftermath of the massacre in 1644 across the bay. Tension between England and the Netherlands was mounting and people on the Shore got suspicious of Dutch residents, thinking they might join a hostile plot with the Indians. The courts issued an order forbidding any Dutch resident from trading with Indians.

On February 16, 1651, members of the militia, including the commissioners who lived in the Upper Parish, met at Nassawadox to consider the peace and safety of the northern part of Northampton County. It was decided that 50 men and 25 horses should be made ready for duty. If not enough men with their own horses volunteered or extra horses were offered, the rest needed could be requisitioned. This alert led to a raid on Indians far to the north of the last English land on April 28, 1651. The incident was reported to the Governor and he summoned the leaders to stand trial at Jamestown on May 10. They were acquitted. On November 28 the Northampton Court ordered William Andrews to be paid one thousand pounds of tobacco for his horse lost in "the late Indian war."

Parliament passed a law October 9, 1651, which eventually brought Northampton County into the war which started in 1652 between England and her old friend the Netherlands. This law was the First Navigation Act of the Commonwealth. It seemed to be drafted to prohibit the Dutch from trading with Virginia and other colonies. It required all goods imported into England or her possessions to be brought in English ships or ships from the country which produced them. In the latter case the ships were to make no trading stops between the home country and England.

Chapter V

1652-1663

On February 16, 1652, a meeting was held at the house of Walter Williams to choose Burgesses to the forthcoming session of the General Assembly. This was the first time in five years Governor Berkeley had ordered such an election in Northampton. The people who met on this day doubtless knew that a commission had been appointed by the Commonwealth Parliament to transfer the Virginia government to its jurisdiction and they might have known the liberal terms of the inevitable change. Governor Berkeley had received a copy of the instructions to the commission on January 19, and the Council had met.

A detachment of soldiers on a heavily armed ship came with the commission. Richard Bennett and William Claiborne must have been called to England to help write the terms for the transfer of the government. The other member of the Commonwealth Commission was the master of the ship. Richard Bennett had been an office holder in Virginia also. Both of these experienced Virginia legislators well knew that time and public sentiment would help ward off the use of force. However, the presence of soldiers in Chesapeake Bay may have shortened the delay.

Obedience Robins headed the list of five Burgesses chosen in Northampton County for this very important session of the General Assembly. The others were Edmund Scarburgh II, Thomas Johnson, William Jones and Anthony Hoskins.

On March 11, 1652, the Virginia government was transferred from Royal Authority to that of the Commonwealth Parliament. The authority was placed in the hands of the

General Assembly as soon as members of the Council and Burgesses who desired to remain in office had taken the oath of allegiance to the new government. The five from Northampton took the oath immediately.

On March 30, 1652, a meeting was held in Northampton County for the purpose of making a protest to the Assembly pertaining to its people having been taxed during the past five years without having Burgesses present when the levies were made. Six men were appointed to write the protest and convey it to the Northampton Burgesses at Jamestown. Stephen Charlton, Levin Denwood, John Nuthall, William Whittington, John Ellis and Stephen Horsey drafted the document which is known as the Northampton Protest, the first written account of Americans speaking out against taxation without representation. The committee asked that Northampton County be exempt from levies due for the current year. No action was taken at this session of the Assembly.

The new form of government had very little effect on Northampton County the first year. Richard Bennett was elected Governor by the General Assembly and William Claiborne was secretary. Those who did not want to take the oath of allegiance to the "government without King or House of Lords," were given a year in which to close out their business and leave the country. Indications are that everybody on the Eastern Shore decided to stay. Ministers were permitted to use the Book of Common Prayer for a year and there is no indication that the rituals for worship, marriages, christenings and burials, adopted by the Commonwealth Parliament were ever used on the Eastern Shore.

The Northampton court ordered a church to be built in the northern part of the county. Presumably it was built on Nandua Creek and it was the first church in the area of the present Accomack County. This was convenient for the settlers who lived as far to the north as Onancock Creek, but they found it inconvenient to attend court so far down the county. The following year the Burgesses took a petition to the General Assembly requesting a court for the upper part of the county.

CHAPTER V — 1652-1663

In January 1653 Governor Bennett received a notice from the Commonwealth Parliament that England was at war with the Netherlands. That country refused to recognize the Navigation Act of 1652. Dutch ships in Virginia waters were to be seized. When the order reached Northampton, there was concern among the Dutch residents here. They were in a precarious position as enemy aliens, although some of them had been born and reared in England. Ann Yeardley and her brother John Custis II and his wife had come to Virginia from Rotterdam where their father had gone to escape the Civil War in England. The Northampton court sent a petition to Governor Bennett asking for an order to give the law-abiding Dutch people here the protection they had the right to expect.

This question regarding the status of Dutch citizens was among several of a local nature which the Northampton commissioners did not want the responsibility of settling even if they had the authority. The General Assembly of 1653 appointed commissioners to sit with Governor Bennett and Secretary Claiborne at a court in Northampton. Argoll Yeardley and Nathaniel Littleton, resident members of the Council, were members of the commisson of five for this special court which, with Governor Bennett presiding, met at Hungars on July 26. The Dutch subjects were assured they would be given the opportunity to become naturalized under conditions set up by the Commonwealth Parliament though Governor Bennett had not received any instructions regarding naturalization requirements to date.

The six men who wrote and signed the Northampton Protest of 1652 were deprived of the right to hold public office or do any public work until they admitted their error and received a pardon from the Governor and Council. This requirement must have been met without delay. By the next election these men were restored to full citizenship.

Another petition which the General Assembly turned over to this court was for dividing the Eastern Shore into two counties. This petition was rejected but the court ordered the commissioners to rotate the court with one meeting at Cherrystone, another at Hungars and a third at Occohannock. Records show that some sessions were held in the area of Old Plantation Creek.

The Commonwealth Parliament failed to function smoothly without an authorized leader. It elected Oliver Cromwell, head of the army, as Lord Protector on December 16, 1653. This step caused the English government to be more like a military dictatorship than a representative government although Cromwell was capable and tactful. Virginia kept her representative government and felt few ill effects of the unsuccessful experiment in England until near the end of the decade.

In the autumn of 1654 the Eastern Shore lost another outstanding citizen by the death of Nathaniel Littleton, a commissioner from 1635 and a member of the Council. He had large tracts of land at Magothy Bay and Nandua which were to go to his two sons when they became of age and a young daughter. On September 4, 1654, he made a deed of gift of livestock which would assure her of money to live on during her minority and an estate to inherit when she was considered old enough to receive it:

> These present witness that I, Nathaniel Littleton, Esquire, devise and make a free gift unto my loving daughter, Hester Littleton, these goods following, vitz. five young cows marked with NL on the right buttocks; two ewe sheep, one is English the other is Dutch; and one bay mare with a white streak down her forehead.
>
> All these goods, with their increase, as belong to my said daughter, are to be carefully kept and looked after. They are to be delivered to my said daughter at the day of her marriage or when she shall attain the age of eighteen years. She is to perform such duty to her mother as expressed in my last will and testament dated August 12, 1654.
>
> And I do hereby devise my loving friend Captain Francis Pott to be the witness of the cattle, sheep and mare to be marked with a swallowed tongue on the right ear, and set apart for her. I hereby empower Captain

cured beef and hog meat, hides, some wool, and livestock for breeding purposes to other colonies. Selling provisions to the masters of small ships which entered the creeks was another source of income. Fur trade was still valuable and skins, such as beaver, otter, wildcat and deer were sold by the pound.

The General Assembly strengthened the law pertaining to standard weights in trade:

> The eldest commissioner in every county shall procure, at the charge of the county, and keep at the courthouse sufficient weights to try as often as shall be desired all steelyards as shall be complained of or brought thither.
>
> The penalty for false weights shall be three-fold damage to the customer, the cost of the suit and a fine of one thousand pounds of tobacco. Half of the tobacco shall be for the informer and the other half for the use of the public treasury.

Mill owners still were permitted to charge as toll one-sixth of the grain brought for grinding. This was determined by weight. Salt, which was made by boiling sea water, was sold by the bushel which weighed seventy pounds. Sugar and molasses from Barbados were among the imported items sold by weight.

The Eastern Shore lost another of its most progressive and influential citizens when Argoll Yeardley died in the fall of 1655. The inventory of his estate presented to the court on October 29 gives some idea of how the eldest son of a Governor, and a member of the Council at Jamestown under both King and Commonwealth, lived. A brief sketch of his life and an introduction to the family he established should make a glimpse at the record of his worldly possessions more revealing.

> Before Argoll reached his eleventh birthday, he went to England to live in the home of his uncle and guardian. Sir George Yeardley died in 1627 and his mother was dead before February of 1629 when Argoll left Jamestown. When he stood on deck of the ship as it neared the Virginia capes he probably looked toward the Eastern Shore where a 3700-acre tract of land

CHAPTER V — 1652-1663

Pott to be a father in trust for her.

In witness wherewith I have set my hand and seal this fourth day of September 1654.

       Nathaniel Littleton
       Seal

Signed, sealed and acknowledged in the presence of:
Edward Littleton
Daniel Baker

Nathaniel Littleton's will was not found in the records. His wife was executrix, and her own will was probated before two of the children reached the age to inherit their property.

When the General Assembly met in March 1655, the question of the location of the Northampton County courts was before it again. The Assembly enacted a law requiring the commissioners to hold court in just two places. One was to be at a place below Hungars Creek and the other was to be above it. The county commissioners were authorized to select a suitable location in each area.

Another Act of the Assembly at this time pertained to Northampton as well as other counties. Each county was to have one place which would be a center of other activities as well as a site for holding court. There was to be a church, a prison and a market. The Northampton commissioners chose a site on the north side of Occohannock Creek in the first bend of the creek beyond the land of Edmund Scarburgh. Richard Kellam had patented the land and it was to revert to him if it ceased to be used for public purposes.

Apparently the church was the only public building erected there. An ordinary, or public house, served as the meeting place for the court, with one room outfitted for a jail. The church was in use by the end of the year, and it continued to be a part of the government like the others in Northampton and Virginia.

Trade within the colony and with other English colonies on this side of the Atlantic increased after the First Dutch War ended in 1654, with the Dutch accepting the terms of the First Navigation Act. Northampton County planters were not only selling tobacco to England, but also butter, cheese, awaited him when he reached the legal age of twenty-one years. He had a brother, Francis, and a sister, Elizabeth, both younger than he. Argoll's formal education was finished and he was trained for business and government by his uncle and the friends of his distinguished father. He returned to Virginia in 1639 with his wife Frances. During 1640 he had his land surveyed and a house built on Mattawoman Creek. He moved to the Eastern Shore, then Accomack County, by the spring of 1641. He was already a member of the Council at Jamestown and he was commissioned commander of the Accomack County Court by May 31, 1642. He served as a commissioner and a member of the Council the rest of his life.

Argoll Yeardley died in 1655 and was survived by his second wife Ann Custis and five children. Frances was in her fourteenth year and Rose, the second daughter, was twelve. Each had had a cow deeded to her in 1643. Argoll II was in his tenth year. Edmund and Henry, sons by the second marriage, were under five years of age.

The inventory shows seven rooms in Argoll Yeardley's house. The hall contained a table and frame and eight leather chairs along with other assorted items. The cooking utensils were in a room called the milk house, presumably the pantry. The hall chamber contained one dozen chairs upholstered in red mohair. This suggests a cross hall. The parlor contained only items belonging to Ann Yeardley and the children so it was not inventoried. A little chamber next to the parlor contained bedroom furniture, including a bed with curtains and valance and a Dutch looking glass. Another little room next to the parlor contained four feather beds, quilts, blankets, and an old looking glass. The parlor chamber contained one feather bed with curtains and valance, bolster and blanket. The supply of towels, table and bed linens stored in this room numbered eighty-four items. Books (in this inventory) owned by Argoll Yeardley included works of William Perkins, a liberal-minded theological writer (1558-1602) and *Lucan's*

Pharsalia, an epic poem dealing with the Roman War between Caesar and Pompey. There were two Bibles. The pewterware for eating, drinking, serving and bathing weighed 120 pounds and was appraised at 510 pounds of tobacco. His silverware included a pot with lid, another silver pot, and tankard, presumably among the furnishings Sir George Yeardley brought to Jamestown in 1619. These items were appraised at 5 pounds 14 shillings sterling, or 517 pounds of tobacco. Ann Yeardley was the executrix and she became the guardian of the children. Argoll II would inherit the land when he became 21 years of age.

Stephen Charlton, another distinguished citizen, died in 1655. He was a member of the first vestry on the Eastern Shore when it was organized in 1635 and continued to be a devoted church leader the rest of his life. He patented the neck of land south of Nassawadox Creek and presumably gave the site for the first Hungars Church in 1643. Charlton was the first host to Henry Norwood after his overland journey through the Shore following a ship mishap in January of 1650. He was a commissioner of the county court and had served as a Burgess.

His will showed that he had made a financial success and that he had a substantial home and the comforts that the times afforded. Too, he and other people in the colony were being spared many of the annoying experiences which people in England were encountering under a government that was no less than a military dictatorship. Charlton left his estate to his second wife Ann and his two daughters. His eldest daughter Bridget was to inherit the home and land now known as Church Neck, after his wife's death. If the time came that he had no legal heirs by either daughter, this land and improvements was to go to the church. The will specified that each daughter was to inherit her property, not otherwise reserved for his wife, when she reached the age of fourteen years. Elizabeth was only six years of age when her father died and she was married at the age of twelve years without the consent of the trustees of her estate. She died the following year in childbirth. The husband sued the trus-

CHAPTER V — 1652-1663

tees for Elizabeth's part of the estate. Even after the Northampton Court ruled that Bridget was to get the estate since Elizabeth was not alive to inherit it, the case was appealed to the higher court at Jamestown. The verdict was again in favor of Bridget and her husband.

The will of Ann Littleton was probated on November 20, 1656. Edward Littleton was named executor. Edward Douglas, Francis Pott and Francis Doughty, minister, were appointed trustees. Edward was already married to the daughter of Edward Douglas, or married her soon after his mother's will was probated. However, he did not reach the legal age of twenty-one years until 1657. He was given the land and house at Magothy Bay with most of the furnishings and all the cattle, horses, mares, sheep and hogs thereon, not otherwise bequeathed. His brother Southey, then under fourteen years of age, was to have the plantation and all the other property on it at Nandua. He was to be kept in school until he reached the age of sixteen years. The bequest to the daughter Hester, then only eight years of age, and plans for her rearing and education can best be described by extracts from Ann Littleton's will:

> Item. I direct that my daughter Hester be with Mrs. Eyre (Susanne, wife of Thomas Eyre) until she is ten years old, and that Mrs. Eyre have eight hundred pounds of tobacco and caske. And afterward it is my request unto my loving and kind neighbor Isabella Douglas (wife of Edward Douglas) that she will take her into her care and tuition until she reaches the age of fourteen years. It is my will that Mrs. Douglas be paid one thousand pounds of tobacco and caske. Further, it is my will that if my daughter shall live unmarried until she reaches the age of eighteen years she is not to sell any part of her estate without the consent of my executor and trustees.
>
> Item. I give her one trunk marked E M containing household and childbed linens (much of it new), and one large new trunk marked N L containing my wearing apparel and another trunk marked S L containing

my wearing linens and small boxes with rings and some jewels and three pair of silk stockings.

Item. I do also give unto my daughter Hester Littleton the room over my usual lodging room at Magothy Bay in which all of her trunks and other goods and the trunks of my youngest son Southey Littleton are to be kept and looked after by my executors until the time arrives for my son Southey and my daughter Hester to possess them. The key is to be kept by one of my trustees.

When the General Assembly met in March 1660, the restoration of government in England under a King and House of Lords was only a matter of time. A strong army from Scotland had marched on London and seized the government there. The leader had plans to recall Charles II from his exile in France and have him crowned. No doubt the people of Northampton County knew something of the trend when the Burgesses were elected for this year. Edmund Scarburgh II, William Waters and John Stringer were chosen.

Virginia had been without a governor since Samuel Matthews, the third chief executive under the Commonwealth, died the previous January. Sir William Berkeley was elected. He accepted with the statement that he would relinquish his power if the English government commissioned another for the office. On July 13 King Charles II issued a commission to the Right Honorable Sir William Berkeley as Governor of Virginia. The transition back to Royal Authority was without undue hardship to the people of Northampton County, but they were destined later to share with the rest of the colony some fifteen years of trouble, unrest and attempted imposition of more Royal Authority than they were willing to accept. A revision of the laws to remove those not pleasing to the Crown was to be postponed for two years.

Among the items of special interest in the revised code of laws which was adopted by the General Assembly of 1662 was the changing of the name of the superior court at Jamestown from Quarter Court to General Court. The title of commissioners of county courts was changed to justices of the peace, and they were given the same authority as justices in England. Every county was to maintain for punishment of law breakers a ducking stool, a pillory, stocks and a whipping post. Although these instruments had been in use on the Eastern Shore from the time of Accomack Plantation, this is the first law requiring a county to have them.

The first law in the new code provided for the Established Church. Rituals in the Book of Common Prayer were to be used; payment of ministers and church expenses were to be by tithes, which was discontinued during the Commonwealth Period, and the assignments of certain governmental duties to the church officers were renewed.

Chapter VI

1663 - 1674

The Eastern Shore was divided into two counties by an Act of the General Assembly of March 1663. The number of tithables, or people on whom taxes were paid, was 707 for the previous year. The division was made so that each county had approximately the same number of tithables rather than by geographical area. From land patents and court records the division line has been located below the present village of Nassawadox. Records of the court since its formation in 1632 had been kept and indexed. The new county carried on the tradition in the same accurate and systematic form. The first page in the court records of Accomack County begins:

At a court held in Accomack County by his Majestie's justices of the peace for the said county on April 21, in the fifteenth year of our Sovereign Lord King Charles the Second, and the year of our Lord God, 1663, were present

Anthony Hodgkins
George Parker   Devereaux Brown
John West   John Wise

Robert Hutchinson was clerk and Edmund Scarburgh II was high sheriff. John Tilney, one of the justices who had been appointed by Sir William Berkeley, was absent at this session. The first item of business was to administer the oath to Wise and Brown, the only justices who were not sworn in at the March meeting of the Northampton Court.

The first court order was for the bill of sale for a mare to be recorded. Then the age of a servant boy was judged by the justices as thirteen years. They ordered this recorded. Certificates for land were issued to five people. Constables, highway surveyors and three of the justices to receive tithes were appointed.

The justices examined written evidence against one Bulbegger Alworth and two associates for Sabbath breaking and ordered the sheriff to summon them to the next court. Each was fined 30 pounds of tobacco. The nature of the crime was not stated but this was the usual fine for a freeman found guilty of playing cards on the Sabbath.

Court met at the house of Anthony Hodgkins, presiding justice and a licensed keeper of an ordinary at Pungoteague, for the next few years. (His house was at the site of Bobtown Crossroad.) Anthony Hodgkins had built an ordinary at Fishing Point when the court began meeting there back in 1640. He was the first licensed keeper of an ordinary on the Eastern Shore. He continued in business at Pungoteague until his death.

In this year of 1663 Virginia became conscious of her boundaries and realized that problems were ahead regarding the Maryland line at the north end of the newly-formed Accomack County. A controversy started which was not settled for many years. Another boundary of concern was with North Carolina, the name given to new patent holders for the area which had been granted as Carolana in 1629, but never settled. The new patent extended to 36 degrees 30 minutes, a few miles farther north than the original one. Also, the Northern Neck of Virginia had been granted to a proprietor by King Charles II while he was in exile and renewed at this time. With proprietary colonies so near, the Crown Colony of Virginia had reason to be concerned about her boundary. The most vulnerable one was on the Eastern Shore. However, in 1663 the settled area did not reach even to the present town of Accomac.

The clerk, sheriff, tithe collectors and surveyor were required to keep books. Apparently they had to pay for them out of their fees. The list of office and personal correspondence supplies in the inventory of a ship, the *Sarah Hatch*, gives some idea of the wholesale cost of such items sent from

England. This list, along with the rest of the cargo of the ship, is in the court records of Northampton County. The office supplies and their wholesale prices were:

Ten ink horns at 8 pence each, 3 dozen black lead pencils at 16 pence each, 2 cases of wax at 6 shillings 8 pence, 6 boxes of wafers at 1 shilling 6 pence, 1 ell of parchment at 13 shillings 6 pence, 3 books in folio folders with parchment at 12 pence, 2 large books at 12 pence, 7 books in gray toned with parchment at 8 pence, and 2 books in quarto with leather at 2 shillings 8 pence. The last books listed were used for the court records and surveyor's reports.

Writing pens were made from the wing and tail feathers of geese, ducks and turkeys. Dry sand was used for blotting purposes. The ink horns presumably contained a dry chemical which could be mixed with water to produce the durable writing of those early clerks.

On April 19, 1664, the Northampton Court issued an order for a courthouse to be erected. Since the court was established in 1632 it had been meeting in the homes of court officials or at public houses. This first courthouse on the Eastern Shore was built at Town Fields on the north side of Kings Creek. It was 25 feet long and 20 feet wide with walls 9 feet high. William Waters, a member of the court, was the contractor. On February 21, 1665, he was paid 6405 pounds of tobacco.

By the summer of 1665 the Accomack County Court was meeting at Folkes Tavern in Pungoteague and an incident at the tavern this year gave this village the distinction of being the scene of the first dramatic performance in the New World.

In the afternoon of Saturday, August 27, 1665, three local men presented a play called "The Bear and the Cub". It was written by William Darby, who directed the play and played the leading part. The members of his cast were Cornelius Watkinson and Phillip Howard. There is no record of the size of the audience, but there is an account of one John Martin, who considered the

CHAPTER VI — 1663-1674

play indecent. He made a statement under oath to that effect to be presented to the court.

On November 16, 1665, the court examined the evidence presented by the King's Attorney for Accomack County and issued this order:

"The court has thought fit to suspend the case till the next session, and orders that Cornelius Watkinson, Phillip Howard and William Darby do appear in those habiliments that they then acted in, and give a draught of the speeches and passages they used."

The sheriff was ordered to hold Watkinson and Howard until they gave bail for their appearance at the next court. William Darby, author of the play (called "The Bear and the Cub"), was to be held without benefit of bail until the date set for the reenactment of the play.

The play was presented before the justices and the verdict was that the actors were not guilty of anything indecent. John Martin, the informer, was ordered to pay all the court cost, including board for Darby while he was in jail.

Regardless of the acquittal, this ended dramatic presentations on the Eastern Shore during the Colonial Period. But it does not mean that there was no entertainment. Horse racing, nine-pins, cards and gatherings of friends and relatives for home entertainment are mentioned as part of the social life of the times.

Although tobacco and livestock raising were the leading sources of income there was some manufacturing on the Shore at this time. Salt was being made both by boiling sea water and by keeping clay-lined vats filled with sea water while the sun evaporated it. The latter method was used for a while on some of the seaside islands and then abandoned. Leather tanning and shoe making were established industries by the mid 1660's.

The establishment of water mills for grinding grain had been encouraged for some time and as settlements moved northward new mills were built. A great deal of ingenuity was involved in making ponds with artificial waterfalls to run the machinery in this almost level country. The law required a mill dam to be twelve feet thick and any road that touched the pond had to be thirty feet wide. The mills were usually built near the heads of the main branches of the principal creeks, and signs of some of the early ponds can still be seen.

The Second Dutch War started in the spring of 1665 and all ships to England were ordered to sail in convoys protected by armed English ships. There were to be only three convoys a year. This meant reduced communication with England and longer periods between new supplies ordered from England. It resulted in a period of austerity for the Eastern Shore. However, the local problem was small in comparison with that of the First Dutch War in the 1650's when a number of Dutch subjects were put under restrictions. Now those Dutch subjects were naturalized citizens and at least one of them was a member of the Northampton County Court. News of the tragic fire in London in September 1666 brought sadness to the Eastern Shore, as well as the rest of the colony of Virginia. Some of the people in both Accomack and Northampton counties had friends and relatives or people with whom they did business in the 450 acres in the very middle of London which had been burned in seven horrible days. Another inconvenience the Second Dutch War caused the Shore was the necessity for constant alert of the militia and keeping a watchman on duty at the entrance to the bay.

Dutch ships did enter Chesapeake Bay and they captured a number of English ships in a tobacco convoy. Although there is no record of the loss this caused Eastern Shore growers, there must have been some. This war ended in July 1667 with a five-year cease fire and a no ship-seizing agreement. The Dutch were still objecting to the English Navigation Acts which restricted trade with the American colonies.

In 1666 a new land patent policy was adopted for Virginia. The headright system was superseded by one in which an individual could patent a large tract and get a clear title for it after he had built a house at least twelve by twelve feet, fenced an acre for an orchard and garden and had someone live in the house for a year. The King's rent on such patents was 2 shillings for each fifty acres per year. Under these terms men with money patented large tracts on the islands and marsh land for cattle raising. The size of a house required for a patent was reduced at this time. Five years earlier the description of a tiny cabin "five and one half feet high, wanting a quarter of an inch, with a door four feet nine and a quarter inches," was recorded. Presumably, the right of a patent was being contested when this little house was measured by two men who testified before the court. Although the terms were easy for getting large patents, only men who could make the land yield a profit could pay the King's rent and hold it.

The Eastern Shore lost one of its distinguished naturalized citizens when Dr. George Hack died in the spring of 1665. His will, proved on April 17, 1665, in Accomack County, shows he had made a financial success and was a scholarly man. He was born in Germany in 1620 but married and started his family in Holland. He and Augustin Herrman of Maryland married sisters. In 1652 George Hack patented 900 acres of land on the south side of Pungoteague Creek next to the bay. He engaged in tobacco growing, cattle raising and trading as well as his medical practice. Among the items in his will showing his scholarly nature were 22 German and Dutch books, 54 books in Latin and 20 books in English. The land he patented is still called Hacks Neck.

In the summer of 1667 an outbreak of smallpox hit the Eastern Shore. The disease is said to have been brought by a seaman whose illness was not diagnosed until it reached its most horrible stage. By that time many people had been exposed. Late in the year the courts took action. The commander of the militia in each county issued the order of the court:

> No member of a family in which there was a case of the disease was to go near other people until thirty

days after the last member of the household with the disease had taken the rash. In other words, the family was quarantined until all members had had the disease or shown an immunity to it. During the reign of King James I a law had been enacted in England requiring thirty days of cleansing and it was to be enforced here.

The acreage of patented land in the northern part of Accomack County increased at a phenomenal rate and most of it was in large tracts. The first patent on what eventually became the Virginia-Maryland line was issued to John Wallop in 1664. Although Maryland claimed all land north of Watkins Point, Virginia patents had been issued north of it by 1670. These patents were in large tracts.

Governor Berkeley and the Council were not pleased with the management of this second Accomack County so a change was made in the government of the Eastern Shore. On October 3, 1670, the General Assembly adopted a far-reaching resolution:

> It is ordered that Accomack County be united with Northampton and that they remain as one county until there shall appear good cause for again dividing them.

This resolution was recorded in the Northampton County Order Book in 1670. The court was to meet in two sections to be known as the Upper and Lower Courts of Northampton County. The order took effect the following month.

> At a court held for the upper part of the county of Northampton, formerly called Accomack, this 7th day of November, in the twenty second year of our Sovereign Lord King Charles the Second, and the year of our Lord God, 1670, were present
>
> William Stringer
>
> William Kendall   Edmund Bowman
> Southy Littleton   John Whitall
> William Spencer   Thomas Rydings
>   Isaac Foxcroft

Daniel Neech served as clerk but in a short time he became deputy clerk for the two courts. John Culpeper had been commissioned by Governor Berkeley as clerk. Apparently the

CHAPTER VI — 1663-1674

latter spent most of his time at Jamestown. The Upper Court continued to meet at Pungoteague.

Early in the summer of 1671 Daniel Jenifer, a surveyor from St. Marys County, Maryland, married Ann Toft of Gargaphia, who had more land than any other woman on the Eastern Shore of Virginia. Lord Baltimore's proprietary colony and Virginia were two nations under the English Crown and this marriage might have had its influence in solving the border question many years later. At least a truce prevailed for some time after the marriage and within a short time Governor Berkeley gave Daniel Jenifer an appointment as a surveyor and as a member of the court.

Daniel Jenifer was a widower who is known to have been in Maryland as early as 1664. He had married Mary Smith who left no children by him. He was a sizeable land holder in Maryland and apparently an officer in the Maryland militia. He was destined to become a large land holder on the Eastern Shore of Virginia before his estate was administered on February 21, 1693.

Ann Toft came to Virginia in 1660 and was issued a patent of 800 acres of land at the north end of the settled area on the bayside. She had three daughters with the intriguing names Arcadia, Atalanta and Annabella. They were living at Gargaphia House, which must have been one of the finest houses on the Shore in 1671. It was located near the Seaside Road a mile east of the present village of Gargatha. This was near her 4700-acre tract of land which reached from Bundicks Creek on the south to Assawoman Creek on the north, and to the present dual highway on the west. In 1669 Ann Toft had bought 3000 acres which extended from the shore of Chincoteague Bay northwestward to the present Maryland line. The village of Horntown is near the center of this tract. She paid 9101 pounds of imported sugar in cask and 708 pounds of indigo.

The year following their marriage Ann and Daniel Jenifer divided this northern tract among the daughters so each had about one third of the waterfront. A stipulation was made that if either daughter married without the parents' consent before reaching the age of seventeen years she was to forfeit her share of the property. Each girl got her property.

On May 3, 1672, a son was born to Ann and Daniel Jenifer. He was christened Daniel of St. Thomas Jenifer. Ann and Daniel received new patents for most of her land and additional acreage. Unlike most patents, all new ones were issued jointly as well as the renewals. Their patents were extensive and two of them were on Chincoteague and Assateague islands. They made some sales as they patented new land. The last joint signature for a deed of sale was dated February 15, 1687. After that Daniel signed alone until his death in 1693. On September 9, 1686, Ann and Daniel had made deeds of gifts to Ann's daughters and their husbands.

The haste of Daniel Jenifer and others to patent the islands and marsh lands was due to restrictions that the General Assembly had placed on letting livestock run wild in the woods. Wild horses had become a menace in some parts of Virginia, including the Eastern Shore. Importation of horses was stopped and anyone catching a wild horse was entitled to keep it under certain conditions. Horse hunting became a sport but it was prohibited on the Sabbath. Horses and cattle were put on the islands as soon as they were patented and rounded up once a year for marking where more than one man owned such an island. Daniel Jenifer was a livestock raiser as well as a tobacco grower, surveyor and importer.

The reference to Gargaphia House on the Seaside Road rather than on the water indicates that locations which had been called "forests" by the Governor and Council at Jamestown in 1627 were no longer looked upon with disfavor. The records show that there were a number of prominent people living on inland sites at this time.

Edmund Scarburgh II died in 1671 after thirty-six years of strenuous business activities and public service. For some years he held the monopoly for selling salt on the Shore and he kept the price reasonable. He was a member of the court, Burgess, collector of customs on the Shore and in

CHAPTER VI — 1663-1674

1666 he was appointed surveyor-general of Virginia. He owned trading ships which plied the waters to New England and southern islands, in which business he was both an exporter and an importer. Although Edmund Scarburgh II patented thousands of acres of land he held but little in his own name at the time of his death. Like many other men of his time, he did a big credit business and a number of judgments were filed against his estate which his wife Mary declined to administer.

Edmund Scarburgh II lived on the north side of Occohannock Creek from the early 1650's until the time of his death. Presumably he had an imposing house and furnishings as elaborate as those of his contemporaries. The area in which he lived and from which he conducted his trading business is the Scarburghs Neck of the present. He left sons and daughters to carry on the traditions of private enterprise and representative government which had characterized the Eastern Shore since 1620.

The five-year truce between England and Holland ended in 1672 and a new shooting war which lasted two years was affecting the Eastern Shore by the following March. Governor Berkeley sent orders for the militia to stand ready to ward off a possible enemy attack and for one of the creeks to be declared a refuge for English ships. It was to be fortified at both sides of its mouth. Apparently, Pungoteague Creek was chosen but the war ended before the fortifications were complete. This war had but little effect on the Eastern Shore, but a large fleet of Dutch ships destroyed eleven Virginia merchant ships before the armed English ships could drive them away. This ended the Dutch menace in Virginia waters.

By 1673 the Shore had two roads over most of the area from Cape Charles to the Maryland line. As settlements moved northward, road surveyors were added to the districts set up by an act of the General Assembly in 1630, and amended as the need arose. The roads were built and maintained by labor requisitioned by the surveyors, who were not necessarily qualified to lay out land boundaries.

When the citizens in a given district saw the need for an added mile or more of road, the surveyor estimated the number of man days of work that would be required to make it. Each freeman was required to provide a part of the labor in proportion to the number of tithables he had. Anyone who failed to supply the workmen with food for the number of days they were to work, was fined by the court.

When a road went through an enclosed farm, the owner was required to provide a fence on each side of the road or a gate at each end. Unpatented land could be used for roads at the discretion of the surveyor and church wardens. After a road was built the owner of the land through which it passed, or the two who owned land on either side, were required to keep it free from fallen trees and limbs.

Early roads were crooked in order to go between land patents rather than through them, to go around fenced fields and to go inland to avoid as many streams as possible. When a bridge was necessary, the owner of adjacent land was required to sell the needed timber to the surveyor. This timber was paid for out of public levies.

Tobacco was hauled over these roads either in carts or rolled in hogsheads (with a gadget which was pulled by oxen or horses). There were roads to the churches and meeting places of the court as well as to the public wharves and mills. Too, there was a network of crossroads connecting those of the bayside and the seaside. The legal width of a public road was thirty feet. Small saplings or the trunks of young trees were sometimes put across low places in corduroy fashion to make the road passable in rainy weather. In summer, carts sometimes got stuck in the sand; but then, as now, people usually were able to travel where they needed to go.

Although the records of the preliminary work have not been found, something must have been done during most of 1673 to get the Shore again divided into two counties. On November 7 Governor Berkeley appointed justices for Accomack County.

In this year of 1673 a map of Virginia and Maryland, which King Charles II had commissioned Augustin Herrman

CHAPTER VI — 1663-1674

of Maryland to make, was published in England and copies were sent to the Eastern Shore. The Herrman Map emphasized large estates by name. The King might have been thinking in terms of a government by noblemen for Virginia as Maryland already had. This map shows the original Maryland line of 1632 located at 37 degrees 30 minutes north latitude.

Chapter VII

1674 - 1700

The Eastern Shore was again divided into two counties when the court for the third Accomack County was held on January 6, 1674. The first court of the Upper Court of Northampton had met on November 7, 1670, after the second Accomack County was deactivated as a governmental unit by the General Assembly. In this year of 1674 the boundary line had not been determined, but outside problems came so fast that there was little time for concern about the county in which people on the potential dividing line were to pay taxes. These outside problems were of mutual concern and the people of the Shore faced them as Eastern Shoremen and Virginians.

The justices for the new court were Southy Littleton, Charles Scarburgh, Edmund Bowman and John Wise who had been justices of the court when the county was discontinued in 1670. New ones were William Custis, Thomas Rydings, Daniel Jenifer and Thomas Brown. Rydings was a son-in-law of Argoll Yeardley II. Thomas Brown was the son of an early settler and at this time he lived in the lower part of the county. William Custis was a younger brother of John Custis II and they had been naturalized at the same court in 1658.

On February 25, 1674, slightly more than a month after the third Accomack County began to function as a governmental unit, which had enjoyed representative government with little or no taxation without representation, the King took a step which was a shocking blow to all freedom-loving Virginians. King Charles granted all of Virginia except the Northern Neck to two of his favorite noblemen who were to collect the quitrents here for thirty-one years. He specified

CHAPTER VII — 1674-1700

that the grant was for the colony of Virginia and the territory of Accomack. Accomack had continued to be the term used in most English documents for the whole Eastern Shore.

Henry Bennett, Earl of Arlington, one of the principal secretaries to King Charles, and Lord Thomas Culpeper were the recipients of the colony of Virginia. They were to receive all rents (one shilling for each 50 acres after seven years of ownership), not only in the future but those which had gone unpaid since 1669. These two men were to have the power over Virginia which the King and Parliament had formerly exercised. Governor Berkeley and the Council were instructed to issue no more land patents. The proprietors would have that authority also. There was nothing in the King's order to assure the people in Virginia that they still owned their land. There is no record of the amount of money Arlington and Culpeper paid the King for this grant, but the King must have received a sizeable amount.

The General Assembly met in September 1674 and drew up a petition to the King asking him to withdraw the proprietary grant to Lords Arlington and Culpeper and let Virginia be subject only to the King as she had been since the Crown Colony was formed in 1624. This Assembly levied a tax to send three representatives to England to plead their cause with King Charles II. A communication from the English government, dated November 19, 1675, confirmed the ownership of the land then possessed by the people in Virginia, but left the people in a state of suspense regarding the other phases of the petition. They wondered what would be the fate of the General Assembly.

In June 1676 a committee of ten representative Eastern Shore citizens was appointed to draw up a petition for their Burgesses to present to the General Assembly. They asked that a new vestry be chosen every three years, that lists of tithables be more carefully examined, that county records be open for any man who chose to see them, that no drinks be sold within a mile of the courts when in session, that no sheriff hold office two years in succession, that five years of residence in the same place be a requisite for holding public office, and that people in Accomack and Northampton counties have the privilege of appealing cases involving less than 3000 pounds of tobacco to the Court at Jamestown. This petition was sent to the session of the Assembly which preceded Bacon's Rebellion, the first civil war in English America.

In July 1676 Sir William Berkeley, with his secretary and some members of the Council, took refuge at the home of John Custis II. The fact that Old Plantation Creek had too much sand at its mouth to be listed among the ports of North America, probably had its advantages when Bacon's forces came to the Eastern Shore for the purpose of capturing Governor Berkeley and his staff. The Shore militia had been called out and the creeks were protected against an invasion. The commander on the ship which brought the detachment of Bacon's soldiers asked for a conference with the Governor. When he came ashore to the temporary capitol at Old Plantation Creek, possibly already called Arlington Plantation, a boarding party captured the ship. Early in September Governor Berkeley led an expedition to resume his duties as Governor at Jamestown. On September 19 Bacon returned with enough troops to take Jamestown which was fortified with militiamen. He burned the town and the church. Most of the early records, except the land books, were burned.

Bacon died on October 26 of an infection. He had waged a strenuous fight against Indians on the fringe of the settled area of Virginia, and he was expecting to make another attempt to capture Governor Berkeley and put the entire colony under his control when death struck him down. Ships and soldiers arrived from England in the fall and the fight went on until Bacon's forces surrendered on January 16, 1677. Governor Berkeley moved his headquarters from the Eastern Shore to Green Spring the last of January. Although Bacon's Rebellion was attributed to neglect of proper Indian defenses by Governor Berkeley, it is now regarded as a step in the long struggle of the people of Virginia to maintain their representative government and to be taxed only when their representatives authorized it.

The people on the Shore were undoubtedly divided into

CHAPTER VII — 1674-1700

Berkeley and Bacon factions, but when the war began there is no indication that any ran the blockade to join the army under Bacon. After the war was over they were united in being disappointed in not being exempt from the quitrents to Proprietors Arlington and Culpeper, and other levies which might have been promised as Governor Berkeley went up and down the Shore to talk with officers of the militia early in the war. No written accounts of such promises have been found.

After making bloody reprisals against Bacon's captured leaders and giving high praise for the favors received on the Eastern Shore, Sir William Berkeley left for England on May 5, 1677, where he died in July. Thomas, Lord Culpeper, one of the proprietors, had been commissioned Governor of Virginia by King Charles II on July 8, 1675, and the commission was to become effective upon the death of Governor Berkeley. The King sent Colonel Herbert Jeffreys with a commission as Lieutenant Governor and an order for Sir William Berkeley to come to England for an audience with his Majesty. Although John Custis II was not paid the sum Governor Berkeley recommended for the use of his house as headquarters, this naturalized citizen was appointed to the Council.

When the General Assembly met in 1677, Accomack County sent its own set of grievances by its Burgesses. Since the tithables had lost much time in guarding the Shore to prevent enemy landings during the late war, and the crops had been neglected by this loss of time, the people of Accomack asked for tax exemptions for quitrents and any levies which might be made to pay the cost of the late war. No action was reported on these and other grievances at the time, but they must have reached the King. In a note to Lord Culpeper he mentioned the loyalty of "The Province of Accomack."

Another Eastern Shore item that came before the General Assembly in 1677 pertained to the boundary line between Accomack and Northampton counties. Consideration was being given to the building of new churches, and possibly courthouses, in both counties and people on the undetermined border line did not want to find themselves assessed for extra taxes in both counties. Governor Berkeley had left this as a local question when the third Accomack County was formed in 1674. The Assembly declined to act on it at this time. The strip of land involved was about a mile wide from bay to sea and the question was to remain unsettled for another decade.

In this year of 1677 the people of the northern part of Northampton County petitioned the court to hold its meetings at a place more centrally located than Town Fields where the first courthouse on the Eastern Shore was built in 1664. Later this year the court was held at a place called the Horns, probably in an ordinary. This meeting place was in the vicinity of the present town of Eastville. A public house was used for the meetings until the "New Courthouse" was ready for use on May 28, 1690.

The churches in Northampton were at Town Fields, Old Plantation Creek and Hungars. The one at the head of Occohannock Creek was in the disputed area and the one farther up the Shore, built in 1652, was no longer appearing in the records. The lower parish of Northampton County had a minister and the Reverend Thomas Teackle apparently was serving Accomack County on week days along with the upper parish of Northampton. Accomack had at least one lay reader licensed to conduct routine worship services.

On July 9, 1679, a contract was made for the building of the second Hungars Church where the present one now stands. The first church had been built after the county was divided into two parishes in 1643. It was in the neck which later took the name Church Neck. No description of the first building survives but the contract for the second is explicit.

>The agreement was made on July 9, 1679, between John Michael and Argoll Yeardley II, church wardens, and Symon Thomas, carpenter.
>
>The building was to be 40 feet long and 20 feet wide with wall plates ten feet high upon the posts. The foundation was to be of locust blocks and all framing,

CHAPTER VII — 1674-1700

including the rafters, was to be of oak. The roof was to be of wood. The outside was to be covered with plank and the inside was to be covered with the ceiling from the old church and as much new ceiling as would be required to complete the interior.

The church wardens agreed to locate the nails and a boarding place for the carpenter and his helpers. He was to take no other work or leave the job except for dire necessity until it was finished.

Symon Thomas was to be paid 10,000 pounds of merchantable tobacco and casks for this job, which was to begin at the earliest possible convenience.

Symon Thomas, carpenter, lived in Accomack County. In 1677 the vestry collected 21,000 pounds of tobacco for some purpose. The following January services were being held at the church at Pungoteague. The name of Henry Parke, minister of Accomack Parish, first appears in the court records in 1678.

The Shore lost a good citizen when John Savage died in 1678. His long and carefully-worded will was probated in Northampton County. Only seventy years earlier his father, who was known on the Shore as Ensign Thomas Savage, came to Jamestown as an apprentice to be trained as an Indian interpreter. John was only nine years of age when his father died, but his estate was kept intact until he reached the legal age of twenty-one years. He was required to furnish headrights for most of the land claimed by his father, but he eventually got a clear title for 9000 acres, extending from the bottom of Savages Neck to the seaside. Although John sold a small acreage at times, he had a large plantation with tenants on it to leave to each of his seven children and to make provision for his second wife, Mary, the daughter of Obedience Robins, by whom he had three sons and two daughters. His first wife was Ann Elkington and they had three daughters. John Savage rendered valuable service as a justice, vestryman and militia officer. He also served one term as a Burgess.

Another good citizen, Southy Littleton of Nandua, died

in the fall of 1679, leaving a place of leadership in Accomack County which was hard to fill. He was the youngest son of Nathaniel and Ann Littleton of Magothy Bay and inherited their entire estate after his brother, Edward, died without children. Southy managed wisely and increased his worldly possessions. His wife was Sarah Bowman of Metompkin, now Bowmans Folly, and she predeceased him. They had seven children.

Southy Littleton made provisions in his will for his children to be placed in the custody of friends until they reached the age for inheriting their property. Each boy was to receive his share at the age of 18 years and each girl was to possess hers at the age of 16 years. The estate was to be in charge of an overseer and supervised by his administrators. His desire was that each child's share would increase in value as well as yield enough revenue to pay expenses. One little girl was placed in the custody of Ann Jenifer and the youngest boy was to be in charge of his nurse at the homeplace. Other children were assigned to friends for rearing and educating.

The inventory of the estate of Southy Littleton, taken January 10, 1680, shows that his house had ten rooms and a milk house. A porch chamber indicates that there was an enclosed entrance porch resembling the one at Bacon's Castle in Surry County. There were a hall, hall chamber, a hall garret, parlor, parlor chamber, porch chamber, back room chamber, new room, kitchen and little room over the kitchen. The new room contained only two large chests and it presumably was the one-story section later known as the colonnade. The hall contained a large table and frame as well as other dining room furniture. There were silver spoons, silver and pewter tableware, household linens, beds and bedding, looking glasses, cooking utensils, milk pans, cheese presses, butchering equipment, twenty-three books and a map of the marshland of Chincoteague.

This large house apparently was built in sections and part of it was built before Southy's mother made her will in 1656. It is doubtful if there was a more imposing house on the Eastern Shore during the seventeenth century.

CHAPTER VII — 1674-1700

The General Assembly of March 1680, following instructions from England regarding a port of entry for each county, enacted a law providing for a town of 50 acres in size to be laid out in each county. The land was to be purchased by the Virginia government and surveyed into lots of one-half acre each. All tobacco shipped from a county was to be loaded at this town and all goods imported for sale in the county were to be unloaded here. In this way export and import duties could be more easily collected. Thus, the prescribed town was called a port of entry.

Town Fields was selected for the Northampton port of entry. In 1682 Daniel Jenifer of Accomack County was allowed 450 pounds of tobacco for "laying out the town." The courthouse had been abandoned and there is no indication that it was restored to use. In fact, there is no assurance that the building of a town here got beyond the surveyor's plat stage.

A site between the two forks of Onancock Creek was purchased from Charles Scarburgh to be a port of entry for Accomack County. The land was surveyed by 1681 and buildings got under way. The purchaser of a lot got a certificate for it and he agreed to build a house at least twenty feet long within four months. Then, upon the payment of 100 pounds of tobacco, he was given a deed to his lot. Although the original plat has not survived, one reconstructed many years later shows the original layout with Market Street as it still is. The present North Street was the boundary line of the original town called Port Scarburgh or Onancock Town.

In 1681 the justices for Accomack County ordered a courthouse built in the "County Town" with all possible speed. The court had been meeting at Metompkin, now Accomac, since it was moved from Pungoteague in 1678. A church was also built here and the earlier one at Metompkin must have been abandoned. Ten years later the court issued the following order to the road surveyor:

> To lay out and cause to be cleared with all possible convenience a good and sufficient road from the Great Neck of Metompkin to Onancock Town for the convenience of his Majestie's subjects to the said church.

Presumably both the courthouse and church were on the site of the present Public Square between Market and King streets. Some of the people on the seaside complained about the inconvenience of getting to court so sessions were alternated between Metompkin and Onancock until it was located at its present site in 1693.

In 1682 the Eastern Shore lost another of its distinguished citizens when Argoll Yeardley II, then high sheriff of Northampton County, died. His two half brothers and his own son predeceased him so the family name became extinct. However, Argoll II left three daughters who reared sons to help the Eastern Shore and the colony of Virginia carry on the ideals of private enterprise and representative government which had been transplanted to America by Argoll's grandfather, Sir George Yeardley, at Jamestown in 1619.

Charles II died on February 6, 1685. Much had taken place in the Virginia Colony and on the Eastern Shore since he was crowned in 1660. The people had lost some of their rights and privileges, but by diligence the General Assembly was still a power of strength. In 1681 Lord Arlington sold his interest in Virginia to his partner, Lord Culpeper, then Governor of Virginia. The latter also bought the Northern Neck proprietary. In 1684 Lord Culpeper surrendered the proprietary rights of all but the Northern Neck to King Charles II for an annual sum which Virginians were taxed to pay. Lord Culpeper made this concession under pressure and he was using pressure to get a perpetual charter for the Northern Neck. This elimination of the proprietors gave the people of the Eastern Shore a feeling of security about their land titles which they had lacked for almost a decade.

James II was crowned King of England upon his brother's death in 1685, but with a general lack of enthusiasm and confidence on the part of people in England and in the colonies. Lord Culpeper made his final departure to England, leaving the government here in charge of a lieutenant-governor. James wanted more power and more money than his brother Charles II had requested. By 1688 there was a general state of unrest in England. Sentiment was growing

CHAPTER VII — 1674-1700

in favor of a revolution to overthrow James II and put his eldest daughter Mary and son-in-law William, Prince of Orange, on the throne. News of such a plan reached the Eastern Shore and precautions were being taken to keep the people loyal to the King. At least one Shore citizen, Henry Pike of Northampton County, was prosecuted for drinking a toast to the "Prince of Orange."

This Prince of Orange was a nobleman in Holland. He was invited by leaders of the two political parties in England to become their leader. He arrived in London on November 5, 1688, with a large army of English and Dutch soldiers. A bloodless revolution was over by December 18. His father-in-law, James II, fled to France.

William was related to the House of Stewart. His mother was a sister of James II. On February 13, 1689, William and his wife Mary accepted a declaration of rights which had been drawn up by those who opposed the autocratic rule of James II. Immediately they were proclaimed King William II and Queen Mary II of England. As the eldest child of the deposed King, Mary II was a joint monarch with her husband. The followers of the deposed King became known as the Jacobites.

People on the Eastern Shore who were aware of the unstable conditions in England after the death of Charles II in 1685, welcomed the proclamation of the new rulers. And, Henry Pike who was punished for drinking a toast to the "Prince of Orange" must have felt heroic.

On March 22, 1688, following an Act of the General Assembly, the boundary between Northampton and Accomack counties was fixed. One commissioner from each county and an appointee of the Governor met and made the survey:

> From an oak tree on the west side of a branch out of Machipongo Creek the line was run and designated by newly unmarked trees to a white oak tree on the east side of the northward branch of Occohannock Creek. (The distance is approximately four miles.) All land, marshes and islands below the said creeks and artificial line to belong to Northampton County. And, all land,

marshes and islands above said line and to the Maryland line to belong to Accomack County. This survey was signed by John Custis II, John West and Edwin Conway.

On March 28, 1690, the Northampton County Court was held in a courthouse at The Horns. This building apparently was erected by an individual who ran a "victualling house," at his own expense rather than lose the court business. Plans were made to build a courthouse a mile south of the present Courthouse Square. The name "The Horns" is said to have been given the place because of the prongs of three bayside creeks which point toward it.

In 1691 the two parishes in Northampton County were combined. A new church to replace the one built at Fishing Point by 1689 was planned and it got under way in 1691 or 1692. A will in 1689 designated 1000 pounds of tobacco for the purchase of "The Lord's Prayer and Ten Commandments" to be set up in the new church when it was built. These were panels as tall as windows, and usually a third panel containing the Apostles' Creed went with the set. These were the only wall or window ornaments allowed in colonial churches. This was Magothy Bay Church and built of brick.

Accomack Parish was planning to build a church at Assawoman at this time if it had not already been started. This was also a brick building. A deed for land for a burial place and a church was given by William Taylor in 1680. Since no contract was found for this or Magothy Bay Church, the building of the brick churches must have been done over a period of years and partly paid for in gifts of time and private gifts of tobacco.

When the Burgesses returned from the General Assembly of March 1692, they brought the gratifying report that King William and Queen Mary were taking a friendly attitude toward Virginia and her problems. Also, they brought new defense orders.

Pirates were operating in the Eastern Shore area as well as in other Virginia waters. At least one raid had been made

CHAPTER VII — 1674-1700

on Smiths Island in which enough cattle belonging to John Custis II were slaughtered to "victual" the pirate ship. Little could be done by the militia to protect the islands but the General Assembly had ordered the militias in Northampton and Accomack counties to be on call to drive off any pirates who attempted to land on the shores of any of the creeks. A watch was to be kept at Cape Charles by members of the militia on a rotating basis. If a fleet of pirate ships was seen entering the bay, the Governor at Jamestown was to be notified. Local militiamen were to keep their arms and horses ready to report at any place which the watchmen directed. This system of coastal defense was continued until the year 1700.

John Custis II died at Arlington on the south side of Old Plantation Creek on January 29, 1696, after a successful business career and a life of public service, including membership on the Council.

John Custis II came to the Eastern Shore from Rotterdam, Holland, in 1649 or 1650. In 1650 he got a certificate for 600 acres of land. The certificate was signed by Argoll Yeardley, and when John exchanged it for a patent he used Ann Yeardley his sister as one of the headrights.

John II married Elizabeth Robinson and they had one son John Custis III, born in 1653. Elizabeth died and John II married Alicia Burdett in 1656. Apparently John went to live at the Burdett home which he purchased from Thomas Burdett some years later. In the meantime he had patented land next to it. He named this Arlington Plantation.

John II and his brother William were naturalized in November 1658 and John immediately became a member of the Northampton Court. He was high sheriff in 1665. Presumably, he enlarged the house as his wealth increased. In 1676 this house was used as a temporary capitol and place of residence for Governor Berkeley and his staff during the civil war known as Bacon's Rebellion.

Alicia Custis died between 1677 and 1680 and John II married Tabitha (Scarburgh) Brown, a woman of wealth, charm and business ability. She had one granddaughter, child of the daughter by her first husband John Smart, and this granddaughter was now married to a nephew of John Custis II. The records show that disagreements developed between John and Tabitha over her property which became his after they were married.

John Custis IV, the eldest grandson, inherited Arlington. He was in England in school and Tabitha was to remain there as long as she chose. Before John IV became of age she married Edward Hill, a former treasurer of the colony. John IV also inherited a diamond ring and a pocket watch. John Custis III, the only child of John II, was a substantial beneficiary of the will of his father.

The Eastern Shore of Virginia was as far advanced as any area of its size in the colony by the end of the seventeenth century. As descriptions of houses gleaned from inventories show, some houses large enough to be called mansions were built. Although no clue to the plan of Arlington has been found, it was large enough to serve as a temporary capitol for the Governor and his staff during Bacon's Rebellion. The house of Southy Littleton in Accomack County had ten rooms and a milk house when the inventory of his estate was taken in 1679. However, the prevailing type of house was a story and a half with two rooms on the first floor. Some of these with unbroken roof-lines, and others with dormer windows, are still in use. (The minimum length for a house in Onancock was 20 feet when the town was planned in 1680.) Tobacco and livestock were the principal money crops. There was some manufacturing. This included salt making (the first industry established on the Shore), butter, cheese, barrels, brick, lime, brewery products, leather, shoes, and hats.

The danger of raids on homes and livestock by pirates was still present and the militia maintained a constant watch at the entrance of the bay. By a relay system the militia

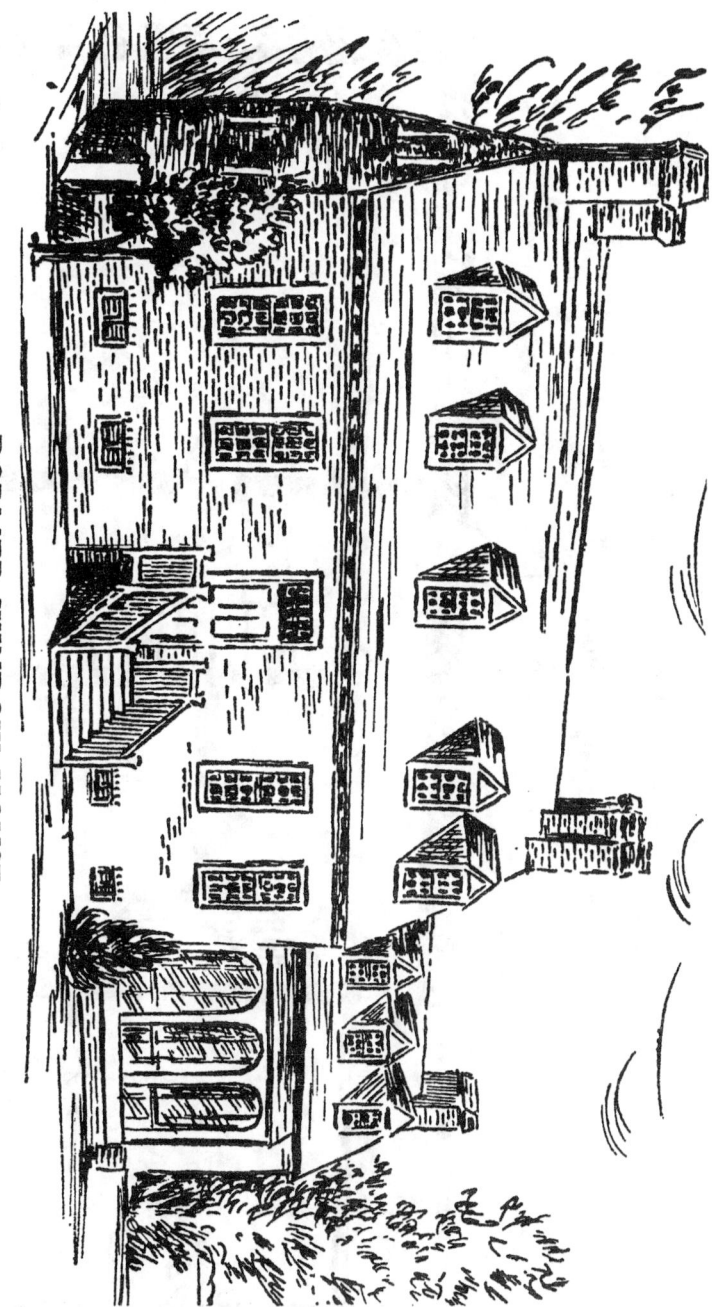

DORMER WINDOW HOUSE
Hills Farm

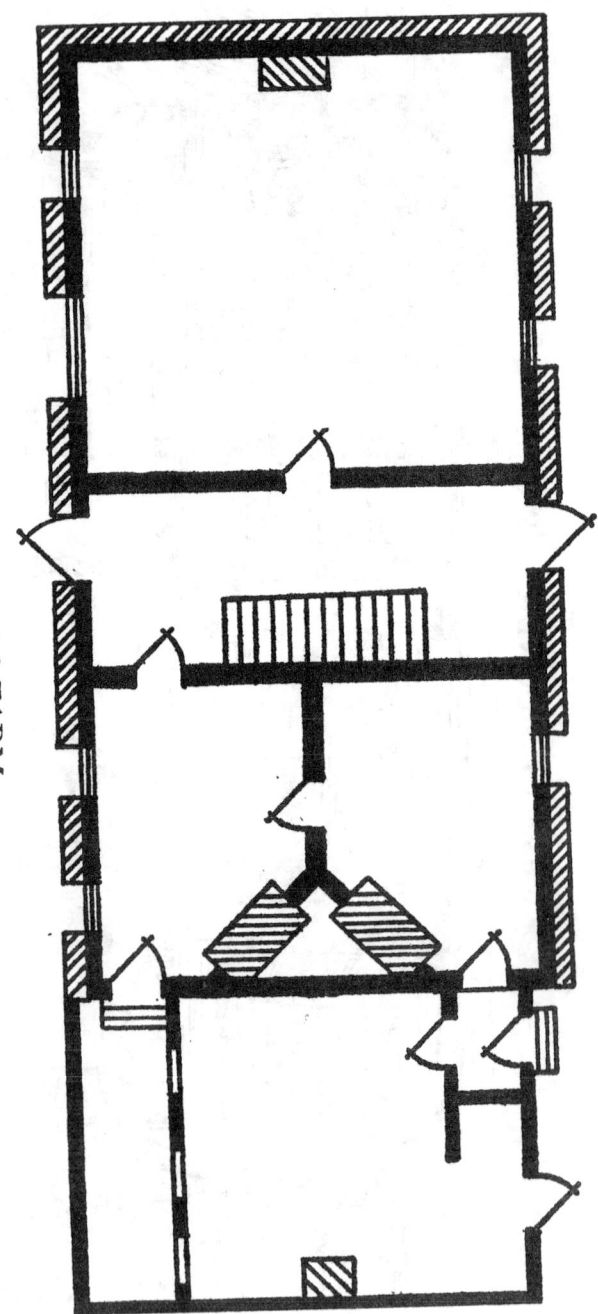

HILLS FARM

Floor Plan 72' Built 1697 and Annex

One Addition with 1942 Restoration Not Shown

CHAPTER VII — 1674-1700

could be called into action on short notice. If outside help was needed to cope with these ships manned by vicious men, the commander of the militia could notify the Governor by a system of intercounty relays in which messengers could be dispatched on a moment's notice.

The Burgesses from the Eastern Shore in 1699 helped select a new site for the capitol and plan Virginia's first incorporated city. John Custis III and Nathaniel Littleton II represented Northampton, while Thomas Parramore and Edmund Allen represented Accomack. This session of the General Assembly enacted legislation to move the capital from Jamestown to Middle Plantation near the site the Assembly of 1693 had chosen for the College of William and Mary. And, this Assembly of 1699 planned the city of Williamsburg with its broad street, almost a mile in length, between the college and the site selected for the State House. Work on the new city was started immediately. By May 10, 1700, all General Courts and Assemblies were to be held in the city of Williamsburg with the college building used as the temporary State House. Incidentally, Charles Scarburgh of Accomack County, a former Burgess, was a member of the original Board of Visitors of the college and served in that capacity while it was the temporary state house and until his death.

At the close of the century the trend on the Eastern Shore was toward more home industries to supply the needs of each household or plantation than had prevailed earlier. This was not looked upon with favor by England who wanted to sell cloth, furniture, medicine and other manufactured products to the colonists. Wool cards, spinning wheels and looms were becoming standard equipment on the larger plantations at this time.

The Shore had produced a number of distinguished men by the end of the seventeenth century. Most of them had sons or grandchildren to carry on the business and govern Accomack and Northampton counties as well as to take part in the government of the Virginia colony.

Chapter VIII

1700-1714

The year 1700 marked almost a century of progress after the fateful landing of Bartholomew Gilbert at the tip of the peninsula. The census figures released bespeak the success the English had made in settling the Eastern Shore of Virginia and organizing it into two of the twenty-five progressive counties in the colony. During this time England was ruled by James I, Charles I, Parliament, Charles II, James II, William and Mary, and Queen Anne who was crowned in 1702. Progress and some disappointments had featured each period on the Eastern Shore, but the two most important goals of private enterprise and representative government had suffered but little.

The census of 1703 showed a population of 2081 "souls" and 99,384 acres of patented land in Northampton County. This was almost 90 per cent of its total area. Accomack County had a population of 2800 and 200,923 acres of patented land, which was slightly under 80 per cent of its total area. Northampton County had 347 men in its militia of which 70 were horsemen and 277 were foot soldiers. Accomack had 101 horsemen and 355 foot soldiers, making a militia of 456 fighting men. Thus, the Eastern Shore at this time had a population of 4881 with a militia of 703 men to protect the homes and cattle against pirates. The patented land covered 300,302 acres.

The Shore had highways extending from the lower part of Northampton to the Maryland line. These highways had been surveyed and cleared by labor contributed by the landowners and tradesmen on the basis of the number of tithables of each. "Every highway was ten feet wide with all

ACCOMACK AND NORTHAMPTON COUNTIES
1700

trees and stumps removed, and all boughs overhead cut down." With minor changes to eliminate curves or to go around farms, the Bayside and Seaside roads are still in use. A middle road through the center of the Shore, surveyed by one John Wallop, and called Wallops Road, was incorporated in the present interstate highway of U. S. 13 through Accomack County. There were crossroads to public wharves, mills, churches and the courthouses.

A political maneuver by Maryland in 1703 is of interest because it laid the foundation for the eventual division of this crescent-shaped peninsula, between the Chesapeake Bay and the Atlantic Ocean and Delaware Bay, among three states. Back in 1683 Maryland surrendered some 2000 square miles of her territory to William Penn. From it three Pennsylvania counties were formed. Thus, the Shore was divided among three English colonies instead of two as it had been since Lord Baltimore got his patent in 1632. The three lower counties of Pennsylvania formed a separate province with its own legislature for the rest of the colonial period. This new province took the name Delaware and furnished the first three letters of Del-Mar-Va, now the Delmarva Peninsula. Overland trade was carried on between the Eastern Shore of Virginia and these northern neighbors.

The General Assembly of 1705 fixed rates for a public ferry from Northampton County to the mainland of Virginia as follows:

> Whereas a good regulation of ferries in this her Majestie's colony and dominion will prove very useful for the dispatch of public affairs, and for the ease and benefit of travelers and businessmen,
>
> Be it therefore enacted by this General Assembly, and it is hereby enacted that ferries shall be constantly kept at the places hereafter named, and that the rates for passing the said ferries be as follows: (More than twenty river ferries were listed and the rates designated before the Eastern Shore was mentioned.) Viz.
>
> From the Port of Northampton to the Port of York, the price for a man shall be 15 shillings. That

CHAPTER VIII — 1700-1714

for a man and a horse shall be 30 shillings. (The charge was the same to the Port of Hampton. Both were covered on the same voyage.)

Previous Acts had provided for the county courts to appoint and license ferry keepers. These courts designated the types of boats, number of crew members, accommodations on a boat and the schedule. Since the contract was included in the bond for each ferry keeper, it was not included in the court books. The name of the ferry keeper from the Port of Northampton in 1705 has not been found. This port presumably was on the north side of Kings Creek where efforts had been made in 1680 to establish a town as a port of entry for Northampton County. Apparently this contract which lasted until 1724 required one boat for men and horses and enough feed and water, food, and sleeping space for the passengers in the event the boat encountered a calm and the voyage required more than a day for the scheduled one-way passage.

Another public utility Act which was amended in 1705 was that for building new water mills. Such mills had been in use on the Shore for more than half a century. Since the branches flowing into navigable streams were dammed to raise the water level enough to get power to turn the mill stones, and such branches were often boundary lines for land, legislation was necessary for a potential mill builder to get land on both sides of the stream. If a mill was considered necessary, a man who desired to build one on his own land on one side of the creek could buy an acre on the opposite side at a price agreed upon by arbitrators if the owner hesitated to sell it. When the mill ceased to exist, this acre reverted to the original tract. The purchaser was required to give bond to start the mill within one year and finish it within three years after purchase of the land and to operate the mill as a public utility. Every customer was to have his grain ground in turn without letting one take another's place in line. The toll by weight of the grain was one-eighth part of wheat and one-sixth part of Indian corn. The mill dam was required by law to be twelve feet wide.

After a permit was issued for a mill on any branch, no mill could be erected upstream from it nor within a mile below it. In this way the water supply was protected as well as the business of the man who invested his money in a mill. A public road was maintained to each mill from the nearest highway. Grain was transported on horseback, with half of one man's supply hanging on each side of the horse behind the saddle, by ox cart, horse-drawn cart and sometimes by men carrying it on their backs. Grinding day was a social event for apprentices who were fortunate enough to be sent to the mill, as well as for small farmers and tradesmen who chose to take their own grain. Although every man put his grain in line when he arrived and moved up in turn, friends had an opportunity to gather in little groups to exchange opinions and gather news.

The fields in this level country had taken on some characteristics of rural England and laws were enacted from time to time to protect the growers of crops from the neighbor's livestock which had the range of the forest for pasturage. An Act of the General Assembly back in 1642 had defined a lawful fence and provided for a man to collect damages if a cow, hog or horse belonging to another broke it and destroyed a crop. In 1705, the law was strengthened. Three types of fences were considered legal:

A fence of split timber, called rails, laid with right-angle corners alternating toward the field and from it, was required to be five feet high and free from gaps through which any domestic animal could crawl. Another type was made of upright timber with one end buried in the ground and the part above the ground 4 feet 6 inches high. The third type was a ditch which served for drainage purposes and land boundaries as well as protection from livestock. Such a ditch was 3 feet wide and 3 feet deep with a hedge or fence 2 feet 6 inches high on one side. For this type of fence to be legal protection, the owner was required to keep the ditch cleaned out and the fence in repair if there was one in the place of a hedge. Some of the ditch fences of 1705 or earlier are presumably still in use.

CHAPTER VIII — 1700-1714

When an animal broke the fence and destroyed a crop, the owner reported the incident to the constable who appointed two reliable men to examine the fence to see if it met legal requirements and to estimate the damage. The owner of the animal was required to pay the damages. Horses were no longer allowed to range in the forests, so any damage by a horse was at the owner's expense. Wild horses had been considered a menace and a man who caught a horse older than two years was allowed to keep it under certain conditions. This resulted in extensive horse hunting by people with time to spare, and a law was passed making "horse hunting" illegal on the Sabbath. Livestock was rounded up once a year on set days for marking the young calves, pigs, sheep and goats. Since the markings were recorded in the court records it was easy for one whose crop had been damaged to identify the owner of the culprits.

In 1705 the law for the election of Burgesses was revised and strengthened. Each county was to have two Burgesses and the sheriff continued to be manager of the elections as he had been since the original counties were formed in 1634. The new regulations were:

Writs were to be signed and the seal of the Colony affixed by the Governor or Commander in Chief of Virginia 40 days before the assembly convened. Within 10 days the secretary of the colony sent them to the sheriffs in the respective counties. The sheriff signed each copy and added the time and place appointed for the election. Elections had to be held at the customary meeting place of the court at this time.

Within three days after receipt of the orders the sheriff delivered a signed and amended copy to every minister or reader with orders to publish it after divine services in the church or chapel every Sabbath until the day set for the election and then endorse it and return it to the sheriff.

If competition among the candidates nominated was close and could be determined "upon the view," presumably by a show of hands, the votes were taken in writing.

Books were provided in the court room in which the names of the candidates were written. The sheriff gave the designated oath to the recorders and to each voter, in turn, to see that only free men voted. The voter then named his choice for two burgesses and his name was written on their pages. When voting ceased the sheriff proclaimed the fact that all free men could vote. If no other voter came after he issued the proclamation three times, he declared the polls closed. If there was a tie between the two candidates with the highest number of votes, the sheriff voted as tie breaker. Then the sheriff proclaimed the results of the election at the courthouse door.

The oath of the voters was: You shall swear that you are a freeholder of the County of_____ and that you have not been before polled at this election.

Penalties were designated for default of duty by anyone concerned with the election. That for the secretary was 40 pounds sterling. Other officers and voters were subject to fines in tobacco. Disabled voters were exempt, but all others were fined 200 pounds of tobacco for not voting. The penalty of the sheriff for failing to carry out his orders was 2000 pounds of tobacco and that of the ministers or readers was 1000 pounds. Any apprentice or nonresident of the county who voted was fined 500 pounds of tobacco.

The Northampton elections were held in the vicinity of the present town of Eastville, then called the Horns. The Accomack elections were held at the site of the present Accomac, then called "Metompkin," in a building erected by an individual when the court was moved from Pungoteague in 1678. Tavern keepers were willing to provide a meeting place for the court in order to get the patronage of those who attended. Joseph Godwin was the court tavern keeper in Northampton and John Cole in Accomack.

The General Assembly of 1710 fixed court days for

CHAPTER VIII — 1700-1714

all counties. Northampton was on the third Tuesday in each month and Accomack was on the first Tuesday. Four justices were the minimum for a session which was to continue until all cases were heard. Both counties were considering better quarters for their courts. In fact, Accomack had one under construction. It was 40 feet long and 20 feet wide on a brick foundation and a loft with a stairway for the use of the jury. It was finished and accepted later this year and remained in use for court, elections and other purposes for almost half a century. The new courthouse in Northampton was 30 feet by 20 feet with a loft covered with planed lumber for the jury. It was first used in June 1716 and served for about fifteen years.

For almost ten years the courthouse of Accomack County was also used for divine services. A court order in 1713 was "to clear the road from the eastern side of Deep Creek to this courthouse and place of hearing of sermons."

Deep Creek probably had something to do with the location of the Accomack Court at its present site back in 1678. The head of its navigation was only five miles from Metompkin Creek on the seaside and people could come from long distances by water to these creeks and go over land, sometimes by foot, to the county seat. The nearness to Metompkin Creek carried considerable weight in keeping the courthouse at its present site.

At the beginning of the year 1714 leaders on the Eastern Shore, as well as the rest of Virginia, were anticipating a change of the head of the English government. Queen Anne had borne seventeen children before she was crowned in 1702 and not one of them lived to be grown. She died on August 1, 1714, and was succeeded by George I, a grandson of Princess Elizabeth for whom a river and a county in Virginia had been named. The news of a peaceful transfer of the head of the government reached the Eastern Shore in the early autumn. There was no immediate effect on the people here or in the rest of the colony, but the new King's policy toward more taxes from the colonies for the English treasury was evident before the decade ended.

The Eastern Shore had the first licensed minister outside of the Anglican church in Virginia. This was Francis Makemie, Presbyterian minister, mill owner, planter and merchant with his own ship. His will, which was probated in Accomack County in 1708, gives some idea of his success as a businessman. His place in the history of the Presbyterian Church of America shows the importance of this Eastern Shore citizen and justifies a brief sketch of his life.

Francis Makemie was born in Ireland in 1658. He was educated in Glasgow, Scotland, and received his license as a Presbyterian minister in 1681. He came to the Eastern Shore of Maryland in 1683 and married Naomi, daughter of William Anderson, a wealthy planter on a creek across the Pocomoke River in Virginia. They lived for awhile in Onancock in the house which his father-in-law built before he secured the first deed on record in the new town in 1682. Francis Makemie served in a Presbyterian church in Maryland and organized at least one new congregation there. He made a number of voyages to Barbados for preaching and mercantile purposes.

Francis and Naomi Makemie had two daughters, Elizabeth and Anne. William Anderson died in 1698, leaving his homeplace of 950 acres near Pocomoke River to Francis and Naomi. He had previously given land below Onancock to them and they inherited the house in Onancock at this time. In 1699 Makemie patented a tract of 850 acres of land, most of which was marsh land or islands near the mouth of Messongo Creek, presumably for raising cattle. In 1701 he bought land on Assawoman Branch near the present village of Temperanceville and erected a mill, which he operated the rest of his life.

While Makemie was accumulating property and rearing a family, he was not neglecting his ministerial duties. He led a movement to get the General Assembly to accept the Toleration Act passed by Parliament and

CHAPTER VIII — 1700-1714

signed by King William and Queen Mary in 1689. This provided for the licensing of ministers other than those ordained in the Anglican church provided they did not represent a sect with political motives or rules that forbade members from being in the militia. This Act was passed by the Virginia General Assembly in 1699 and Makemie immediately got a license to preach in his house in Onancock and the one on Holden Creek where his father-in-law had lived.

In January 1706 Francis Makemie met with the other Presbyterian ministers of North America in Philadelphia. The meeting is said to have been arranged by Makemie and it goes down in history as the beginning of organized Presbyterianism in America.

In his lengthy will, Makemie left his estate to his daughters. Elizabeth died later in 1708 and Anne became the sole heir. Almost twenty years later she and her first husband, Thomas Blair, sold the mill which was operated by successive owners under their names into the twentieth century.

As a licensed minister, Makemie received notices for the election of Burgesses from the sheriff and was required to announce them after divine services. People who attended his services were exempt from attending those of the Anglican Church. However, Makemie and his members were required to pay taxes for the support of the regular church and the poor in the parish. Mill owners had certain tax exemptions and this might have been one incentive for him to build the mill.

When the report was sent to the Bishop of London in 1705 Accomack and Northampton counties were without Anglican ministers. Northampton (Hungars Parish) probably had part-time services by a minister from across the bay. Accomack Parish had the services of a minister from Maryland on some week days every other month. Accomack Parish bought a glebe farm of 250 acres in 1704 and there was a house on it at the time, or one was built immediately. Services were being held by readers at Pungoteague Church, the Courthouse and at Assawoman Church. Northampton had services at the second Hungars Church and at Magothy Bay Church. It, too, had a glebe farm. In 1709 the Reverend William Black, from the part of southern Pennsylvania which became the state of Delaware, became minister in Accomack Parish and remained the rest of his life, which was almost thirty years.

In the year 1710 the upper part of Accomack County received a large bequest for the education of poor children. Samuel Sandford, a London merchant and Virginia farmer, who had served in the General Assembly and was sheriff in Accomack County for the year 1693, left 3400 acres of land with buildings and livestock to provide revenue for the education of poor children between Guilford Creek and a line to the Atlantic Ocean and the Virginia-Maryland line.

The will was written and probated in London in April 1710 and a copy was recorded in the Accomack County Court Records in January 1711. The vestrymen of Accomack Parish were designated as trustees, and the land was to be divided into tracts suitable for leasing to good advantage. No lease was to be for more than a period of seven years. In the same paragraph of this will Samuel Sandford left a trust fund of 200 pounds sterling for the education of poor boys in his native parish of Avening in Gloucester County, England. He gave instructions for the use of the interest on that fund as follows:

> I give for the learning of six poor male children, whose parents are esteemed incapable of giving them learning the interest on said 200 pounds sterling. The children are to be put to learn when past five years of age, and when one has learned to read his primer and say his catechism without a book, he is to have a brown colored cloth coat with buttons of horn, one pair of shoes, one pair of stockings and a hat. Fourteen shillings are to be spent for these items for each child. No child is to be kept learning with this fund for more than two years but the number of boys to be kept learning is to

CHAPTER VIII — 1700-1714

always be kept at six.

Although no record has been found of the subjects taught in Accomack County by the schoolmaster paid from income from the Sandford land, it is safe to assume that it was used to teach the children how to "read, write and cipher." Boys had the preference for free schooling.

A school was being operated with the Sandford funds in 1724, and John Morough, an Irishman, was the schoolmaster when the Reverend William Black made his report to the Bishop of London. Since the area designated by Samuel Sandford as Upper Accomack County, covered an area of some 200 square miles, only a boarding school or an itinerant teacher who spent a few weeks in each neighborhood would have been practical. For more than 160 years the Sandford or "Free School" land remained free from taxes and the income was used as designated by the donor. More than half of the "Free School" land was "sea meadow" or marsh land, now in the Saxis Marsh Wildlife Refuge.

The year 1714 was the one hundredth anniversary of the first English settlement on the Eastern Shore of Virginia and Accomack and Northampton were as prosperous as any counties in Virginia.

Chapter IX

1714 - 1752

March 25 was New Year's Day on the Eastern Shore in 1715 as it was in England and all of her colonies. The tax reports submitted to the Governor and Council in 1714 give some idea of the importance of the Eastern Shore as a part of the Virginia colony. Nothing had been recorded about making the Eastern Shore of Virginia a separate nation for at least twenty-five years.

The report made in 1714 showed that Accomack and Northampton counties had 334,302 acres of patented land. Of this 230,462 were in Accomack and 103,840 were in Northampton. The number of people on whom taxes were paid was 1886. In general this represented one-third of the population which is calculated at 5658 men, women and children. Of these Accomack had 1055 tithables and Northampton had 831. The small difference in the population in contrast to the much larger acreage in Accomack may be explained by the fact that much of the upper part of Accomack County was in large patents, with a high proportion of the islands and marsh lands being used for cattle, sheep and horse raising.

The vast areas in the ocean islands of Assateague, Chincoteague, Wallops and smaller islands had been patented more than three decades earlier. In order to hold his patent, the owner was required to keep only four men on it and pay the King's rent. This small number of men could tend a large herd of livestock where no fences were required.

Where two or three men owned a whole island, they prorated the breeding stock put on the island, then prorated the increase. In this manner there was no need for a spring roundup to mark the young while they were with their mothers as was the case on the mainland. The men employed to serve as livestock rangers presumably did some slaughtering and curing of meat and prepared the hides for market. Such products required inspection at one of the ports on the mainland before they could be shipped out of the colony.

The General Assembly had enacted rigid inspection laws and authorized each county to appoint as many meat packers as necessary. These men were sworn in with a prescribed oath and they watched the packing of every hogshead. Each man had a seal for labeling the hogshead after it was closed. This label designated the type of meat it contained and the contents. Each hogshead had to contain at least 220 pounds of pork or beef. In case of pork the label stated whether it was from large or small hogs. The penalty for a packer, who was actually an inspector, to let defective meat go into a hogshead for shipping was 5 pounds sterling. The packer received 6 pence for each hogshead upon which he placed his seal.

Skins of wild animals were a good source of revenue. The cattle rangers were allowed to do some trapping and share in the profits from their catch. Later in this century an export duty was collected on hides and skins to help support the College of William and Mary. The hides were rawhides, tanned hides (cow), dressed and undressed buck skins, and dressed and undressed doe skins.

The fur-bearing animals from which skins were marketed were otter, beaver, mink, fox, raccoon, wildcat and muskrat. The duties on the otter and beaver skins were the highest, while that on the muskrat was the lowest. Skins were shipped in hogsheads and each shipper was required to take an oath before a justice regarding the contents of each hogshead and to put his name and the contents on it. There was a heavy penalty for a false statement.

Each port from which boats entered and departed had a collector of customs and the ship master was responsible for seeing that nothing was put aboard his ship without the proper inspection labels. A certificate from the collector of customs was required before a ship could leave port.

Among the islands that were being used for livestock ranges at this time were the Russell Islands group in Chesapeake Bay which appeared on Captain John Smith's Map of 1608. They were patented and given individual names as early as 1670. However, the name Tangier did not appear until 1713. It remained under the ownership of two families and was used as a cattle range until after the Revolution. Chincoteague, Assateague and Wallops islands on the seaside also had been used for livestock ranges from the late 1600's. Since no mention of shipping from these islands is in the records, it is assumed that all products were delivered to the owners on the mainland for packing and shipping.

In the spring of 1722 the Eastern Shore ports, as well as those in the rest of the colony, required a new kind of inspection and protection. There had been an outbreak of the "plague" in several cities in Europe, and precautions were taken on orders from the Governor to prevent its spread into Virginia. Members of the militia were called out to see that the orders were obeyed when a ship arrived from an infected city. They were:

> Nobody was to land from the ship, no goods were to be transferred to other boats, and nobody was to go aboard without a permit from the master of the port. After the period of quarantine was over all goods were to be aired under the supervision of a designated person. The penalty for breaking any one of these rules was 20 pounds sterling.

Although large ships could not enter the Eastern Shore creeks many small ones came, but happily no plague reached Virginia during this outbreak in Europe.

Since the militia numbered more than 800 back in 1703, it must have been considerably larger by the 1720's. Virginia had no standing army as such but every able-bodied man was a trained soldier and the General Assembly had a pay scale for men on duty. There was no remuneration for drilling. A man had to be on duty more than two days at a time to be eligible for any pay. Watches were being main-

CHAPTER IX — 1714-1752

tained at the entrances to Chesapeake Bay. Piracy was still a dreaded menace and England was constantly on the verge of war with some European nation, and the first blow might be struck at Virginia, her wealthiest Crown Colony. The Eastern Shore was the most vulnerable part of the colony. The two branches of the militia were "the horse" and "foot soldiers." The daily pay was slightly higher for the "horse soldiers" as the following rates show in pounds of tobacco:

Horse		Foot Soldiers	
Colonel	60 lbs.	Colonel	60 lbs.
Lt. Colonel	50 lbs.	Major	50 lbs.
Major	50 lbs.	Lieutenant	30 lbs.
Lieutenant	30 lbs.	Corporal	22 lbs.
Corporal	25 lbs.	Quartermaster	25 lbs.
Quartermaster	25 lbs.	Sergeant	18 lbs.
Trumpeter	22 lbs.	Drummer	18 lbs.
Trooper	20 lbs.	Soldier	15 lbs.

Each county had these officers who were under the county lieutenant commissioned by the Governor.

A ferry had been making two round trips a week, weather permitting, from the Port of Northampton to York and Hampton since 1705, but the accommodations were such that officers of the militia, Burgesses and other officials who had business in the capital city of Williamsburg, went in private boats. The Port of York was the debarkation point for passengers, horses, freight and official mail consigned to Williamsburg.

On September 14, 1724, one John Masters gave bond for operating ferries from the Eastern Shore to the ports of York and Hampton. The terms of his contract were written and filed with his bond for 20 pounds sterling in Northampton County where it still is on file. George Harmanson, son-in-law of Argoll Yeardley II, signed the bond. The port was moved to Mattawoman Creek, the main prong of Hungars, where Harmanson had kept a public warehouse for storing tobacco for some ten years. The terms of the contract were:

To keep a ferry from Hungars Creek in Northampton County to the ports of York and Hampton on the Western Shore of Virginia, and to provide one good and sufficient boat to transport foot passengers and another for men and horses. He is to give speedy passage to all express which shall be sent from either port for the next seven years.

John Masters could have been the operator of the original ferry and Harmanson merely got the port moved to Hungars. The contract for 1705 has not survived. Masters was not found among the land owners on the Eastern Shore and he left no property in Northampton.

On March 12, 1731, Elias Roberts and Michael Christian gave bond for operating the ferry from Hungars to York and Hampton. George Harmanson sold an acre of land for a public wharf and warehouse, presumably the land which was already in use for that purpose. Michael Christian married a niece of George Harmanson's wife and a granddaughter of Argoll Yeardley II. This public wharf was in the present Old Town Neck and it remained in use until the twentieth century. The ferry terminal was destined to make two more changes. The bond for Elias Roberts covered the same contract as that of Masters.

By an Act of the General Assembly in 1745 the government at Williamsburg resumed the right to grant the franchise for the ferry across Chesapeake Bay. Littleton Eyre, who married a great-granddaughter of Argoll Yeardley II and inherited land in Old Town Neck, got the franchise. The following session of the General Assembly fixed the charges for ferry service across the bay:

    For a man or horse, passing singly, 20 shillings

    For a man and horse, or if there be more, for each 15 shillings

    For a coach, chariot or wagon and the driver the same as for six horses (4 pounds 10 shillings)

    For every cart or four-wheel chaise and the driver, the same as for four horses (3 pounds)

    For every two-wheel chaise, or chair, as for two horses (2 pounds)

CHAPTER IX — 1714-1752

For every hogshead of tobacco as for one horse (20 shillings)

For every head of cattle as for one horse (20 shillings)

For every sheep, goat or lamb, one fifth part of the ferriage for one horse (4 shillings)

For every hog, one fourth part of the ferriage of a horse (5 shillings)

As public wharves, or ports, increased in number, legislation was enacted by the General Assembly to protect the channels leading to them. Sailing vessels brought in quantities of sand, gravel and stone as ballast. This was material with considerable weight to balance the vessel when the cargo was not heavy enough to do it. When a vessel entered a port with a light load and took on a heavy load, the ballast had to be emptied. In order to keep this from being dumped into the water near the wharf, each county court was ordered to appoint overseers. The law enacted is as follows:

> Since casting stones, gravel, sand or other ballast into rivers or creeks must prove dangerous and destructive to navigation, the court of every county adjacent to any navigable stream shall immediately appoint one or more persons, residing conveniently to places where ships ride, to be overseers and directors of the delivering and bringing on shore all ballast to be unloaded. The shipmaster is to notify the overseer when he has ballast to bring ashore and the overseer is to direct the placing of the ballast where it will not be washed into the stream.
>
> The shipmaster is to pay the overseer of the unloading of ballast 5 shillings. The penalty for unloading ballast other than in the presence of the overseer shall be 50 pounds sterling.

When a shipmaster could utilize the space with building materials including limestone, chalk, bricks and stones cut for building purposes, he not only got the freight charges on it but also saved the overseer's fee. The overseers were sworn in by one of the justices and were under oath to answer the call of a shipmaster as soon as he conveniently could after receiving the call. The collector of customs at the port sometimes served as ballast overseer also.

The Shore ports for which ballast overseers were appointed at this time were on Pocomoke River (Pitts Wharf), Messongo Creek, Guilford Creek, Hunting Creek, Deep Creek, Chesconnessex Creek, Onancock Creek, Pungoteague Creek, Nandua Creek, Craddock Creek and Occohannock Creek on the bayside and Machipongo, Wachapreague, Metompkin (Folly) and Chincoteague (Mosquito) creeks on the seaside in Accomack County. Those on the bayside in Northampton were Occohannock, Hungars, Mattawoman, Cherrystone and Old Plantation creeks. Those from Cape Charles northward on the seaside in Northampton were Hawleys Creek and Machipongo Creek.

This list of ports gives some idea of the extent of trade by sailing vessels in the second quarter of the eighteenth century. However, only small craft could enter most of these ports and they rendered shuttle service from the larger ports.

King George I died on June 11, 1727, and was succeeded by his son who was crowned as George II. The news was proclaimed in Virginia and prayers were offered at all Divine services for the new King as they had been for his predecessor. George II was 44 years of age while his father had been 54 when he became king.

The General Assembly of 1732 provided for the licensing of attorneys. Physicians and surveyors had been licensed for some years. The procedure for an attorney to get a license was as follows:

> A petition setting forth the qualifications of the applicant was submitted to the Governor and Council. They referred the application to a person, or persons, learned in the law. If the qualifications were considered acceptable, the Governor and Council issued the license. Then the attorney took the oath prescribed by law before the court where he lived. After November 10, 1732, no attorney was to practice without a license and the penalty was 5 pounds sterling for each case in which he appeared. In 1748 the law was amended to require an

CHAPTER IX — 1714-1752

applicant to be examined and recommended by the justices of the county in which he resided before submitting his application to the Governor and Council.

By the time the Act for the licensing of attorneys was passed, Northampton Court was meeting in its first brick courthouse. The contract had been awarded to John Marshall on February 9, 1731, two months after the justices instructed the sheriff to give public notice to prospective builders in both Northampton and Accomack counties. Several bidders appeared on February 9 and Marshall, "being the fairest proposer for the undertaking of the building of a brick courthouse in Northampton at a charge of 50,000 pounds of tobacco," was awarded the contract and ordered to give bond in the sum of 100,000 pounds of tobacco. He was to finish the work by the last day of December 1751. This is the building known as the Old Courthouse - Restored. (It was torn down and rebuilt on its present site after being used as a store when another brick courthouse superseded it.)

The first brick clerk's office was built near the brick courthouse after the courthouse was finished in 1751 and is now used as a museum. A brick prison, later known as the Debtors Prison, was built at an unknown date and it is still standing.

In 1722 Accomack County built a frame church near the present Accomack Wayside Park and called it the Middle Church of Accomack Parish. Divine services had been held in the courthouse for the middle part of the parish since the church in Onancock went out of use before 1708.

An entry in the court records on October 3, 1738, shows that taxes were being collected to pay for a new church at Pungoteague, and the sum indicates that the church was of brick. A floor plan made in 1959, after extensive excavation, shows that the building was shaped somewhat like a Greek Cross with a semicircular apse at the east. The dimensions were 65 feet 3 inches east and west and 57 feet 4 inches north and south. The latter is the surviving part of the church. Tradition says the original building was irreverently called "the ace of clubs church" because of its unusual shape.

HUNGARS CHURCH
1742

CHAPTER IX — 1714-1725

In 1742 Northampton County built the second brick church in Hungars Parish, which then covered the entire county. This new brick building replaced the second Hungars Church which was started in 1679 and finished by July 1681. It is still in use although it has had slight alterations. The original building was 45 feet by 95 feet, with one large door at the west end and doors near the centers of the north and south walls. More than a hundred years after this charming edifice was built it needed considerable repairs, and it is said to have had a narrow escape from being torn down and replaced. However, a skilled workman saw a way to repair it. The west end was removed and the building was shortened by about 15 feet. The side doors were replaced with the windows. The brick work is in the Flemish bond pattern and the mason who did the repair work was as skilled as the original builder. Hungars and three other churches on the Eastern Shore had communion silver which is still in use.

Prosperity on the Eastern Shore was recorded for posterity in the lives of sons who were sent to the College of William and Mary and by imposing homes that were built or increased in size and architectural features. The story-and-a-half house with a cross hall and dormer windows was still fashionable. But in the 1730's this type of house inspired more spacious rooms on the second floor and the gambrel roof appeared. Dormers were visible from the outside but were surrounded by shingles between slanting sides joining the roof. In that manner the gable end had seven segments instead of the traditional five of the high-pitched roof of earlier times.

The story-and-a-half house was increased in size by the addition of a colonnade one story high and a kitchen end of a story and loft. This was known as the twin house. The one room and loft type of house was made into a twin house by the addition of a colonnade and another section. Sometimes this was a story and a half and had dormer windows. The traditional two-room-and-loft house continued to be popular with people of limited means. Those who inherited the quaint little houses usually added dormers and a colonnade and kitchen section. Surviving houses of each type and inventories of the estates of owners show that people on the Eastern Shore had the same comforts and luxuries for gracious living as the people in Williamsburg and Yorktown. The house at Arlington had been destroyed by fire before John Custis IV died at Six-Chimney House in Williamsburg, and was buried on the Eastern Shore. Daniel Parke Custis, who had married Martha Dandidge earlier that year, inherited Arlington. The life story of John IV is a part of Eastern Shore history and the inscription he wrote for his tomb is an oddity.

    John IV, the eldest son of John III and Margaret Michael, was born in 1678 and received his grammar school education, along with his brothers and sisters, under private tutors at the home of their father. Then his grandfather sent John IV to a school in England. Although John III was one of the most prominent men on the Eastern Shore during his lifetime and held all the elective offices that existed at one time or another, he did not attempt to send nine children away to school. John IV went to Arlington to live when he reached the legal age of twenty-one years and engaged in tobacco growing and trading.

    After the only seven happy years of his life, as his tombstone indicates, he married Frances Parke who was regarded as a beautiful lady and supposed to be wealthy. (John IV became the brother-in-law of William Byrd II, who was married to Lucy Parke.) John IV and Frances had two children who died and were buried at Arlington. Two other children, Frances and Daniel Parke, lived to be grown but Frances predeceased her father and left no children.

    When John IV's father-in-law died, it was learned that his estate was a liability rather than an asset. William Byrd, John IV and even his son Daniel Parke spent the rest of their lives clearing the debts. If John IV and his wife were ever congenial, this financial strain ended their happiness together and blotted out John's memory of it. They moved to Williamsburg some time before

CHAPTER IX — 1714-1725

Frances died on March 14, 1715.

John IV finished rearing his children at Six Chimney House in Williamsburg. After his daughter married and Daniel went to live at his Pamunkey River Plantation, he lived alone and managed his home with a group of loyal servants. He became a member of the Governor's Council in 1733 and served in that capacity until the last few weeks of his life.

He was a plant scientist and imported many plants and shrubs from England. The letters which he and Peter Collison of London wrote each other while they were exchanging plants have survived and they furnish valuable botanical information of the time. Although this exchange of plants took place long after John IV left the Eastern Shore, presumably some of the plants he imported were propagated and eventually found their way to the Shore. Scotch broom was one plant that received careful attention in his correspondence.

At least one love letter written to Frances Parke the year before their marriage, shows that John Custis IV was a romantic dreamer and finding himself married to a human being, rather than one who approached the status of an angel in his imagination, was probably enough of a shock to inspire the pathetic inscription that was put on his marble tomb at his positive order. The seven years at Arlington were before his marriage. He lived as a widower thirty-four years at Six Chimney House in Williamsburg.

In his will written in Williamsburg on November 14, 1749, he ordered his executors to pay 100 pounds sterling for a handsome tombstone of the most durable marble, engraved with his coat of arms and the following inscription:

Under this Marble Tomb lies the Body
of the Honorable John Custis Esqr.
of the City of Williamsburg, and Parish of Bruton.
Formerly of Hungars Parish on the Eastern Shore of
Virginia and County of Northampton the
Place of His Nativity.
Aged 71 Years and Yet liv'd but Seven Years

which was the space of time He kept
a Bachelors house at Arlington
on the Eastern Shore of Virginia.

Neither Daniel Parke Custis nor his descendants ever lived at Arlington but the plantation remained in the family for a quarter of a century after Daniel's grandson built the mansion now called the Custis-Lee Mansion, at Arlington on the Potomac River. The Custis cemetery is owned by the Association for the Preservation of Virginia Antiquities.

In the autumn of 1751 a communication from Williamsburg stated that an Act of Parliament had provided for a change in the calendar after the last day of December 1751. For almost two centuries other European countries and their colonies had been using the Gregorian (New Style Calendar) and the Act of Parliament had adopted it for England and her colonies. The year 1752 would begin on January 1 instead of March 25, which was New Year's Day by the Old Style Calendar. Thus there would be no court records on the Eastern Shore for January 1 through March 24, 1751.

Moving New Year's Day to January 1 was not the only change necessary to bring the English calendar in line with those in the rest of Europe. Easter and other church festivals were eleven days later than those on the Continent. When Parliament enacted the law for the calendar it designated a time for dropping the eleven days when there was neither a Holy Day nor a church festival on the church calendar. This was between September 2 and September 14.

When new calendars arrived from England there was a mild protest about the change by some people. January 1 was New Year's Day and March 25 was a Holy Day. September 2 was followed by September 14. People whose birthdays came between January 1 and March 24 had to move them up eleven days and add a year in order to make them authentic by the New Style calendar. A person born on February 11, 1750, would be officially recorded as if he were born on February 22, 1751. However, to keep the records clear, both dates were retained for those born between January 1 and March 24, 1750, and 1752. No boy was deprived of his inheritance when he reached the legal age because of the loss of ninety-four days in 1751 and 1752.

Chapter X

1752-1790

When the Burgesses were elected for the General Assembly of 1752, business was good and life was as near stable as it had ever been on the Eastern Shore. The watch at the entrance to Chesapeake Bay had been maintained by militiamen for such a long time that it was accepted as a part of the routine rather than as a symbol of danger from enemy ships. Littleton Eyre, ferry owner, and a Burgess since 1745, was reelected and Matthew Harmanson was his colleague from Northampton. Ralph Justice and George Douglas represented Accomack County. These Burgesses served until 1755 and drastic changes which affected the Shore and the colony took place while they were in office.

In the spring of 1754 the General Assembly enacted a tax law to pay militiamen to join an army to drive the French from Virginia's western frontier then called the Ohio Country. The French soldiers from Canada had built some forts below the Great Lakes and their commander had disregarded an appeal from the Governor of Virginia to withdraw. A corporation known as the Ohio Company had been formed in 1749 to develop this country and presumably some Eastern Shore businessmen had bought stock in the company. It was a colony-wide corporation.

The Colonial army which attempted to drive the French away in 1754 did not succeed in its mission. Then in the spring of 1755 a British army of 1000 men was sent to fight with the Colonial troops. This help would have been welcome if the British had not been put in complete charge of the campaign. Every Colonial officer above the rank of captain was demoted to that of a captain. Some officers, including

BIG HOUSE, LITTLE HOUSE AND KITCHEN
Drummonds Mill Farm

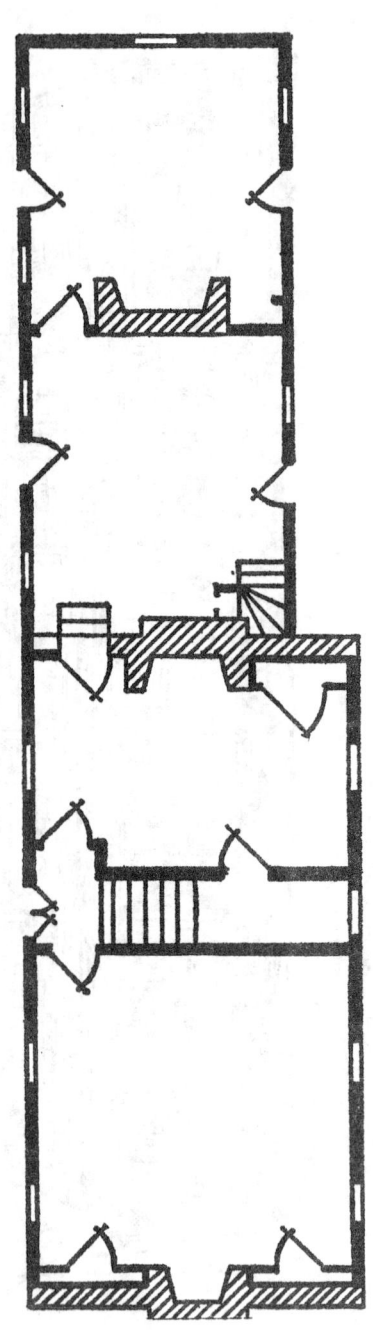

DRUMMONDS MILL FARM

Floor Plan   Length 77'   1753-1800

Partitions Added in 1957 Restoration   Brick End

George Washington, who had led the 1754 campaign, resigned their commissions. General Edward Braddock who was in charge of the British troops engaged Washington as a member of his staff in order that he might have the benefit of his experience in frontier fighting. When the campaign failed and General Braddock was killed, Washington led the soldiers in the retreat. At least three commissioned officers and an undetermined number of soldiers from the Eastern Shore fought on the frontier at this time.

When the General Assembly met in August 1755, the frontier war was a Colonial war. All the colonies had been asked to send men and to help finance it. On August 5 a draft law was passed by the General Assembly. Every county was assigned a quota of men, and county courts were given the power to draft members of the militia if there were not enough volunteers to fill the quota. This frontier war in which colonial troops were drafted went down in history as the French and Indian War. By the end of the second year it was almost a global war and the Eastern Shore was in a vulnerable position.

England and France had been on unfriendly terms for some time and England declared war against France on May 17, 1756. In English history it is known as the Seven Years' War, but Virginia had nine years of it. The French were driven out of the Ohio country and eventually out of Canada. While England was fighting for supremacy on the North American continent, the ports on the Eastern Shore were guarded against enemy landings. So many men were on guard duty or in the army of occupation on the frontier that production of tobacco was reduced and trade in general was curtailed. Although economic conditions grew worse as the nine years of war progressed, the people of the Shore developed initiative and skills which made them more and more independent of England.

On January 6, 1759, the people of the Eastern Shore became interested in George Washington for reasons other than as the hero of the early years of the French and Indian War. He became the step-father of the potential owner of

Arlington Plantation. Daniel Parke Custis had died on July 8, 1757, leaving a son, John Parke Custis, born late in 1754 and a daughter Martha born in 1756. Martha Dandridge Custis married George Washington while he was a member of the House of Burgesses. John Parke Custis and his sister went to live at Mount Vernon.

When the General Assembly met in November 1762, the Seven Years' War between England and France was pointing toward a victory for England and the fighting was practically over in North America. Although the mouths of navigable creeks on the Eastern Shore were still guarded, and some Shore militiamen were on duty in the string of forts which had been built to protect the western frontier, civilian life was back to a nearer normal state than it had been since the fighting began in the West in 1754.

The making of cloth and other necessities on the various plantations had increased during the time when trade with England was hampered by enemy ships on the high seas and crops had been reduced because of militiamen on active duty. Traveling weavers, tailors and shoemakers went from place to place to make the necessary items to supply the family and servants for a season. Virginia-made linen sheets and pillow cases were found in increasing numbers in inventories, and weaving equipment was becoming a necessity on plantations. While the people were getting to be more self-reliant, the leaders of Accomack County were considering some changes in order to make it easier for people to get to church. So, a petition was presented to the General Assembly for the creation of a new parish with the following results:

> It was enacted by the General Assembly of November 1762 that from January 3, 1763, the Parish of Accomack shall be divided into two distinct parishes by a line to begin at the mouth of Parkers Creek (on the seaside), then to run up the said creek to the head of Rooty Branch, and from thence by a direct line to be run to the head of the branch called Drummonds Mill Branch, and thence down the said branch to the

mouth of Hunting Creek (on the bayside). All that part north of the said bounds shall be a distinct parish and retain the name Accomack. All the part below the said bounds shall be another distinct parish and known by the name of St. George.

All freeholders in the two said parishes shall meet on February 5, 1763, for the choosing of vestrymen. The sheriff is to notify the said freeholders of the time and place of each meeting by January 5.

The glebe land of Accomack Parish is to be sold by the vestry of the new Accomack Parish to the individual or individuals who will pay the best price for it. The money is to be divided according to the number of tithables in Accomack and St. George parishes and applied toward the purchase of glebes for the respective parishes for the use and benefit of the ministers forever.

St. George Parish bought a glebe farm of 349 acres on Occohannock Creek and built a house. This parish also bought a four-acre tract of land a mile south of the courthouse and erected a brick church with a floor plan 86 feet in length and 40 feet in width. Although no further information has been found about the building, it seems logical to assume that it resembled Hungars Church. Upon its completion in 1767, it was called the New Church in St. George Parish. Some thirty years later it took the name St. James. The vestry planned a work house for the indigent, but the church was relieved of the duties of caring for the poor before the house was built. There was no town around the courthouse when St. George Parish was formed and the site chosen was near the road from the seaside to the bayside at its junction with the Middle Road.

Although Accomack Parish got the frame building known as the Middle Church, it was too near the parish line for the convenience of the people. It was replaced with another frame building, some two miles north of the present Accomack Wayside Park, and was called the Lower Church in Accomack Parish. Another frame building was erected on the Middle Road near the Maryland line. It was called New Church and the village that was built up around it perpetuates the name. The brick church at Assawoman was the principal church in the parish. The new Accomack Parish bought the glebe which had belonged to the county-wide Accomack Parish.

Some people considered the creation of two parishes in Accomack County a step toward forming a new county to be called St. George County. When the General Assembly met in 1770, a petition was presented as follows:

> Since the tithables in Accomack County are so numerous and the business of the court is so multiplied, the persons whose names are hereunto subscribed request that the said county be divided into two counties.

Another petition with as many signatures was presented asking that the two parishes be kept as Accomack County. No action is on record in the Journal of the House of Burgesses so the first one must have been disposed of by the committee which reviewed such petitions. There were more urgent questions for Accomack and Northampton counties, as well as the rest of Virginia and other colonies, than minor local affairs.

King George III succeeded his grandfather as ruler of England in 1760. The new King, 28 years of age, had met with favor during the final years of the war with France, which ended in 1763, leaving England in possession of the Ohio country and all of Canada. However, George III began to exert his authority over the colonies as soon as the treaty was signed with France. On October 7, 1763, the King signed a proclamation which set the Virginia boundary at the Allegheny watershed on top of the mountains. No new settlers were to cross these mountains and those who had gone to the Ohio country were ordered to move back to the eastern side. This was of concern to men on the Eastern Shore and elsewhere who had been promised land in the West if they helped defend the frontier, and those who had invested in the Ohio Company back in 1749. Little effort was made to enforce the proclamation, but this and other dictatorial acts of George III put the people on the alert.

When the General Assembly met in 1765, Burgesses from the Eastern Shore joined the others in indignation over the Stamp Act which was to become effective on the following November 1. Every legal document, newspaper or pamphlet handled in an American colony was to have a stamp attached to it. Such stamps would cost from 1 penny to 4 shillings, English money, and they could not be purchased with tobacco. The revenue from the Stamp Act was to pay the expenses of British soldiers who were left in the colonies after the war with France ended and any surplus was to go into the English treasury. With a normal volume of business, the necessary stamps would have taken all the English money out of circulation within a few years. Thomas Parramore and Southy Simpson from Accomack and John Harmanson and Thomas Dalby from Northampton represented the Eastern Shore at this time. They were present when Patrick Henry submitted resolutions against taxation without representation and the General Assembly adopted them to be sent in a petition to Parliament.

Both Accomack and Northampton County courts adopted resolutions opposing the Stamp Act, and they agreed to refrain from prosecuting people who did legal business without using the stamps. The Northampton Court met on February 11, 1766, with these justices present: Littleton Eyre, John Wilkins, John Bowdoin, Nathaniel Savage and John Stringer. The justices in attendance at the Accomack Court on February 25 were: Edmund Allen, William Bagge, Isaac Smith, James Arbuckle, John Wise and Henry Fletcher.

Virginia and other colonies not only sent petitions to the English government but they sent representatives to plead their cause. Purchase of English-made goods was so drastically reduced that English merchants and ship masters exerted their influence on Parliament. An Act to repeal the Stamp Act was passed by Parliament and signed by George III on March 18, 1767. At the same time Parliament adopted an Act claiming the right to make the laws for the colonies and denying them the right to petition the King or Parliament in matters displeasing to them. Parliament imposed heavy import duties on certain items which the colonies were buying from England. Items on which the import duties applied and the charges were:

    For every hundredweight avoirdupois of:

Crown, plate, flint and white glass	4 shillings 2 pence
Green glass	1 shilling 2 pence
Red lead	2 shillings
White lead	2 shillings
Painters' colors	2 shillings
For every pound of tea	3 pence
For every ream of paper,	
Atlas fine	12 shillings

    Sixty-six grades of other paper carried
        duties according to the grade.

These import duties were to become effective in the colonies on October 1, 1767.

    The high duty on the best grade of paper was an alternative for collecting revenues from stamps on local documents and the lower duty on cheap paper got revenue from newspapers and almanacs printed in Virginia and the other colonies. The duty on painters' supplies touched boat builders as well as people with houses which required paint for their preservation. Having the paint supply taxed so heavily was of deep concern to the home owners of the Eastern Shore and other areas where dampness is a characteristic. However, most people valued their right to self-government above material conveniences and joined in an embargo on these revenue-raising imports. A group of Burgesses met as private citizens in Williamsburg after the General Assembly adjourned in 1769 and signed an agreement to refrain from buying items covered by the import duties. Parliament removed the import duties on all the items except tea in 1770 and trade with the mother country was renewed. However, the news had not reached Virginia when the Assembly met. The presence of British soldiers in the colonies kept the people on the alert for the next intrusion on their liberties as

English subjects. A small minority of Eastern Shore people objected to resisting the arbitrary laws handed down from England.

Littleton Eyre I, who presided when the Northampton Court took the action against the Stamp Act, died in 1768. His will, written May 7, 1768, was probated July 12, 1768. He was the son of Severn Eyre who had married Gertrude Harmanson, a granddaughter of Argoll Yeardley II. He lived on former Yeardley land for some years and operated a ferry from a port on this land for more than two decades. He became a justice of the Northampton Court in 1740 and served the rest of his life. He was the presiding justice in 1766 when the court passed the resolution not to enforce the Stamp Act. He served in the House of Burgesses from 1748 to 1758. He had one son, Severn, who inherited Eyre Hall.

Littleton Eyre is best known for the ferry service he rendered. He got the ferry franchise in 1745 by an Act of the General Assembly and he might have held it under a county franchise from the death of Neech Eyre in 1737. In 1755 Littleton Eyre purchased two fast sailing boats and added the Port of Norfolk to those of York and Hampton. John Bowdoin II, who was his associate in the ferry business, got the franchise after Littleton's death in 1768. The franchise stayed in the Eyre and Bowdoin families, who had become related by marriage, for more than a hundred years.

The Eastern Shore enjoyed a brief interval of peace and prosperity between the resumption of trade with the mother country and the next Act to keep the colonies in a state of submission rather than partners in the English nation. Incidentally, Maryland and North Carolina, which had been settled as proprietary colonies, and the Northern Neck of Virginia, which paid levies to a proprietor rather than to the Virginia government, were just as eager to preserve their rights as free Englishmen as the rest of Virginia and other colonies. The present state of Delaware was a part of Pennsylvania, but had its own General Assembly. Each small farm or large plantation in Accomack and Northampton counties was rapidly becoming a production factory for the bare necessities of life. Only luxury items had to be purchased from off the Shore.

Tobacco was still the principal money crop. Pork, beef, hides, shoes, corn and wheat, salt and sea foods were among the principal exports. Later records show that castor oil was produced extensively. This product was used for medicine and in a number of other ways, including soap, axle grease for wheeled vehicles and artists' paints. Flax was produced to make linen and the seed were used in the manufacture of house and boat paint.

In 1773 the owner of a twenty-acre tract of land next to the Northampton Courthouse had it divided into forty lots of one-half acre each and offered them for sale. The settlement had been called the Horns since the court began to meet there. The colonial postoffice was called Northampton. No record was found of a town being chartered at this time but the name Peachburg replaced the Horns and continued in use until the end of the century when it became Eastville.

When the report reached the Eastern Shore that the port at Boston had been closed by an act of Parliament of March 31, 1774, the people were divided in their sentiments. They had heard about the "Boston Tea Party" on the previous December 16 when Boston citizens, disguised as Indians, went aboard a ship and destroyed a large cargo of tea to keep the citizens from paying the prescribed 3 shillings a pound import tax. They expected some retaliation but nothing so drastic as closing the port and removing the personnel of the Customs House. This meant that no ships from Virginia or other colonies could trade with Boston. Those who sanctioned the Act of Parliament became known as Tories. However, they were in the minority as later incidents show. When news reached the Shore that Parliament had annexed all the land north of the Ohio River and east of the Mississippi to the Province of Canada, Eastern Shoremen who had fought in the French and Indian War, or had an interest in land in Virginia's Northwest Territory, were enraged. No doubt some Tories became Patriots when this and other moves touched their pocketbooks.

When the General Assembly met in 1774, it called for "a day of fasting and prayer" as an expression of sympathy for the people of Boston. Lord Dunmore dissolved the Assembly in protest of this action, but the Burgesses did not leave Williamsburg until they met in Raleigh Tavern and provided for a meeting of Delegates from the counties in August to conduct business for Virginia in the event Lord Dunmore ceased to call the General Assembly. Local Committees of Safety were appointed in the various counties and local companies of volunteer soldiers were recruited in some of the counties. Lord Dunmore did call the Assembly in session on June 1, 1775, but he left Williamsburg on June 8 never to return. The ex-Burgesses went home. The same people met as Delegates in Richmond on July 17, 1775. The convention voted to raise two regiments for the army which had already been organized with George Washington as commander in chief. Patrick Henry was chosen as commander of one regiment.

The Delegates met for the fifth time on May 15, 1776. Records do not show how much work had been done toward a Constitution for a free Virginia, but early in July one had been written and adopted by the Assembly of Delegates. It provided for the House of Delegates and a Senate. The House was to be composed of one member elected in each county. The Senate was to be made up of members elected by districts formed according to population. There were twenty-four senatorial districts in the Constitution of 1776. The Convention was still in session when the Declaration of Independence was signed on July 4, 1776. Patrick Henry was elected Governor of Virginia. Instructions were sent to the counties for transferring the county courts from Colony to Commonwealth. The declaration read by the sheriffs of Accomack and Northampton counties was:

   The Continental Congress has declared the thirteen United States of America free and independent. The convention of this Colony of Virginia has found a new plan of government in the name of the Commonwealth. All justices on the present list may continue to serve by taking the oath of fidelity to the State and the oath of office.

Delaware and Maryland were among the thirteen states, so the Delmarva Peninsula became divided among the three states. The entire peninsula played an important part in the American Revolutionary War although it was not a major battlefield.

The Eastern Shore of Virginia supplied seven companies of soldiers, one captain, two lieutenants, one ensign, four sergeants and a drummer who marched overland to join the Ninth Virginia Regiment. John Cropper was the highest commissioned officer from the Shore. As reenforcements were needed, it was necessary to draft some men. A large number of militiamen and some regular army soldiers were required to guard the creeks and inlets of the two counties.

Some people were not in favor of the Declaration of Independence. They were watched by the loyal majority and tried for treason if found engaged in acts unfavorable to the Commonwealth and the American Army. John Cropper's diary, which has survived, indicates that a man lost the title of "Mister" if he showed a tendency to be a supporter of the British. Tory Tom _____, Tory John _____ and others were mentioned. After a court martial a convicted man was sent to the Governor for sentencing. Presumably some Tories went to England or English colonies early in the war.

The ministers of the Anglican Church were in a precarious position since they were subject to the Bishop of London, who was an official of the English government. Although taxes for their support were not provided in the new government of Virginia, a minister was privileged to live in the glebe house and carry on the work of his parish for volunteer contributions. He did not have to take an oath of allegiance to the new government, but he was required to leave out the prayer for the King of England in the services. One minister adjusted himself to the new situation and served his parish while another on the Shore was sent west of Richmond to stay until the Revolutionary War was over. Then he came back and served his parish the rest of his life.

The beginning of the Commonwealth government did not bring about the separation of Church and State. The vestries were still required to collect taxes to care for the poor in the parishes and to look after the moral behavior of the people. This responsibility continued into the next century.

After British warships took possession of the mouth of Chesapeake Bay, the ports of Accomack and Northampton counties became a part of the main supply line between France and other neutral counties and the Commonwealth of Virginia. Medicine, munitions and other needed supplies from overseas were brought to Metompkin and Chincoteague Creeks, then taken overland for reloading on small vessels which went toward the head of Chesapeake Bay, then down the western side to escape the small craft, called barges, which operated in the bay. A fort was established on Parramores Beach to protect incoming ships and to intercept British raiding barges entering Metompkin Creek.

In 1779 the Eastern Shore and the entire lower part of Tidewater Virginia were in danger of being seized by the British. The General Assembly of that year completed its business in Williamsburg and voted to move the seat of government to Richmond.

Early in the Revolutionary War the British established an operating base on Hog Island. Small ships called tenders and barges raided the Eastern Shore to get food and livestock which were used to replenish the supplies of British warships in the area. In most instances they made such raids at night when all the poultry was on the roosts and they captured the entire flocks along with cattle in the pounds, hogs, and cured meat and grain. If there was any sign of resistance, or knowledge that the man of the house was in the United States army, the raiders usually took the silver and other valuables and set fire to the house. The Hog Island base was in command of Captain John Kidd.

Ferry service to the mainland was discontinued before the British got control of the lower part of the Chesapeake Bay and the ships were leased to the new government. The ships in the ferry fleet, and others owned by people on the Eastern Shore of Virginia and Maryland, presumably helped transport Washington's army from the head of Chesapeake Bay to the area north of Yorktown in 1781. And some Eastern Shore of Virginia men fought in the decisive battle there which ended on October 19, 1781. However, the war was prolonged for another year.

The last naval engagement took place on the Eastern Shore side of the Chesapeake Bay on November 30, 1782. It is known as the Battle of the Barges. Commodore Whaley of Maryland, whose name has been recorded as Zedekial Walley, Whalley, or Whaley, was in charge of a fleet of barges engaged in the protection of Maryland shores from Commodore Kidd's marauders. He came into Onancock Creek and appealed for Virginia volunteers to help man the barges for a battle with enemy craft up the bay. John Cropper and a number of others volunteered. Commodore Whaley was killed and his body was buried in the graveyard at Scott Hall in Onancock. Many years later the United States government placed a marker on his grave. John Cropper and other Virginians were captured but they were soon exchanged for British soldiers who had been captured earlier.

During the interim between the adoption of the Virginia Constitution in 1776 and the adoption of one for the United States, the Eastern Shore featured in trade agreements and a navigation contract with Maryland. The question arose regarding Virginia's right to charge toll on ships going between the Virginia Capes to and from Maryland. Also, the question had been raised regarding the right of people on the south bank of the Potomac River to build piers and fish in that river. On March 28, 1785, a commission of three men from Maryland and two from Virginia met at Mount Vernon to work out an agreement. At the head of the Maryland commission was Daniel of St. Thomas

CHAPTER X — 1752-1790

Jenifer, a descendant of Ann Toft and Daniel Jenifer who had made a diplomatic marriage between Maryland and Virginia in 1671. An agreement was reached for Maryland ships to use the entrance to Chesapeake Bay without charge in exchange for Virginia citizens to use the Potomac River for commerce and fishing.

In October 1786 the General Assembly acted favorably on a petition of seven people who lived near the Accomack Courthouse for the establishment of a town to include the houses of the petitioners and ten acres adjoining this built-up area as follows:

> Be it enacted by the General Assembly that ten acres of land, the property of Richard Drummond, adjoining Accomack Courthouse, shall be laid out into lots of half an acre each, with convenient streets, and together with twenty other half acre lots already improved shall form a town by the name of Drummond. John Cropper II, Thomas Evans, John Teackle, Thomas Bailey and Thomas Custis shall be trustees. The trustees or the major part of them shall sell the lots at public auction after the time and place of the auction have been advertised for two months at Accomack and Northampton courthouses. The purchaser of each lot is to build a house 16 feet by 16 feet at least within two years of date of purchase. The house is to have a brick or stone chimney. The trustees are to convey the deed when the conditions are met and pay the money to Richard Drummond, or his legal representative.

The kitchen ends of some of the imposing houses still in use were built to secure the deeds for lots purchased as soon as they were offered for sale in Drummondtown. One surviving unit of this type is 16 feet by 18 feet with a brick chimney 9 feet wide at the base. The charter designated brick or stone chimneys, and an added precaution against fire was taken. These chimneys which formed part of a brick end were separated from the gable several feet below the top of the roof.

Drummondtown was built on a site that had been pat-

TWO ROOM AND LOFT HOUSE
Debtors Prison

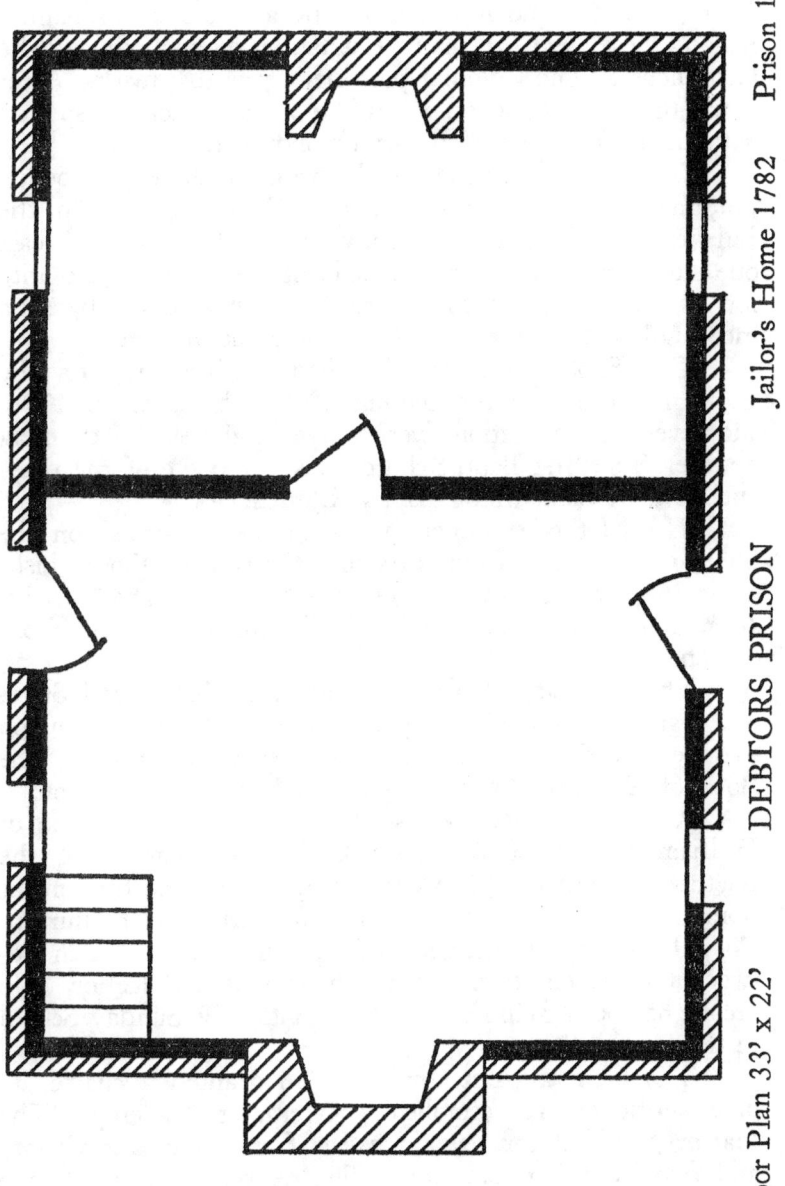

ented by 1664, and it was called by a succession of names. Among these were Freeman's Plantation, Metompkin and the Courthouse. The Colonial post office was Accomack. After more than two hundred years the name Accomac, spelled without the K, superseded Drummondtown.

In 1786 the settlement had a brick courthouse, a wooden jail, and a brick house (now called the Debtors Prison) for the jail keeper and his family, a tavern, a saddle shop, at least one store and seven houses outside of the land divided into lots when Drummondtown was laid out. A Presbyterian meeting house stood just south of the corporate limits.

The Baptist denomination had its beginning on the Eastern Shore with the coming of Elijah Baker in 1776, and several congregations were active by the end of the next decade. The first Baptist church was at the site of the present Lower Northampton Baptist Church.

The Methodist denomination is first recorded on the Shore in 1779, and Francis Asbury, the first Methodist bishop in the United States, visited the Shore in 1784. In his *Journal* he mentioned Guilford, Downings and Garrisons churches.

The Protestant Episcopal Church of the United States was organized in 1789 as a part of the Anglican Communion to supersede the Established Church of colonial times. The Book of Common Prayer was adapted to the new nation.

A Sunday School was started in 1785 in the home of William Elliott of Accomack County, a member of the Methodist Church. After conducting it for some time in his home, he transferred the infant organization to Burtons Chapel and it was later moved to Oak Grove Church between the present towns of Wachapreague and Keller. No record has been found of an older continuous Sunday School in the United States.

The General Assembly of 1786 granted a charter to nine petitioners for establishing Margaret Academy. The charter provided for seven trustees from Accomack County and five from Northampton. The petitioners were George Corbin, Isaac Avery, Thomas Evans, Littleton Savage, Levin

CHAPTER X — 1752-1790

Joynes, George Parker, John Harmanson, Edward Kerr and John Cropper. They were among the original trustees. The charter placed the full responsibility for raising funds, acquiring property, erecting buildings and employing teachers in the hands of the trustees. Some funds were raised immediately but the opening of Margaret Academy and its story belong to the next century.

John Parke Custis died in 1781 and his only son inherited Arlington. He had married Eleanor Calvert and four children were born to them. George and Martha Washington adopted the son George Washington Parke Custis and the youngest daughter. George Washington Parke Custis built Arlington on the Potomac, now called the Custis-Lee Mansion, and his only child was married to the future Confederate general, Robert E. Lee, when he sold Arlington on the Eastern Shore in 1832.

Chapter XI

1790-1800

The Eastern Shore of Virginia had 3 per cent of the population of the present state when the first United States census was taken in 1790. There were 6889 people in Northampton County and 13,959 in Accomack. If the county planners in 1674 had three counties in mind for the Eastern Shore, and there are indications that they did, they put the dividing line where one third of the population was in Northampton when the 1790 census was taken. No figures were found for St. George and Accomack parishes, but ten years later the figures were published separately. Each parish had approximately one half of the Accomack population.

The county seat of Northampton had the characteristics of a town at the end of this century but no charter was found for the Horns, Peachburg or Eastville. The present name Eastville came into use around the year 1800. This town is within the 9000--acre tract which the son of Ensign Thomas Savage left to his children in 1678. Northampton had been the colonial post office and it remained Northampton Court House P. O. well into the next century.

Hungars had some characteristics of a village spread over the 3700-acre tract of land originally patented by Sir George Yeardley. The ferry terminal and an ordinary, last kept in the brick end building with a gambrel roof and still known as The Ferry House, were important business enterprises. The tobacco warehouse was near the ferry landing and a physician built a house in this area in the eighteenth century. John Bowdoin bought land and developed a plantation which he called Bowdoin Hungars, and John Mapp

CHAPTER XI — 1790-1800

bought a tract of land in the area and lived there for many years. Littleton Eyre inherited a house and land on the tract. He lived there until he inherited Eyre Hall from his father. At least seven historic houses built on the original tract, many times subdivided, are still in use. At some undetermined date the neck part of the Yeardley land acquired the name Old Town Neck.

Other places had names which were destined to develop into villages. The present village of Hadlock is an example of an eighteenth century village in its infancy. A large area around this site was called "T B" from about 1669 until the name Hadlock came into use in 1795. The name "T B" came from one Thomas Bell who burnt his initials on large white oak shingles with his cattle branding iron and fastened them to trees and ditches with fences to mark them.

In 1794 one Robert Hadlock, merchant, bought sixteen acres of land on the Bayside Road, about two miles below the Accomack County line, and built a store and residence. Hadlock sold half of his land for another home site two years later. Other small tracts were purchased but no small building lots were found on the records. Dr. John Tankard bought Lumber Hall, now called Tankards Rest, in the vicinity in 1796 and engaged in medical practice for the next forty years. A tobacco warehouse stood on Nassawadox Creek and there was a wheelwright shop in the area.

Joshua Robins, a planter and tradesman, lived on the road below the Hadlock Store site. The record of the settling of his estate in 1793, some four years after his death, according to terms in his will which provided for each of his six children to get an equal share of his property, gives a vivid picture of his house and furniture, work implements, home industries and farm products in this area.

Robins was a younger son and his father had died when he was a child but he had made a success in business. He married Sarah Green in 1768 and seven years later he bought land and built the imposing house called End View. The name came from a brick end with two chimneys facing the road. There were two rooms and hall extending the length

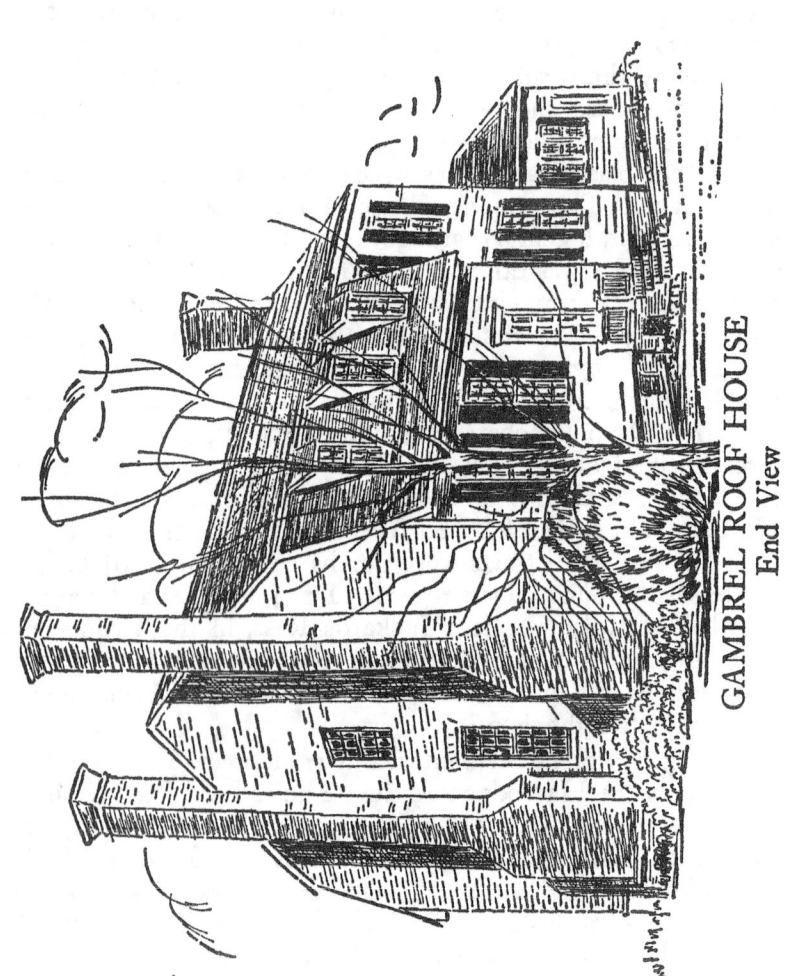

GAMBREL ROOF HOUSE
End View

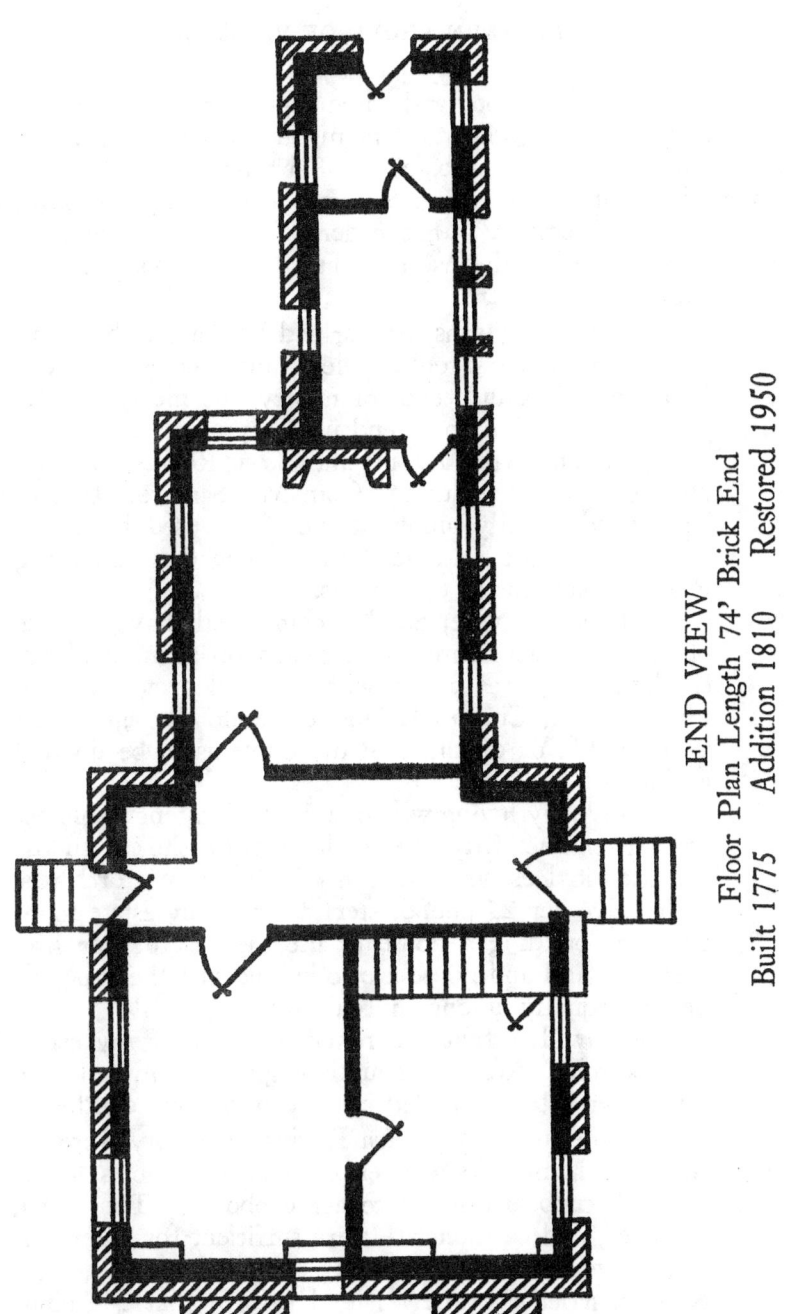

END VIEW
Floor Plan   Length 74'   Brick End
Built 1775   Addition 1810   Restored 1950

of both on the first floor and three rooms and a hall under the gambrel roof. Joshua Robins made his will on October 13, 1788, and it was probated on February 10, 1789. In the will he stated that he was "sick and low in body but sound of mind and memory." He ordered his debts to be paid and then designated the use and disposition of his property in the following manner:

> I give to my sons, Arthur and William Robins, my joiners and turners' tools. I lend unto said Arthur and William 70 pounds each of money due me from Mr. James Sanford. Also I lend unto my eldest daughters, Rosey Robins, Sally Robins and Betsy Robins, the balance of the money due me from Mr. Sanford. It is to be divided equally among them to be used by them. When my estate is divided the money they are using is to be taken out of their parts.
>
> My loving wife, Sarah Robins, shall have the use of the remainder of my estate to support as many of my children as choose to stay with her and obey her until my little son, Charles Robins, comes to the age of 14 years in life or death, then my estate is to be divided as follows:
>
> I give my loving wife one third of my moveable estate. I lend her fifty acres of land which she can choose provided it does not contain my buildings and orchards. I also give her 25 pounds sterling from my estate to be used for building a house to use the rest of her life, then the land and house are to be sold and the proceeds divided equally among my children.
>
> My will is that the remaining part of my estate is to be sold. After 25 pounds is given to my wife the remainder is to be divided equally among my children.

Among the items in Joshua Robins' inventory were six beds and two hammocks, sixteen chairs, three tables, three chests, a dish cupboard and a corner cupboard. The china, silver, pewter, and earthenware were sufficient for entertaining large crowds. A coffee pot and a tea pot were also listed.

Sarah married Matthew Floyd before Charles Robins

CHAPTER XI — 1790-1800

reached the age of 14 years when Joshua's estate could be settled. The house was sold in 1793 and the settlement was completed. Matthew Floyd bought the house and all the land except the 50 acres in which his wife had a life interest. Floyd sold End View and the land to John Addison in 1810. The new owner added the spacious dining room and made other improvements to keep this the most imposing house in the Hadlock area.

Franktown was the nucleus of a village before the Revolution. It got its name from one Frank Andrews who opened a store there in 1764. A Quaker meeting house was in use on the site of the present Methodist Church before 1717. A brick house was mentioned in a will in 1716. Franktown is on the Bayside Road between Hadlock and the original Nassawadox, now Bridgetown. Magothy Bay was another area with a name at the turn of the century and there might have been others in Northampton.

A record of places with names has been preserved in the census of 1800 for Accomack County. Head of Machipongo Creek, Belle Haven, Head of Occohannock and Scarburghs Neck were the places next to the Northampton County line. Bradfords Neck, Hacks Neck, Pungoteague, Sleuthkill Neck, Deep Creek, Folly Creek, Drummondtown and Onancock were other places named in St. George Parish. Onancock was the largest settlement on the Shore at this time.

Place names in Accomack Parish were numerous for the times. Some have survived while others have been superseded by two or more settlements with new names. Metompkin, Hunting Creek, Middle Road, Seaside Road, Wallops Road, Glebe, Gargatha, Muddy Creek, Guilford, Kegotank, Assawoman, Messongo, Pocomoke, Church Town, Swansecut, Gores Neck and Horntown were place names on the mainland. People were living on Jobes, Watts, Tangier, and Sykes islands on the bayside, and Chincoteague, Assateague and Wallops islands on the ocean side. Horntown and Guilford were the oldest places with the characteristics of villages at this time. Horntown was a place with a name in 1744.

Guilford is the oldest village with its original name near the center of Accomack County. The name presumably came from a town in England and it appeared in the Accomack County records in 1683 in a deed given to six trustees for:

> One acre of land where there is a small house by the name of the Meeting House, where the people of God, called Quakers, shall have the right to meet at their pleasure and to bury their dead.

The house was burned in 1694 and Quaker meetings were held in a private home in Onancock until a new one was built at Guilford and remained in use until 1728. The change of the meeting place to Onancock was recorded in the Court Records as required by law.

The first tobacco warehouse on Guilford Creek was built in 1725. It was called a "rolling house" and the court ordered a rolling road to be cleared from the bayside crossroad to this site. Tobacco was transported over such roads in hogsheads attached to a frame which provided for a hogshead to roll when pulled by an ox or a horse.

The storekeeper from 1780 to 1802 was one William Young and his account book has survived. He also operated a boatbuilding establishment and a shoemaking shop for which he employed workmen by the day or by the year. Through the years the village store has been a social center on the Eastern Shore and before the days of the telephone, radio, and television it was the principal means of getting the news. If a doctor was in the community he would stop at the store after administering to the patient for whom he was called to get other calls that were left for him when the report got around that he was to be in the area. William Young of Guilford was a typical storekeeper and an accommodating neighbor. Guilford had a Methodist congregation in 1785 when Francis Asbury visited the Eastern Shore. In 1789 a half acre of land between the branch and the crossroad was deeded to the trustees:

> That they shall erect thereon a place of worship of the Methodist Episcopal Church and it shall be used

CHAPTER XI — 1790-1800

for no other purpose.

Horntown is another village which had its name by 1744. (It was originally called the Horns.) The keeper of an ordinary was licensed there in 1759 and before the end of the century it was a place for travelers to rest and feed their horses. This village is located on the Seaside Road less than four miles from the Maryland line. Corbin Hall, near Horntown, is an imposing Georgian house which was started by 1787.

The settlement called Pocomoke was near the present village of New Church. A Baptist congregation is said to have been organized here in 1786 by Elijah Baker and the land on which Chincoteague Baptist Church now stands was donated in 1790. However, the name of the village came from the last Anglican church built in Accomack County during colonial times. The Anglican Church never appeared in the records after the Revolution.

This sampling of villages gives some idea of their beginnings, getting names, growing into service centers and forming a connecting link between succeeding generations as civilization advanced and the people of the Eastern Shore built for posterity.

In 1795 Northampton County built a second brick courthouse which was larger and more comfortable than the first, which was sold to be used for a store. It was torn down and rebuilt on its present site more than a century later. Part of the Eastville Inn was then in use. It was a successor to at least two taverns at the Northampton county seat. Coventon, Park Hall and possibly Ingleside were started before the end of the century.

Drummondtown was the scene of considerable building from the time it was chartered in 1786 until the turn of the century. One of the houses that best illustrates the traditional Eastern Shore type of architecture known as Big House, Little House, Colonnade and Kitchen got an addition in the 1790's. This house was built by Dr. Fenwick Fisher on Main Street. The one room and loft section with the large outside chimney had a colonnade and another story and a loft

ONE ROOM AND LOFT
Seymour Kitchen

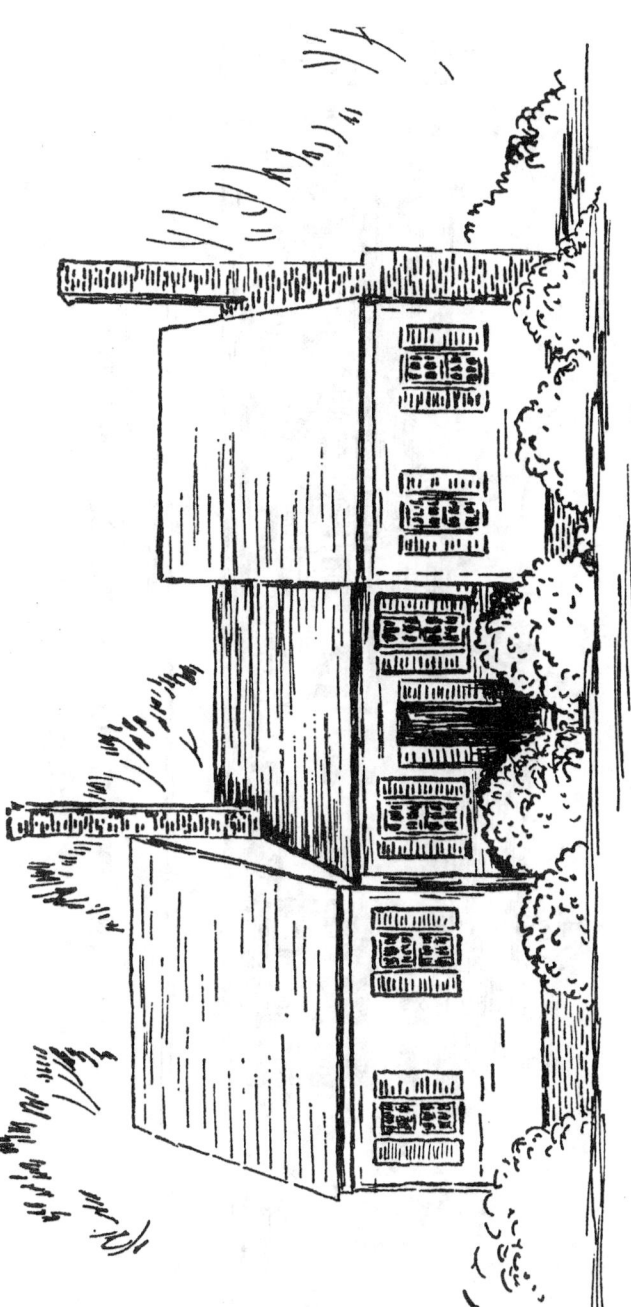

SIAMESE TWIN HOUSE

Little Room, Colonnade and Kitchen of Seymour House

BIG HOUSE, LITTLE HOUSE, COLONNADE AND KITCHEN

Seymour House

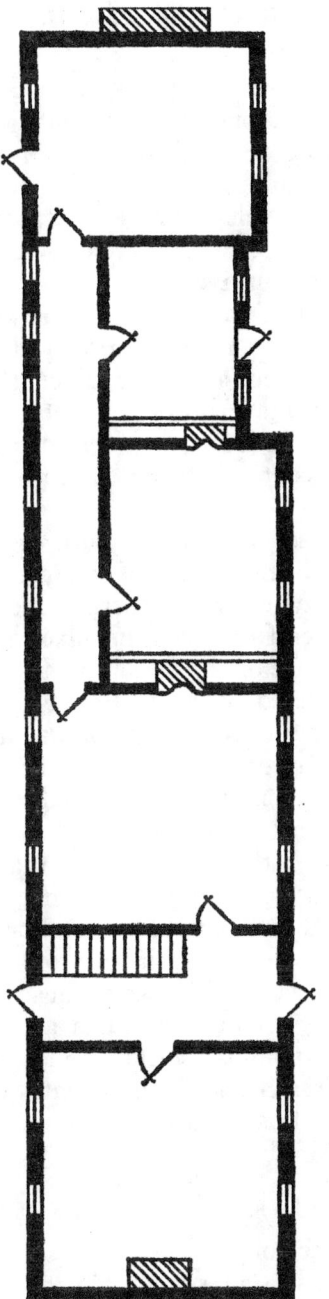

SEYMOUR HOUSE

Floor Plan 104'   Built 1791-1816

Big House, Little House, Colonnade and Kitchen

section added. This made what is known as a Siamese twin house on the Shore. Other one-room sections got additions with the colonnade joining the back of the story-and-a-half section forming an "L" while others were joined to form a "T". The varying roof levels prevailed regardless of the shape of the outside. Still other early houses with two sections and a colonnade have survived.

Among the houses in Onancock that were built in the eighteenth century and still in use are Scott Hall, completed by 1779, but now modernized, and Kerr Place, the home of the Eastern Shore of Virginia Historical Society. This handsome mansion was started in 1797, and completed, with the exception of the more recent annex, by the turn of the century.

While mansion houses were being built by the people who had accumulated the most wealth, many small houses of the story-and-a-half type, which characterized the 17th century, were built for comfort and some luxuries by people of moderate means. Because of the various winds and tropical hurricanes which have passed over the Eastern Shore at intervals like rigid building inspectors, substantial houses have dominated the landscape from the beginning. The story-and-a-half house of the 18th century usually had two or more dormer windows and small windows. The fact that most of the clapboard houses of the 18th century that have survived have brick ends incorporating the chimneys, indicates that brick ends reduced the hazard of destruction by fire.

Tobacco and livestock were the principal sources of money but numerous other items were sold in small quantities. Some merchants continued to keep their accounts and price their merchandise in English pounds, shillings and pence while they got their pay in French and United States coins, or in items for resale. This is illustrated by a page in the leather-bound account book of William Young.

January 8, 1796   Charges
    Charge for building a vessel of 64 tons
        at 4 pounds per ton   250-0-0
    Additions to the vessel (presumably

CHAPTER XI — 1790-1800

sails, ropes, anchor and sand box
for cooking) 50-0-0

Total 300-0-0

January 8, 1796   Payments
  By cash forty dollars ($40)   12- 0- 0
    105 lb. sugar   4-10- 7
    14 lb. coffee at 0-1-9   1- 4- 6
    32 gallons molasses   4-18- 0
    4 bushels of salt at 0-7-6   1-10- 0
March 25
  By cash 10 French crowns   3- 5-10
April 11
  By cash   1- 4- 0
April 14
    3 barrels pork at 0-6-0   18- 0- 0
  415 lb. iron at 36-0-0 per thousand   7- 9- 4
April 15
  By cash   30- 0- 0
  300 lb. spikes at 0-0-16   18- 0- 0
  1 sack of salt   1-10- 0

Total 103-12-3

Balance due 196- 9-9

Saw Mill Charge
For getting logs to table   0- -6
  Cutting 500 ft. plank   0- 7-6
  Cutting 346 ft. oak plank   0- 6-5
  Sending the plank by vessel   0-11-1

Small Items
1 curry comb   0- 1-6
1 paper of ink powder   0- 1-0
1 paper of pins   0- 1-0
1 hat (for a man)   0- 8-0
1 yard fine linen   0- 4-9
14 yards linen at 0-2-0   1- 8-0
3 lb. feathers 0-0-6   0- 1-6

5 yards shirting	0-12-0
2 handkerchiefs 0-6-0	0-12-0

Food

1½ bu. wheat at 0-5-0	0- 7-6
1 bu. peas	0- 1-0
Fish	0- 1-3
1 lb. coffee	0- 2-2
3 lb. sugar	0- 3-0
1 gallon molasses	0- 4-6
1 barrel pork	6- 0-0
1 bu. corn	0- 6-0
273 lb. beef at 0-0-3	3- 8-3
Making of 1 pr. shoes	0- 1-0
Making 1 pr. shoes and leather for making	0- 9-0
1 pair half soles	0- 0-8

Flax was grown on large plantations and small farms to provide linen cloth, boat sails, thread for fishing lines and nets, as well as for rope. In the month of August 1796 fourteen people sold flax seed in quantities ranging from a half-bushel to three bushels at the store at Guilford. The seed was a source of income as a byproduct of producing the plants for the fiber. They were used in making medicine and linseed oil for paint. The production of linen fiber was a long and tedious process and required more hand labor than any other product at the time.

The seed were sown in rows in early spring and cultivated to keep weeds out until the slender stalks, two or three feet high, were at the right degree of maturity to harvest. Each stalk had little branches with seed near the top, but the best fiber was made from plants harvested before the seed were fully ripe. The plants were pulled up and placed across the rows to dry. Then they were formed into small bundles to be drawn over a block with spikes like a comb to remove the seed. This step was called rippling. Then the stalks were spread out for rain and dew to rot the woody part of the stalk. This was called retting. The flax was then passed through a brake or pounded to crack the woody part

CHAPTER XI — 1790-1800

of the stems. The Guilford storekeeper had a brake and charged customers for putting flax in it. It consisted of two grooved boards, one of which was on hinges and worked up and down like a hand printing press. Wooden mallets were used by some people for braking. Then the fiber was put on wooden blocks and scraped with wooden blades to remove the remaining woody portions. This process was called scutching. The next step was heckling, or combing with combs to separate the long fiber from the short fiber, or tow. The next step was to spin the fiber on a flax wheel into thread of the desired size. The weaving or rope making came last.

The making of wool cloth was another home industry on the Eastern Shore in the early years. Large farmers raised sheep to produce wool for home use and for market while smaller ones bought wool. In the spring, sheep were herded together in a small pasture and taken one by one to a shearing table where the wool was cut off. The sheep had time to grow a new coat before cold weather. Athough there was some bleating at shearing time, sheep put up little resistance to this annual ritual. The wool was washed, carded into rolls of fiber about ten inches long and spun into thread on spinning wheels about twice as large as flax wheels. Some people wove cloth to sell but no record was found of a weaving factory on the Eastern Shore.

The woman at the head of a home was as busy as her money-earning husband and her hours were longer than from sun to sun. On a large farm there were servants to do the various kinds of work, but the lady of the house was the overseer, instructor and coordinator. The woman in the small house with few or no servants did the work with the help of her children. All the girls were trained to be homemakers and in homes where there was time, the daughters were taught to do fine needlework as an expression of their artistic talent. Stockings and socks were knit from yarn and the woman kept some knitting in reach when she sat down to rest or to chat with her family at night. When a woman went visiting she usually took along her knitting.

Visiting was the principal recreation for women and

family gatherings were frequent. Even with travel by boat or on horseback and horse-drawn vehicles, families managed to get together for a day or for a week. People kept open house, so to speak, and friends and relatives were welcome at any time they could come. The housewife made certain that the table was laden with food and that there was sleeping space although it was crowded by present standards. Pallets on the floor were frequently used for older children on such occasions.

The men took part in family gatherings and it has been said that some candidates for office owed their election to these social events where friends of a candidate could influence their kinsmen. The men also found sociability at the county seats on court days and election time. In 1797 Thomas Evans of Sunderland Hall in the Kegotank area, now Modest Town, was elected to the United States House of Representatives. He had been county surveyor for two decades when he was elected to Congress and was a trustee of Drummondtown when it was chartered. After serving two terms he returned to his position as surveyor until he was appointed Circuit Court judge.

The Eastern Shore furnished the Speaker of the House for the Virginia General Assembly in 1798-1799. This was John Wise, a descendant of the first John Wise who came to Virginia in 1635, and was destined to be the father of a governor of Virginia in the next century. General John Cropper was a State Senator in this decade.

During this interim of peace and prosperity, defense was not neglected. Both Accomack and Northampton counties had militias with designated officers and scheduled drill periods, which were held monthly at eleven o'clock in the morning on the drill fields in Accomack and Northampton counties.

When ferry service was renewed after the Revolution, the first port on the mainland was Hampton where passengers transferred to James River boats for Richmond. From Hampton the ferry went to Norfolk and then to Yorktown on the return voyage. The latter was never a profitable port for the ferry after the capital was moved from Williamsburg. Peter Bowdoin kept the franchise although others tried to get it from him through political maneuvers. The mail contract which went with the ferry franchise was equivalent to a government subsidy. The ferry with two boats sailing together continued to make two round trips a week from the port of Hungars.

There were post offices at Accomack and Northampton courthouses. An overland mail route was provided to Philadelphia during the Revolution and apparently it was continued under the United States postal service. Newspapers, personal correspondence and official documents made a large volume of mail from Richmond to the Eastern Shore, especially when the General Assembly was in session. Some items were sent postpaid, but the general rule was for the recipient to pay the postage.

When the report reached the Eastern Shore that George Washington died on December 14, 1799, a memorial service was held at the Protestant Episcopal Church near Drummondtown, which had taken the name St. James. John Cropper was a vestryman and one of the greatest admirers of General Washington.

At the end of the century the people of the Eastern Shore had good houses, food in abundance, equipment for manufacturing cloth and other necessities, and tobacco to sell as a cash crop for paying taxes and ordering luxury items from Europe. Potatoes had probably been grown as table vegetables since the English first came, but the first record was found at the end of this century. A workman collected 2 shillings for plowing a "pertater" patch and making the holes.

Chapter XII

1800 - 1840

The Eastern Shore entered the nineteenth century on the wave of prosperity that blessed the new nation. Large planters, small farmers, watermen, tradesmen, merchants, lawyers, doctors, and surveyors were alert to the opportunities to accumulate property and money to lend out on interest. When the Second United States Census was taken in the year 1800, the Shore had a population of 22,456 with 6763 of the people in Northampton County.

The Accomack County census rolls for the year 1800 are presumably the only such rolls for a Virginia county which have survived. This census was taken separately for Accomack and St. George parishes. Chincoteague and Wallops islands were in Accomack Parish while all the bay islands now in Accomack County were in St. George Parish. Only the heads of families were listed by name, but the ages of dependents show whether they were children or adults. Likewise, the records show whether they were women and girls or men and boys. Accomack Parish had a population of 8479 and St. George had 7214.

Chincoteague Island had a population of 60 including 23 people under sixteen years of age. Joseph Sharpley, Joseph Jr. and Thomas Sharpley, and their dependents, accounted for 13 of the population. Other heads of families were John Burch, Occro Brima, William Bowdoin, Lemuel Johnson, Parker Lewis, Edward Mumford, Isaiah Mears, John Stroks, and George York. Wallops Island had a population of 30 with only 14 of them above sixteen years of age. Thomas Hancock, William Pruitt, William Read, Michael Read, Revel Read and Kendall Thornton were the family

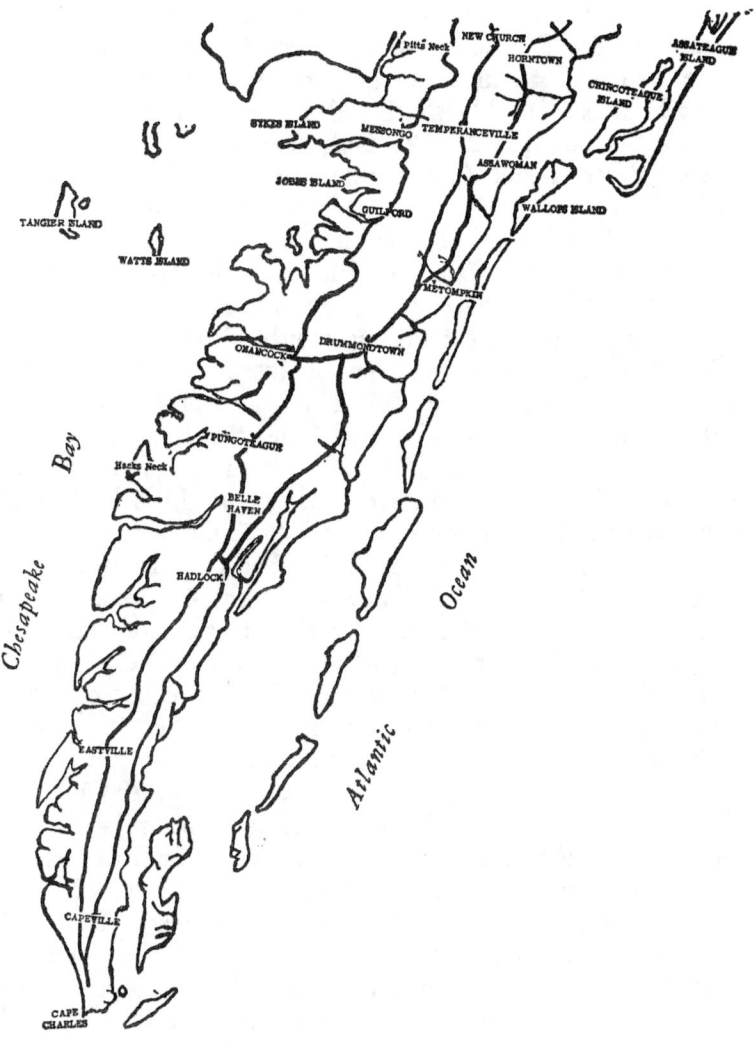

THE EASTERN SHORE OF VIRGINIA 1800

heads.

Sykes Island, now Saxis in Chesapeake Bay, had a population of 35 and 20 of those were under sixteen years of age. The heads of families were Sampson Marshall, Abraham Marshall, Samuel Marshall and Molly Sterling. Jobes Island had a population of 27 and 10 of these were under sixteen. Watts Island had a population of 15. Of these 10 were in the family of Robert Parker and the other five were employed by him. Tangier Island had a population of 79 and it was one of the first places on the Shore to transact business in the currency of the new nation.

One of the earliest wills in which a bequest was made in United States dollars was that of Joseph Crockett of Tangier Island made on July 18, 1805, and probated on April 29, 1806, in Accomac. This will and the Accomack County census roll for the year 1800 provide some revealing details of the settlement on Tangier. Although this island in the Russell Islands group on Captain John Smith's Map of 1608 was patented in 1670 the name Tangier was first used on the records in 1713. Joseph Crockett bought 450 acres of land there in 1778 from the heirs of the original patentees. He was the first Crockett to own land on the Eastern Shore of Virginia, although the family name had appeared on Maryland records for more than a century. Of the 79 people on Tangier 33 were Crocketts. According to Joseph Crockett's will all of these were descendants or daughters-in-law of Joseph. There were 20 people in the Evans family with Richard and Richard Jr. as the heads of the families. One of these could have married a daughter of Joseph Crockett. The Parks family with Job and Zorobabel as the heads of families numbered 13. The wife of one of these was presumably a Crockett daughter. Joshua Simpkins, James Sparrow and Joshua Thomas were the other heads of families on the island in 1800. No occupations were listed but later records indicate that the seafood business was a thriving business with Philadelphia and New York among the markets.

Joseph Crockett had five sons and five daughters, but the son Jesse predeceased him and left at least one grandson.

CHAPTER XII — 1800-1840

Zachariah, the eldest son, received the home place of 250 acres in fee simple and shared the livestock, other unbequeathed property and furniture with a maiden sister, Tabitha Crockett. Zachariah was named the executor. Thomas Crockett got 200 acres where he was living in fee simple. John got $100 and Joseph Jr., who lived on the mainland of the Eastern Shore, got $100. Zachariah was given the use of South Point for life and then it was to go to a grandson John Crockett. All the sons were listed as heads of families in 1800. The five daughters got cash bequeaths. Tabitha Crockett, Sally Dunton, Leah Hopkins, Rachel Parks and Molly Evans received $20 each.

The first inventory in which the property was appraised in dollars was that of Dr. James Lyon, of Northampton, dated January 24, 1812. The items in this inventory brought $4014.53 at a public auction. Some items in the inventory show the value at this time of basic furnishings in comparison with similar items in seventeenth century inventories while others duplicate those found in museums depicting rooms of the early nineteenth century. A mahogany bedstead with curtains and furnishings sold for $73, a child's bedstead and furnishings for $12 and a large looking glass for $50. A set of breakfast china brought $10, a set of blue and white dining china brought $40 and the remainder of the dishes brought $20. The glassware, including 2 cut glass salt cellars, sold for $25, 2 cases with knives and forks brought $12 and flat silver and hollow ware brought $336.

Among items of special interest in this inventory are a new mahogany wardrobe, 6 carpets and 24 yards of entry carpeting, 20 black and gilt Windsor chairs, 1 clock on a stand, 12 botanical pictures, a portable writing desk, a spy glass, a mahogany bookcase with 100 books including a Prayer Book and Bible, and the *Encyclopedia Britannica* in 3 volumes.

The supply of household linens was large. It included imported linen, Virginia linen and two large cotton counterpanes. A cotton wheel with a reel and winding blades in the inventory indicates that the thread was spun in the household of Dr. Lyon and sent elsewhere for weaving. This was the first cotton wheel found in an inventory on the Eastern Shore. Cotton was rapidly replacing flax as a home-grown fiber.

Cotton required less labor than flax after the invention of the cotton gin in 1793, but more than two decades passed before gins were in general use. A gin propelled by a mule hitched to a pole which was attached to the gin created enough demand for cotton to cause Eastern Shore farmers to use part of their tobacco land for cotton. Before the gin was invented the seed had to be separated from the fiber by hand and one person with nimble fingers could produce no more than one pound of fiber in a long day. The seed were sown quite thick in rows in the early spring, then thinned with a wide hoe after the plants were strong enough to stand alone. The plants were cultivated and kept free from weeds until July when they produced white blooms. When these dropped off, little green bolls were left to grow and open into white puffs in the early autumn. These puffs were picked by hand. In some cases flocks of geese were used to pick the grass from the cotton plants. These same geese yielded feathers for market and for home use when the soft feathers were removed each spring at sheep shearing time. Thus, the geese reduced the hand labor and provided an extra source of income through the sale of the feathers.

After the seed had been removed, the fiber was pressed into bales of about five hundred pounds. One thousand pounds of seed were a byproduct of each bale. They were pressed to extract oil. The hulls were used for livestock feed and the residue after the oil was clarified was made into a yellow powder, known as cottonseed meal. This was also used for livestock feed. Cotton was replacing tobacco as a money crop early in the nineteenth century.

The most widely discussed public issue of the times dealt with completing the task of separating church and state. The Protestant Episcopal vestries still had the responsibility of collecting taxes to pay for the support of the poor, although the church had been supported by voluntary

CHAPTER XII — 1800-1840

contributions since 1776. Other denominations did not object to the vestries having this task but they did object to the glebe farms and other property, bought while the church was an arm of the government, remaining in the possession of the Episcopal Church. Some people thought that denominational jealousy would end when the property acquired in colonial times was disposed of.

The General Assembly of 1802 enacted a law authorizing the county courts to appoint overseers of the poor. These new officials were to sell the glebes as soon as the ministers then in the parishes ceased to serve. Part of the money from the sale of the church property was to be used for the care of the needy. Church buildings and furnishings, other than those which were known to have been private gifts, were to be sold when they ceased to be used for divine services. St. George Glebe was sold in 1804 and the one in Accomack Parish was sold the following year. The brick church at Assawoman was used for a school.

Margaret Academy was opened in an imposing brick building on the Bayside Road, north of Pungoteague, in the autumn of 1807. Part of the proceeds from the glebes were added to the donations which had been accumulating since the institution was chartered by the General Assembly in 1786. Margaret Academy was a boarding school to give students an elementary classical education.

When Congress declared war against Great Britain on June 18, 1812, the Eastern Shore was again in a vulnerable position for enemy raids and possibly enemy occupation. An undetermined number of men from Accomack and Northampton counties joined the armed forces and the militia was strengthened for home defense with Thomas M. Bayly as the highest militia officer. Drills were held on scheduled days and detachments of militiamen rotated at watch duty at the mouths of the bayside creeks. In so far as the records show the enemy did not bother with the seaside, which got the worst punishment during the Revolutionary War.

Ferry service was discontinued across the bay as soon as British ships appeared in the Hampton Roads area. Members of the General Assembly went north to cross the bay and then journeyed overland southward to Richmond. Trade with northern cities was hampered but it was not paralyzed. Home industries provided most of the necessities of life so there was money for some luxuries from New England manufacturers, France and other friendly European countries when ships succeeded in evading the British warships. During the first ten months of the War of 1812 the British were engaged in war with France. When the war was over, preparations were made to attack the nation's capital. The place chosen for the operating base was on Accomack County soil. This was destined to be mostly a naval campaign and the site chosen was out of reach of the Eastern Shore militias.

On April 5, 1814, a British force under the command of Rear Admiral George Cockburn occupied Tangier Island and used it as an operating base until the end of hostilities. The number of troops landed there before the end of the summer has been estimated at 14,000. They cut trees and pitched their tents and commandeered the livestock on the island for their own use. The British also built a fort there. Through the efforts of the Reverend Joshua Thomas (a Methodist evangelist who was listed in the 1800 census as head of a family and later brought fame to the island), the trees on the Camp Meeting site were spared. The inhabitants of Tangier were practically prisoners of the army of occupation.

The first recorded attack on Virginia from this base was near Pungoteague on May 30, 1814, and is known as the Battle of Pungoteague. A summary of the report made to the Governor of Virginia on May 31 is as follows:

> At seven o'clock on the morning of May 30, an enemy tender and seven barges fired some cannon at the mouth of Onancock Creek to draw the militia there while the fleet proceeded to Pungoteague Creek. The enemy crossed the bar of Pungoteague Creek in eleven barges and launches. Two tenders, a sloop and a schooner remained in the bay. Rear Admiral Cockburn's ship, the *Albion*, was in full view from the guard on the south

CHAPTER XII — 1800-1840

side of the creek.

The enemy landed on the north side of the creek and advanced about a mile with a force of more than 450 men. Plans were made to draw them inland as far as possible then to attack from both the front and the rear. Militiamen under Major Finney took a position behind a ditch on one side of an open field while the enemy took a position on the other side of the field where the ditch had a bank with a fence on it. The two ditches joined some distance inland. Each advanced toward the angle of the field under continuous artillery firing. When the militiamen and the enemy were about one hundred yards apart a bugle from the barges sounded a retreat order. Some eighty marines covered the retreat. Six wounded men or dead bodies were seen to be carried in blankets to the barges. The militia loss was one private badly wounded. The British set sail to their fort and camp on Tangier Island.

The war ended in February 1815 with little material damage to the Eastern Shore, but the people shared in the loss in Washington, D. C. The White House had been burned and the unfinished Capitol had been damaged by fire.

When ferry service across the bay was resumed in 1815, the Hungars Ferry, which had been operated since 1724, had competition. A franchise with duplicate service was granted from the Port of Pungoteague across the creek from the site of the only Eastern Shore of Virginia battle on record against a European nation. The Battle of the Barges during the Revolutionary War was actually fought in Maryland waters.

The Eastern Shore lost one of its best known citizens when John Cropper died on January 15, 1821, at Bowmans Folly. A summary of his life and public service not only preserves the memory of a useful man but it provides a digest of the Shore's history during his active years.

John Cropper was born at Bowmans Folly on December 23, 1755. He was a descendant of a John Cropper who married the daughter of Edmund Bowman who patented Bowmans Folly Plantation in 1664. (In the seventeenth century the word "folly" meant a clump of trees rather than lack of wisdom.) Sebastian Cropper inherited the plantation and in 1721 he left it to three sons. His namesake Sebastian got the tract with the house on it and the John Cropper born in 1755 inherited it. John's mother was Sabra Corbin Cropper.

John Cropper was educated by private tutors. In August 1776 he married Margaret Pettit. He had been a member of the local militia for some time and late in 1776 he was commissioned captain of a company of soldiers which left in December as part of the 9th Virginia Regiment to join General Washington at Morristown, New Jersey. In 1777 John Cropper was commissioned major of the 7th Virginia Regiment. He took part in the battle of Brandywine. In 1778 General Lafayette commissioned him lieutenant colonel in command of the 11th Virginia Regiment. In June he took part in the Battle of Monmouth. In the fall of 1778 he got a furlough for six months and returned home. His first child Sarah Corbin Cropper was born the following autumn.

In March 1779 John Cropper received a commission as a lieutenant colonel of the 7th Virginia Regiment, signed by John Jay as President of the Congress. However, he was permitted to remain in Accomack County on an indefinite furlough. Shortly after his arrival at Bowmans Folly in 1778 a British raiding party landed, took the food they could find, removed his wife and daughter to a small building in the yard and were preparing to blow up the residence when John and an aide intercepted them. John Cropper moved his family to Latin House near Accomac until danger subsided. In 1782 John Cropper was one of the volunteers who took part in the Battle of the Barges in which he was wounded. His wife died later in 1782, leaving two daughters.

John Cropper's second wife was Catherine Bayly. John's admiration for George Washington was so great that he commissioned Charles Wilson Peale, a traveling

CHAPTER XII — 1800-1840

artist, in 1792 to paint a portrait of Washington for him. He also had portraits of himself and his wife Catherine painted. Two of the six children by John's second wife had Washington as a middle name.

John Cropper continued to render public service in peace and in war while he managed his plantation and looked after his shipping business. One entry in his diary mentioned a ship leaving for France. He was a member of the Virginia House of Delegates from 1784 to 1792 and he was a member of the State Senate from 1813 to 1817. His service in the War of 1812 was recruiting men and inspecting the drills of the militia. In 1815 John Cropper was commissioned brigadier general of the 21st Brigade, Virginia Militia. This accounts for his being known as General John Cropper.

Sarah Corbin Cropper married John Wise of Accomac and in 1806 they became the parents of Henry A. Wise who was destined to become Governor of Virginia.

In 1815 John Cropper had the original Bowmans Folly house torn down and numerous tons of dirt hauled to the site. Then he built the three-story Georgian house with a little house, colonnade and kitchen attached. John Cropper left five daughters and three sons, and legacies to all. His wife chose Latin House, which had been renamed Edge Hill, as her share of the property.

In the fall of 1824 Peter Bowdoin sold his ferries to one John K. Floyd, and he reopened the port on Kings Creek. Floyd had bought the Secretary's Land in 1800. The port of Hungars which had been the ferry terminal for at least a hundred years continued to be a public wharf but with little business after the tobacco warehouse was closed in 1824 or earlier.

In 1833 Henry A. Wise, a grandson of General Cropper, was elected to Congress. He was educated at Margaret Academy and Washington College in Pennsylvania before going to a private law school in Winchester. After finishing law school he went to Nashville, Tennessee, and married a girl he met while he was at Washington College. When he was elected to Congress, as the third Eastern Shore citizen to win that distinction, he and his family were living at Edge Hill, near Accomac.

In 1835 articles about Accomack and Northampton counties were published in *A New and Comprehensive Gazetteer of Virginia and the District of Columbia.* Brief historical sketches were followed by a description of each county, the crops grown, some local customs and a description of the towns and villages which then had post offices. Since the United States Census up to this time did not cover agriculture, these articles furnish the earliest recorded information on agricultural products which replaced tobacco in the early part of the nineteenth century:

> The Shore is almost as level as a bowling-green and the ancient hospitality of Virginia is unimpaired. The people have a high relish for good living which they are able to indulge in because the soil and climate are so suitable for growing food and the waters abound in excellent fish, oysters and crabs. Huge fig trees laden with fruit, and some pomegranates are to be seen. There are few places where more food can be produced for the man or horse.
>
> The principal crops are wheat, Indian corn, rye, oats, peas, beans, cotton and potatoes. Crop rotation protected the soil from wearing out. In Northampton when a field is not cultivated it is soon covered with a sort of wild vetch, called the Magothy-Bay bean, which shades the land while it is growing, and returns to it a rich coat of vegetable manure.
>
> There is here an article of culture seldom found in other parts of the state. It is the castor bean and many farmers grow from eight to ten acres. The income from an acre is about as much as for an acre of corn. Each bushel of beans yields two gallons and a half of oil and sells at the press for $1.25 a bushel.
>
> The castor bean plant was an annual, planted in the early spring and grew from six to eight feet high before the burs

CHAPTER XII — 1800-1840   167

were ready to be picked and the seed threshed out. The plants had large leaves which served as umbrellas for the flowers and seed pods or burs.

There were five castor oil factories, or presses, in Northampton in 1835, and parts of one have survived. It is at Brownsville, a seaside plantation still owned by descendants of John Brown, who patented the land in 1652 and his granddaughter who married Arthur Upshur II about 1690. The building which housed part of the operations was converted into a barn but the twelve-inch beam from which the scales were suspended is still intact. A large copper boiler with a flat bottom, straight sides and a three-inch rim at the top has survived. Another item of equipment in the possession of the owners of Brownsville is a five-gallon jug with a little pitcher-shaped top above the place where the cork stopper goes in. One family used this for its supply of oil and sent it to the factory each year.

Castor oil was made by pressing the fluid from the beans, then heating it over boiling water until the sediment formed a solid mass. Then the clear oil was poured into jugs or pots ready for sale. The sediment was poisonous to animals, but it made an excellent fertilizer. A ledger with the list of customers and the price for a gallon of castor oil has been preserved at Brownsville. It also shows that salt was being made and marketed on that plantation but salt was not mentioned in the *Gazetteer* article.

The information about towns and villages with post offices seems important enough to quote. Apparently a post village was one served by a stage coach which carried passengers and mail. Mail to post offices only was carried by a gig or a two-wheel cart, or on horseback. The towns and villages described were:

> Capeville P. O. situated 12 miles south of Eastville, the county seat, 6 miles north of Cape Charles and 176 miles from Richmond. It is a small village containing 12 houses, 2 mercantile stores, 1 boot and shoe factory and several other mechanical shops. It is a place of great resort for the neighbors of several

miles around to obtain early possession of the news from vessels arriving on the coast. Population 25.

Eastville P. V. (Post Village) and seat of justice is in about the middle of the county and two miles from the Chesapeake Bay and the Atlantic Ocean. Eastville has 2 principal streets running at right angles to each other. Besides the usual county buildings it contains 21 dwelling houses, 4 mercantile stores, 2 taverns, 1 new and handsome Episcopal church, 1 common school and 1 Bible society. The mechanical pursuits are: 1 coach factory, which completes about $6,000 worth of work annually; 1 harness maker, 1 cabinet maker, 2 blacksmiths, 2 boot and shoe manufacturers, 3 tailors, 1 house and sign painter and 1 hatter.

There are in Eastville 3 castor oil manufactories and 2 others in the county. The county exports about 20,000 gallons of oil annually. The principal commerce is with Baltimore, Philadelphia and New York.

The population is 217 persons, of whom 2 are attorneys and 3 are regular physicians. The inhabitants are not to be surpassed for their morality and hospitality to strangers.

Accomack Court House, or Drummondtown, besides a brick courthouse and jail, contains a Methodist house of worship, 39 dwelling houses, 1 common school, 3 mercantile stores, 1 tannery, 2 saddle and harness makers, 3 tailors, 3 cabinet makers, 1 watch and clock maker, 1 carriage maker, and 2 boot and shoe factories. There are 3 grist mills in the vicinity. The population is 240, including 4 attorneys and 2 physicians. County courts are held on the last Monday of every month, quarterly courts are held in March, June, August and November. Judge Upshur holds his Circuit Superior Court of Law and Chancery on May 12 and October 15.

Belle Haven P. O. is situated in the southeastern part of the county, 20 miles from Drummondtown. Pungoteague P. O. is 12 miles from Drummondtown. There are 20 dwelling houses, 1 Methodist house of wor-

CHAPTER XII — 1800-1840

ship, 1 Episcopal house of worship, 1 common school, 1 tavern, 1 mercantile store, 1 tannery, 1 boot and shoe maker and 1 blacksmith shop. The trade from Pungoteague Creek employs 5 regular coasting vessels. The population is 100 including 1 physician.

Onancock P. O. is situated on the creek next to the Chesapeake Bay and is southwest of Drummondtown.

Modest Town P. V. is 10 miles northeast of Drummondtown. It is 2 miles from the tide water, and 3 miles from the Atlantic Ocean. It contains 6 dwelling houses, 1 Baptist and 1 Methodist house of worship, 1 Sabbath school, 2 mercantile stores, 1 boot and shoe maker and 1 blacksmith shop. The population is 43 including 1 physician.

Horntown P. V. is 16 miles northeast of Drummondtown and is on the Post Road leading to Snow Hill, Maryland. It is within a mile of a navigable stream for vessels which draw from 6 to 8 feet of water. It has 15 dwelling houses, 1 Methodist house of worship, 1 common school, 2 taverns, 4 mercantile stores, 1 house carpenter, 1 hatter, 1 wheelwright, 1 tanyard, 2 shoe and boot factories, and 1 mantua maker (dressmaker) and milliner. The population is 150.

The Episcopal church in Eastville in 1835 was Christ Church. It was built in 1826 to replace the old Magothy Bay Church which was condemned as unsafe and beyond repair. The absence of an Episcopal church in Drummondtown is explained by the fact that the colonial church was a mile south of the courthouse. In 1838 it was torn down and rebuilt on South Street in Drummondtown. Classical revival architectural design was used for the new edifice and the interior was painted with murals with Christian symbols and perspective lines to give the effect of a chancel extending beyond the back wall. (This is St. James Church in the present town of Accomac.) Francis Makemie Presbyterian Church was built on Back Street in Drummondtown in 1837. It, too, is in the classical revival style of architecture. Methodist and Baptist churches had been built in many sections of the Shore by this

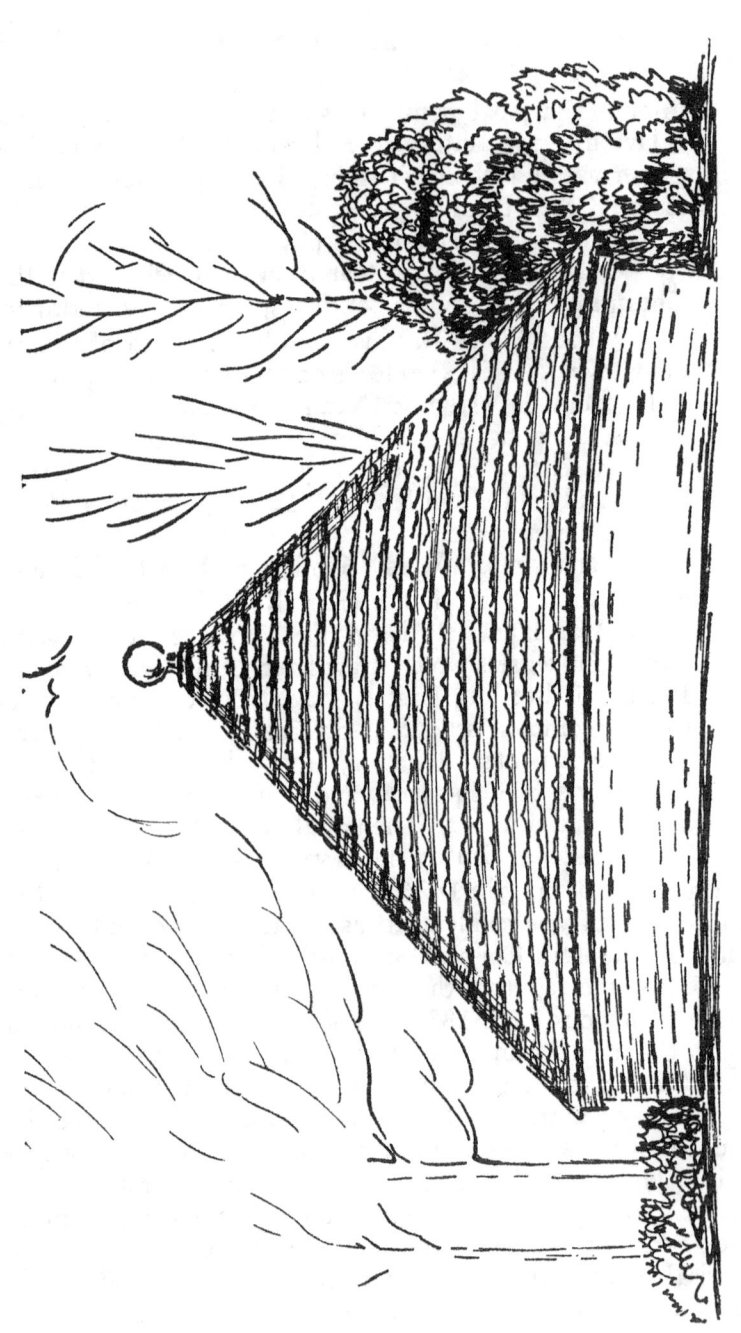

ICE HOUSE

time, but apparently no buildings in use in the 1830's are still in use. Most of those early ones were frame buildings and were replaced with brick structures.

Many plantations and town houses had ice houses. This was not a new practice, for references were found of harvesting ice and storing it for summer use at Jamestown in the seventeenth century. It is safe to assume that the early planters on the Eastern Shore provided themselves with the same conveniences. However, the ice houses which have survived were built in the early part of the nineteenth century. They remained in use until mechanical means of making ice for sale and delivery provided a supply at a reasonable cost.

The typical surviving ice house is a well about 20 feet in diameter and from 15 to 40 feet deep. The brick curb with mortar made of oyster shell lime makes the ice house waterproof even when nearby cellars are flooded. The curb extends from 3 to 4 feet above the ground and has a door 4 feet wide. The cone-shaped roof is of wood shingles and the top is ornamental but with holes for ventilation.

One of the best preserved of these ice houses is at The Folly, a plantation on the south side of Folly Creek near its head. It even has the ladder used to place the ice between layers of sawdust or carefully chosen leaves and to attach blocks of it to a pulley when it was to be removed for use. The owner of The Folly remembers when a dam was placed across a fresh-water branch to form a pond for harvesting ice. When the water froze to a depth sufficient to cut one-hundred-pound blocks, it was harvested with an ice saw pulled by a mule. When the weather was too mild for ice to be harvested locally, boatloads were brought from the Hudson River and other northern ice fields to be stored for summer use.

The need for lighthouses on the Eastern Shore had been evident since colonial times, but the actual building got under way in the 1830's. Cape Charles Lighthouse, on Smiths Island, was completed in 1828 at a cost of $7,398.82, appropriated by Congress. One on Assateague Island was completed the following year and land was purchased for one on

Watts Island in Chesapeake Bay. A study was under way for a lighthouse on Hog Island between Cape Charles and Assateague on the ocean side, but some years passed before Congress appropriated the money. Dwellings for the keeper and assistant keeper were built along with the lighthouses. The lights were oil lamps in front of reflectors so the lamps required daily care and the reflectors had to be cleaned at regular intervals. The lighthouse keeper was an important part of Shore life by the end of the 1830's.

Chapter XIII

1840-1870

Accomack and Northampton were wealthy farming counties when the first agricultural figures were officially recorded with the Sixth Census of the United States in 1840. The transition from staple crops to commercial vegetables was under way. The steamboat era was in sight and this new form of transportation got Eastern Shore products to market more rapidly than sail boats. Farm products and by-products were in demand in Washington, Baltimore, Philadelphia and New York. The completion of the Chesapeake and Delaware Canal across the fourteen-mile neck of the Delmarva Peninsula in 1829 shortened the distance from Chesapeake Bay ports to the northern cities.

The population of the Shore was 24,811 in 1840 and the people chose to live in the open country, or small villages, rather than in towns. No place had a population of 500 at this time. Post offices were opened at Franktown, Bridgetown, Messongo, Locustville and Locust Mount (now Wachapreague) after 1835. This made a total of thirteen for the Shore in 1840. Mail was still being sent with the word "prepaid" written by the address if the sender chose to pay the postage. Otherwise the recipient paid the charges. Newspapers presumably came to the Shore from northern cities as well as from Richmond. Merchants were interested in news from the places where they did business.

Agricultural products recorded in 1840 were in quantities produced rather than acres planted. The sweet potato was the commercial vegetable of greatest importance and 165,000 bushels were produced the year before this census. Corn, wheat, peas, and beans, including castor-oil beans, were among the staples. The census report included 10,254 pounds of cotton, 107 tons of flax and only 112 pounds of tobacco. Other items sold were 173 pounds of beeswax, 4598 bushels of salt and 3372 cords of firewood. The wood is called a by-product since it presumably was cut from land being cleared for farming.

Mills for grinding corn and wheat were among the early public utilities and the Shore had seventy-five in 1840. There were five lumber mills and one brick-making plant. Sixty-four stores were recorded. Some of the owners were post-masters, traders, importers and exporters.

The seafood industry was a going concern and oysters were being marketed in northern cities. Legislation had been enacted by the General Assembly prohibiting the sale of oysters between May 1 and September 1 as a conservation measure. It was unlawful to use seines or nets at the mouths of streams or in them between March 1 and October 1. No turtles were to be marketed during the same period and it was unlawful to disturb the eggs of turtles. Anyone convicted of breaking any of these laws forfeited his nets, seines, tongs and boat, and paid a fine. One half of the fine went to the informer. Although these conservation laws were in force, the census barely touched the seafood industry. Only one item, 234 pounds of salt fish, was recorded.

In 1841 Abel Parker Upshur was appointed Secretary of the Navy. He was the first Eastern Shore man to serve in a President's Cabinet. The Secretary of the Navy was well known on the Shore and in Virginia long before he received this appointment.

Abel Parker Upshur I was born June 17, 1790, at the spacious and artistic family home known as Vaucluse in Church Neck, Northampton County. He was the fifth of nine children born to Littleton I and Ann Parker Upshur. He attended Princeton University and then studied law under a tutor in Richmond.

He practiced law in Northampton County and began his political career as a member of the General Assembly from Northampton County in 1812. From 1818

CHAPTER XIII — 1840-1870

to 1823 he served as Commonwealth Attorney for the city of Richmond. He returned to Vaucluse and represented Northampton County in the General Assembly in 1824. Two years later he was appointed to the General Court by Governor John Tyler. Judges of the General Court also served as Circuit Court Judges. Abel Parker Upshur was a member of the Constitutional Convention of 1830. He continued to serve in the General Court and the Circuit which included Accomack and Northampton Counties until President John Tyler appointed him Secretary of the Navy in 1841. On June 24, 1843, he succeeded Daniel Webster as Secretary of State.

Secretary Upshur was killed accidentally on February 23, 1844, along with another Cabinet member and several others on the battleship *Princeton*, in the Potomac River. President Tyler, members of the Cabinet and others were on the ship to witness the firing of a new kind of cannon called "The Peacemaker." The first firing was without incident, but late in the afternoon a second firing resulted in an explosion of the gun and the end of the life of Abel Parker Upshur I, one of the Eastern Shore's most distinguished citizens. His brother George Parker Upshur was a naval officer of distinction and became Superintendent of the United States Naval Academy in 1847.

Steamboat ferry service began between the Eastern Shore and Norfolk, Hampton and Yorktown in the early 1840's. Either before or immediately after the death of John K. Floyd, who had operated the ferries from Kings Creek for two decades, a steamboat company got the franchise for both Accomack and Northampton counties. The terminal was moved to Cherrystone Creek in Northampton and two round trips a week were made to the ports on the mainland. Once a week the boats went to Pungoteague. The steamboats used on this route for many years were the *Star* and the *Joseph E. Coffee*.

In 1845 the General Assembly enacted a law permitting

communities to form school districts and to levy taxes for free schools. If a proposed district desired to take advantage of this regulation, the County Court appointed three election commissioners. All men who were entitled to vote in an election for a member of the General Assembly were entitled to vote. If three-fifths of the votes were in favor of a free school, it was established and the election commissioners served as the school commissioners until the following January 1. Thereafter three commissioners were elected by the voters for a one-year term to begin in January. Chincoteague Island was among the first communities in Accomack County to vote for a free school and some details are on record:

The Board of School Commissioners appointed a superintendent, who acted as treasurer and clerk. He collected school taxes in the district as the sheriff did in the county. He attended all meetings of the Board and kept a record of the proceedings. He kept a register of all children enrolled at the school and supplied them with books, stationery and other items authorized by the School Commissioners. The superintendent was required to give a bond in the amount of $1000 and his compensation was not to exceed $50 per year.

The School Commissioners selected the teachers and fixed their salaries. A member of the commission visited each school once every three months and examined the register of the teacher.

The teacher was required to teach reading, writing, arithmetic, English grammar and geography. When the commissioners considered it practical it designated other subjects to be taught. All children between the ages of six and twenty-one years living in the district were permitted to attend the school. Any pupil of incorrigibly bad habits or guilty of gross misconduct could be suspended.

In 1850 Accomack County had twenty-seven one-room schools with an enrollment of 1260 pupils. Northampton had thirteen such schools with an enrollment of 622. In addition to the taxes collected by the superintendent in the district,

CHAPTER XIII — 1840-1870

each county got a part of the State Literary Fund income. Upper Accomack had an annual income from land left by Samuel Sandford back in 1710 and Charles Piper who left 75 acres near Horntown for free school use in 1818. Private tutors were still serving many families.

The General Assembly of 1850 passed a law dealing with the marketing of sweet potatoes:

> Be it enacted that in the County of Accomack sweet potatoes shall be purchased and sold by weight and the standard weight of a bushel shall be 65 pounds and a barrel of sweet potatoes shall weigh 150 pounds. Any person who shall sell or purchase sweet potatoes in this county in any other manner shall pay a penalty of $21 for each offense upon conviction in any court having jurisdiction to try the case. But nothing in this act shall be construed to prohibit any person in said county from selling his crop of sweet potatoes by the gross, patch or hill.

When the Virginia Constitution was revised in 1851, a provision was made for the division of all counties into districts. Accomack was to have six districts and Northampton was to have three. No district was to have more than two voting precincts and one was to be at the Courthouse. The districts were numbered rather than named. Commissioners in each county were appointed by the Governor to lay out the districts and to designate the voting precincts. They were paid $2 per day.

The new Constitution extended the right to vote to every white male citizen over 21 years of age (except criminals, paupers and insane), while formerly a voter was required to own or hold a lease on real estate. The Governor, Lieutenant Governor, members of the Board of Public Works, Commonwealth Attorneys, county clerks, sheriffs and judges were to be elected by the people. Governor and Lieutenant Governor had been elected by the General Assembly, and other officers were appointed by the Governor and approved by the General Assembly. The Shore had not furnished a governor for the state of Virginia, but it had not been without public officials.

During the first half of the nineteenth century six Eastern Shore men represented their district in Congress. In 1801 Thomas Evans was succeeded by John Stratton of Northampton who served one term. Thomas M. Bayly of Accomack served from 1813 to 1815, Severn Eyre Parker of Northampton served from 1819 to 1821. Henry A. Wise served from 1831 to 1843. He was succeeded by Thomas H. Bayly of Accomack.

Henry A. Wise was the Democratic candidate for Governor of Virginia in 1855. During 1843, his last year in Congress, he built a house on Onancock Creek in Accomack County and named it Only. He served as Minister to Brazil from 1844 to 1847 and then returned to his native county to practice law and take part in political affairs. After Candidate Wise secured the nomination in a convention he canvassed the present area of Virginia and West Virginia and made speeches wherever people could be assembled to listen. The opposition candidate also covered the vast area throughout which voters lived.

Votes were still cast by voice. Magistrates who served as election judges sat on high benches with the clerks who called the names of the voters and recorded their votes at a low table in front of them. A judge repeated the name and asked, "For whom do you wish to vote for Governor?" The voter named the candidate of his choice. After the judges saw the vote written in the proper place, one of them announced the candidate for whom the vote had been cast. A representative of the fortunate candidate rose and thanked the voter. Voting was leisurely and time-consuming since this procedure was followed for every office to be filled by the election and for every person who appeared to cast his vote. More than two weeks passed before all the precincts got their reports to Richmond to show that Henry A. Wise was elected. He took the oath of office in the Capitol on January 1, 1856, and never returned to the Eastern Shore to live. He was a Brigadier General in the Confederate army and then practiced law in Richmond until his death in 1876.

CHAPTER XIII — 1840-1870

In 1855 a survey was made through the Shore for a railroad and the map which was published gives some interesting information although the railroad was not built. The title is *A Map and Profile, Experimental Survey, Virginia Section, New York and Norfolk Air Line Railway, May 1855.* The term air line was used to indicate a straight line. The proposed railroad was to extend from Snow Hill, Maryland, to Eastville in a straight line, then one branch was to terminate at the steamboat landing at Cherrystone and another was to go to the tip of the peninsula. In the northern part of Accomack County the proposed railroad was east of New Church, called Church Town on the map, on the west side of Drummondtown, through Belle Haven, Hadlock Town and Eastville. Hadlock Town was one of the important places on the map. The east branch was drawn through Capeville, west of Sea View then to Cape Charles. Among the unusual names of villages that have disappeared were Turkey Pen and Chinch Town.

The Eastern Shore had twenty-three post offices when the *Postal Guide* was published in 1856. The post offices and the names of the postmasters were:

Accomack County:
Accomack Courthouse (Drummondtown)
                              Samuel E. Lilliston
Belle Haven   Joshua E. Humphreys
Chincoteague   John W. Corbin
Guilford   Samuel Andrews
Horntown   John Henderson
Locust Mount   Nathaniel B. LeCato
Locustville   Emmanuel Binswarger
Messongo   Thomas A. Northam
Metompkin   John L. Snead
Modest Town   George W. Widgen
New Church   William H. Marshall
Onancock   Samuel L. Carmine
Pungoteague   Walter Raleigh
Temperanceville   William S. Byrd
Wagram (Northwest of New Church)

180   THE EASTERN SHORE OF VIRGINIA

Wiseville   Irvin W. Merrill
Northampton County: Oliver P. Drummond
Bayview
Capeville   John C. Dalby
Cherrystone   Thomas Hallett
Eastville   Edward T. Robins
Franktown   Leroy Oldham
Johnsontown   Thomas B. Fisher
Sea View   Albert G. Holt
                                 Edmond T. Nottingham

Postage stamps were first issued by the Government in 1847 and the charge for sending a piece of paper a distance of thirty miles or less was five cents, up to eighty miles 10 cents, to 150 miles was 12½ cents, to 400 miles was 18½ cents and any distance beyond that was 25 cents. When postage stamps were first issued they were in solid sheets to be cut apart with scissors and they had no glue on them. Prepayment of postage became mandatory the year the government issued its first stamps.

While the number of post offices was increasing, business was expanding and records were kept to show if an enterprise was yielding a profit, as well as to keep account of the purchases and payments of credit customers. The account book of Spencer D. Finney from 1852 to 1860 includes items imported, produce bought and sent to cities for sale and local customers' purchases. Among these are:

6 boxes soap, 28 lb. each at 7c per lb. $11.76
936 lb. sugar at 6c per lb.   56.16

The book gives the account of the cargo and profits of the Schooner *Magnolia* on a trading trip to a northern city in the fall of 1858:

Sold the loose potatoes for $348.00
Paid for them   293.75

    Profit from them $ 54.25
Second trip:
Sold loose potatoes for $337.02
Paid for them   277.32

CHAPTER XIII — 1840-1870

Profit from them	$ 59.70
Sold in barrels 4 barrels for	17.62
Total Profit	$ 77.32

The same account book, with another Finney name, listed the retail charges to some customers:

1 lb. coffee	$ .25
1 lb. bacon	.05
14½ yards of checked osnaburg at 35c	5.08
10 yards of domestic at 26c	2.60
1½ ounces of thread	.15
3 dozen buttons at 3c	.09
2 pounds butter	.62
14½ yards striped osnaburg	3.60
5½ yards satin	3.41
1 comb	.28
5 lb. sugar at 15c	.75
1 pair shoes	1.50
2 oz. indigo	.25
2 lamp chimneys at 12c	.24
20 lb. flour	1.00
2 bu. potatoes	2.00
2 gallons molasses at 50c	1.00
1 shovel	2.50
1½ yds. calico	.31
1 pair boots	5.00
1 tin basin	.31
1 broom	.25
2½ lb. of rope	.40
3½ lb. cheese	.53
3 boxes of lye at 20c	.60
½ gallon vinegar	.10
1 paper of pins	.10
Candy	.05

Some of the items were used for home industries to supply the needs on the farm. Soap for bathing was usually purchased, but that for laundry and cleaning was made at home.

From the earliest times of the English in America, lye for soap making was extracted from wood ashes by placing them in a hopper with a trough at the bottom. Water was poured over the ashes until the lye dripped in the form of a reddish liquid. This was boiled with fat until it was of the right consistency for liquid soap. Then it was strained and stored in large gourds or pottery containers. When lye crystals came on the market much of the labor of making laundry soap was eliminated.

Calico, satin, thread and osnaburg were materials for making clothing. This was done by hand at home. A traveling tailor, who lived with a family while he made the best clothes, was part of the commercial services during the 19th century, but most of the clothes were made by members of the household.

The census figures for 1860 show that the Eastern Shore was producing more food than formerly, less cotton, and no flax. The crop of Irish potatoes was 62,807 bushels while that of sweet potatoes was 305,525 bushels. The corn crop exceeded 1 million bushels and oats were produced in the amount of a half million bushels. Some of the corn and oats were used for food and feed on the farms, but a substantial surplus was exported.

At the beginning of the year 1861, the Eastern Shore was an important farming and maritime area with scheduled steamboat ferry service to the mainland. Steamboats were making regular stops on both bayside and seaside ports to deliver goods and to take on cargoes of farm produce and seafoods. Fleets of sailing ships owned by local people were trading with Cuba and other nearby islands, and with northern cities of the United States. The survival of sailboats in the steamboat era was due to the fact that the sails and rigging had been improved for more speed and smaller crews than in earlier times. The wind was free and wood or coal was required for the steamboats. Too, the initial cost of a steamboat was far more than that of a sail boat. One firm which had been in business since 1842, and the only one known to predate 1861 and still in business in 1963, is Hop-

CHAPTER XIII — 1840-1870 183

kins Brothers at the wharf in Onancock. It had a half dozen sailing ships to import goods and export produce in 1860. Many farmers owned small boats to use like farm wagons and several hundred watermen owned work boats.

Lighthouses were standing as sentinels in strategic places to guide the outgoing and incoming vessels. The most important one was built in 1832 on Smiths Island at the mouth of Chesapeake Bay. One on Assateague Island had been in service from 1833 and one on Watts Island in the bay was started that year. The Hog Island lighthouse was completed in 1852. Small lighthouses marked the entrances to Occohannock and Pungoteague creeks.

In 1857 a new brick tower was built for the Assateague light and it is still in use. The bricks were brought in by boat and hauled to the top of the sand ridge in carts pulled by oxen. The oyster shell lime was made near the building site. Tons of broken stone were hauled in to be put under the concrete foundation before the building was started. The red brick tower is more than 27 feet in diameter at the base and the wall there is 28 inches thick and it tapers gracefully to 129 feet in height where the lens is attached. A spiral stairway leads to the lens which was once lighted by oil lamps but was equipped with electric lights a century after the land for the lighthouse was purchased in 1832. Assateague light is located at 37 degrees 54 minutes and 40 seconds north latitude and 75 degrees 31 minutes and 23 seconds west longitude. Its importance in maritime history is extensive.

These lights were burning bright in February of 1861 when the delegates from Accomack and Northampton counties went to Richmond to the Convention which had been called to consider a referendum in which the people would decide whether to remain in the Union or secede and join the Confederate States of America. A referendum was ordered for May 23, 1861, in which the people of Accomack and Northampton counties were to accept or reject the action of the Convention to join the Confederacy. Before the date arrived, federal ships had taken possession of the lower Chesapeake Bay. The lighthouses were blinded by the Confederate

ASSATEAGUE LIGHTHOUSE
Brick Tower 142'

soldiers as soon as ferry service was stopped between the Eastern Shore and the mainland. Assateague light was not put out. Both counties, with the exception of Chincoteague precinct, voted to join the Confederacy.

The courts in both Accomack and Northampton counties authorized funds for arms and ammunition, and a recruiting program, between June and September 1861, resulted in an army of 800 men, divided into eight companies of infantrymen, two of cavalry and one of light artillery. Every able-bodied white man between the ages of 18 and 45 years was already a member of the local militia and there had been three drills a year. After the 800 were put into the army, drills for the militiamen were held weekly. The Shore militia was in three regiments with one in Northampton County, and one each in St. George and Accomack parishes in Accomack County. This had been the arrangement for drilling the militia since the War of 1812 while an era of peace prevailed.

Colonel Charles Smith of Ingleside, Eastville, was put in command of all the forces on the Shore. Lieutenant-Colonel Louis C. Finney of Meadville, near Onancock, was second in command, and Major R. R. Cary was third. Dr. Peter F. Browne of Accomac was assistant surgeon with the rank of Captain, and Richard B. Winder was assistant commissary with the rank of Captain. These officers received their commissions from President Jefferson Davis. Each company of infantry, cavalry and artillery was in charge of captains, first and second lieutenants and non-commissioned officers.

Major General John A Dix, a native of New York, was put in command of the defense of Maryland on July 23, 1861. Baltimore was known to have Confederate sympathizers. General Dix immediately saw the necessity of occupying the Eastern Shore of Virginia in order to keep Maryland supplies from being sent to the Confederates through Accomack and Northampton counties, and to keep those counties from influencing Maryland people to join the Confederate States. He worked out a plan for occupying these Virginia counties and the War Department approved it.

Brigadier General Henry H. Lockwood, a native of Kent County, Delaware, and a West Point graduate, was selected to head the army of occupation. He was a professor of mathematics when hostilities began but resigned immediately and enlisted. He was stationed at Cambridge. After he got a report of the Confederate activities in Accomack and Northampton, he requested an army large enough to show the Confederates that there was no need to fight. By November 15, 4500 troops were stationed at Newtown, now Pocomoke, Maryland. On that day General Dix sent a proclamation through General Lockwood "To the People of Accomack and Northampton Counties, Virginia." He offered assurance of protection of private property if the people would not resist the army of occupation. He promised to reopen trade with these counties and to restore the lights in the lighthouses.

When the troops began to arrive at Newtown, General Smith ordered his army of 800 men and about 1200 militiamen to the northern part of Accomack County to defend it. Breastworks, forming three sides of a pentagon, were built between New Church and the present intersection of the Chincoteague Road. General Smith had a way of keeping informed of what was taking place at Newtown. When the proclamation reached him, there was no alternative but to order a retreat. Before the Union Army had complete possession of Accomack and Northampton counties, 44 officers and 64 enlisted men escaped to the shores of Gloucester and Norfolk counties to join other units of the Confederate Army. Young men from the Shore who were in college enlisted and still others ran the blockade to join them. A total of 197 men from Accomack and 255 from Northampton served in the Confederate Army away from the Eastern Shore. Many letters written in camp to relatives on the Shore have survived.

General Lockwood occupied the home of Dr. Browne in Accomack and used the medical office in the yard for a telegraph office, as soon as lines were strung from Maryland. Property of people known to be in the Confederate Army

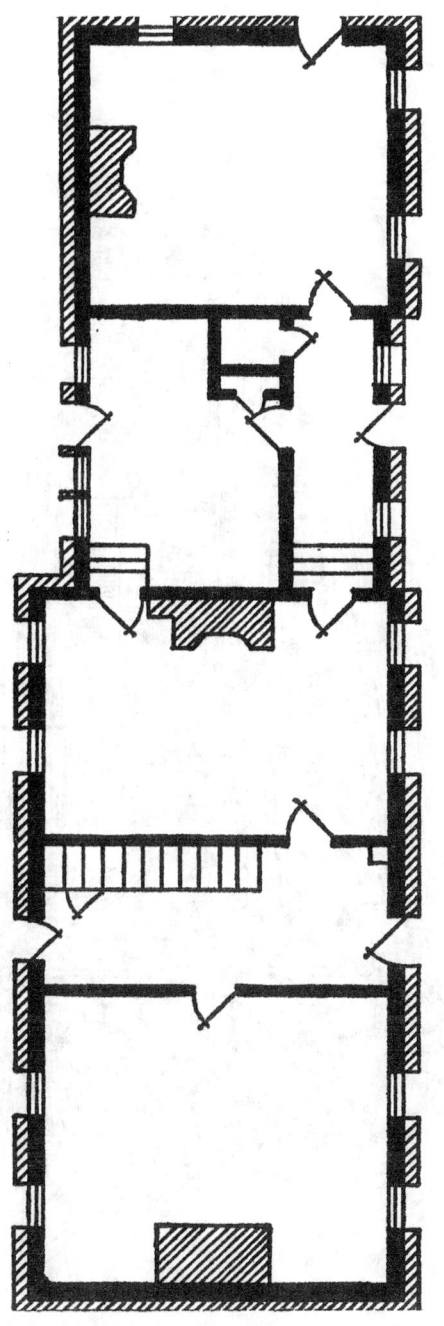

THE RECTORY

Floor Plan 86'   Built 1798-1811

The Rectory 1885   Union Army Hdq. 1861-65

BIG HOUSE, COLONNADE AND KITCHEN
The Rectory

CHAPTER XIII — 1840-1870

was confiscated, or commandeered. (It was eventually returned to the owners.) A camp near Accomac which had been used by the Confederates was occupied by the Union Army. Staff Headquarters for Northampton were established at Cessford in Eastville and the Union Camp for soldiers was in Old Town Neck where breastworks which probably date to the Revolutionary War are still visible.

On December 21, 1861, General Lockwood issued an order which shows that the occupation of Accomack and Northampton counties without bloodshed did not mean that the task was completed. Since several attempts had been made by men to run the blockade, guards were to be placed at the mouths of sixteen streams and landings. They were:

Cape Charles, Cherrystone Inlet, Chesconnessex Creek, Craddock Creek, Guilford Creek, Hungars Creek, Hunting Creek, Messongo Creek, Nandua Creek, Nassawadox Creek, Occohannock Creek, Old Plantation Creek, Onancock Creek, Pungoteague Inlet and Smiths Inlet.

The order directed that no trade should be permitted between soldiers and natives except under strict regulations. A portion of every article of food offered for sale to soldiers should be eaten in the presence of an officer before a soldier was permitted to buy it. The penalty for violating this order was to be punished by hard labor for one month. If hard labor was not practical, then the guilty soldier was to be imprisoned for one month with a diet of bread and water. Horses which had been purchased for the Confederate Cavalry and those owned by officers were taken over by the Union Army. The other horses on the Shore were undisturbed.

The Union soldiers used some churches for barracks or stables. Among these were Downings, near the Maryland line, Francis Makemie Presbyterian Church in Accomac, and the Methodist and Episcopal churches in Pungoteague. Through the influence of a tactful lady in Accomac, plans were abandoned to occupy St. James Episcopal Church and the commanding officer granted permission for services to be held there provided a prayer was said for the President of the United States.

Civil officers who took the Oath of Allegiance were permitted to carry on their work. The courts were restricted in the cases they could try during the first few months of the occupation. Everyone who practiced a profession, engaged in mercantile business, shipped produce, or left the Shore was required to take the Oath.

For administrative purposes the Federal government grouped Accomack and Northampton with the western counties that chose to stay in the Union when the referendum was held. However, there is no record of the Eastern Shore having been represented at the General Assembly in Wheeling, now in West Virginia. The Assembly provided for Accomack and Northampton to have a referendum for becoming a part of Maryland, but no record of a vote has been found.

The Eastern Shore of Virginia became an important link in the communication system between Washington, D. C. and Fort Monroe. A telegraph line was built through the Shore to Cherrystone and a cable was laid to Old Point. Troops were moved through the Shore to reinforce Fort Monroe. Steamboat service from Cherrystone was established by the army.

The state of West Virginia was formed from the counties that declined to join the Confederacy and was admitted to the Union in 1863. After the surrender at Appomattox in 1865, Virginia was given the status of a territory and was designated as Military District Number 1. Accomack and Northampton were a part of that District. A new Constitution acceptable to Congress was a requisite for Virginia's readmission to the Union.

A Constitutional Convention met in 1867 and finished its work in the spring of 1868. Congress accepted the Constitution but it was not presented to the voters for ratification until July 1869. Some of the objectionable clauses were to be voted on separately. The document known as the Underwood Constitution was accepted by the voters. The General Assembly met in October 1869 and Virginia was readmitted to the Union early in 1870.

Chapter XIV

1870-1900

The people of the Eastern Shore rejoiced with the rest of Virginia when self-government was restored early in 1870 and the last of the Union soldiers were withdrawn. They had been under military rule for more than eight years and Accomack and Northampton counties had been encouraged to join Maryland. The Constitution of 1869 required some changes in county government and the General Assembly met in March 1870 to provide for the changes.

On April 2 an Act was passed to divide the counties into townships as units of county government to replace the magisterial districts which had been created eighteen years earlier. The Governor appointed commissioners for Northampton and Accomack counties on April 21, and they were instructed to divide their respective counties according to area and population, and to include at least thirty square miles in each township.

The commissioners appointed for Northampton County were: Thomas J. Hallett, Leonard B. Nottingham, A. W. Downing, Edwin Goffigon and John W. Tankard. They were sworn in as required by law and met in the office of Severn P. Nottingham in Eastville with all the commissioners present except John W. Tankard. They divided Northampton County into three townships as follows:

> The township of Capeville was laid out to include all that part of the county which lies south of Salem Crossroad, including Mockhorn and Smiths islands. From the terminus of Salem Crossroad it extends on a straight line eastward through Dr. Thomas J. L. Nottingham's land to the creek, and from the western

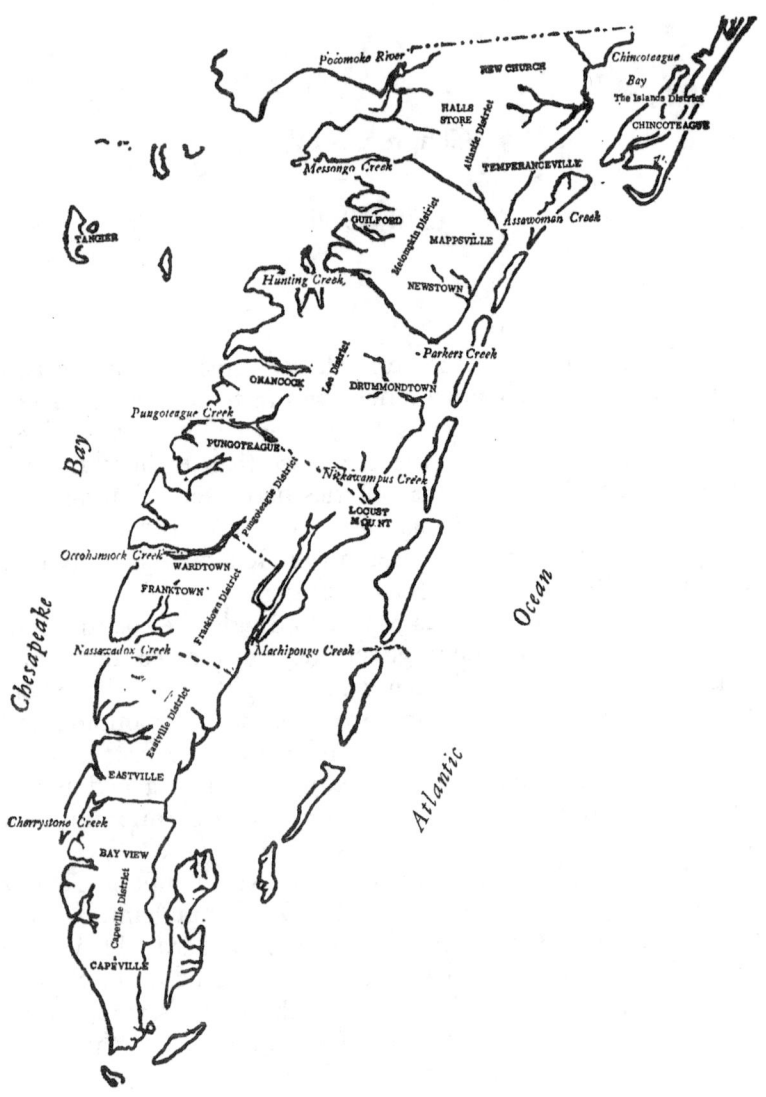

MAGISTERIAL DISTRICTS
AND BOUNDARY CREEKS 1870

CHAPTER XIV — 1870-1900

terminus of said crossroad in a straight line with Severn Eyre's riding-in way to Cherrystone Creek, and thence down said creek by Sandy Point to Chesapeake Bay, leaving Severn Eyre's house north of said line.

Eastville Township was to start at the line just designated and to include Sand Shoal Island which is between that line and one running from Red Bank Creek at the southeast corner of the land belonging to the estate of Jacob Nottingham, deceased. Then the line follows the Red Bank Road to Red Bank Church. Then it runs westwardly along said crossroad to the intersection of that road with Jacob Branch and down said branch to Parramores Mill. From there it runs down Church Creek to its mouth and thence down Nassawadox Creek to Chesapeake Bay.

Franktown Township was to include Hog Island and all of the area of the county between the Eastville Township line and the Accomack County line. The road dividing Capeville and Eastville townships is attached to Eastville Township and that road dividing Eastville and Franktown townships is attached to Franktown Township.

Capeville and Bayview were appointed as election precincts for Capeville Township; Eastville and Johnsontown were chosen as election precincts for Eastville Townships; and Franktown and Wardtown were designated as the election precincts for Franktown Township. The time required was one day each for four commissioners.

The report was accepted and recorded in the Deed Book of Northampton County in April 1870.

The commissioners for dividing Accomack County into townships were Thomas P. Copes, John E. Wise, William S. Byrd, J. W. Gillet and John R. Reade. They received the notice of their appointment on April 21 and on April 23 they took an oath before a justice of the peace "faithfully and honestly to discharge the duties required of them." The commissioners met on April 26 and 27 and after due consideration divided the county into five townships.

The Islands Township consisted of Chincoteague, Assateague, Piney Island and Popes Island. The Tavern House on Chincoteague Island was designated as the place for opening polls (in the said township for all elections in the commonwealth).

Atlantic Township was to begin at the Maryland line at the north with the east boundary in the middle of Chincoteague Bay, including Wallops Island and extending to Assawoman Inlet. The south boundary was placed through the said inlet and up Assawoman Creek and to a branch emptying into a prong of the creek, to the head of the branch. Then a right line was designated to a stone placed by the commissioners at a point where said line intersected Wallops Road, then to the head of a ditch and following the said ditch to the point where the ditch emptied into Messongo Branch, then through Messongo Creek to Pocomoke Sound. The line passed to the west of Sykes Island to the Maryland line. New Church, Temperanceville and the Store House of Henry Hall were designated as the places for opening polls.

Metompkin Township was to begin at the southeast corner of Atlantic Township and passed east of Assawoman, or Gargatha, and Metompkin beaches to Metompkin Inlet. Then it turned at a right line across Metompkin Bay to the mouth of Parkers Creek, then followed the line known as "the Parish Line" to the mouth of Hunting Creek, then in the bay west of Jobes Island and Bennett Island to the southwest corner of Atlantic Township. Mappsville, Newstown and the Store House at Guilford occupied by William H. Bloxom were designated for opening polls.

Lee Township was to begin at the southeast corner of Metompkin Township then extended southward along the Atlantic Ocean east of Cedar Island to Wachapreague Inlet. Then on a line through the said inlet and up Wachapreague Creek to Nocks Branch and up it through the big ditch to a sycamore tree near the head of the

CHAPTER XIV — 1870-1900

ditch, then to the northern end of the store house. Then along the Public Road leading toward the main road from Accomack Courthouse to Pungoteague until the first mentioned road reached Bull Branch. Then the line went down Bull Branch to Pungoteague Creek and through it to Chesapeake Bay, up the bay so as to include Tangier, Big Watts, Little Watts, Fox and Half Moon Islands, and any part of Smiths Island in Virginia, then to the mouth of Hunting Creek and along the southern boundary of Metompkin Township. Polls were to be opened at the Courthouse of Accomack County, in the town of Onancock, and on Tangier Island in the Store House formerly occupied by John Thomas.

Pungoteague Township was to begin in the Atlantic Ocean at the southeast corner of Lee Township and pass east of Parramores Beach to Machipongo Inlet, then through the inlet and up Machipongo Creek along the line dividing Accomack and Northampton counties and through the mouth of Occohannock Creek, then up Chesapeake Bay to the Lee Township line. Pungoteague and Locust Mount were designated as places for opening the polls.

In November 1874 the word "township" was changed to magisterial district by a Constitutional Amendment. The magisterial districts in both counties have retained their names and boundaries. But the big ditch between Atlantic and Metompkin districts was filled some years later, and an Act of the General Assembly in 1892 was required to have it opened and again accepted as a part of the boundary.

The modern school system began on the Shore on October 7, 1870, when the Governor of Virginia commissioned superintendents for the two counties. James C. Weaver held the office in Accomack County for the next fifteen years and John S. Parker served in Northampton for eleven years. A brief sketch of the life of the former is as follows:

James C. Weaver was born in 1822 at Portsmouth, Virginia, and educated at Richmond College. After graduation he came to Northampton County to teach.

After one session he went to Kentucky and qualified to practice law. After three years in that profession he returned to the Shore and married Sallie Pope Sturgis of Accomack County. He engaged in farming until 1861 when he enlisted in the Confederate Army. From 1865 to 1870, when he was appointed Superintendent of Accomack County Schools, he taught a private school near Onancock. His home was in Onancock, on Kerr Street, and his office was presumably in his home, his buggy or saddlebags and in his coat pocket. In 1885 James C. Weaver became associated with the *Eastern Virginian*, a newspaper published in Onancock. In 1887 he made an unsuccessful bid for the office as floater delegate to the General Assembly from Accomack and Northampton counties. He was appointed keeper of the Customs House in Onancock and held that office until his death in 1900. Some of his descendants are now teaching in Accomack County.

Three trustees were appointed for each magisterial district and these trustees composed the county school boards which met once a year. Accomack County had fifteen trustees and Northampton had nine. They qualified for office on January 1, 1871, and public schools went into operation on February 1. Since the labor of many children who should attend the public schools would be required on the farms of their parents at harvest time, the school term opened on February 1 and closed on June 30, during the first decade at least. Some existing schools with one or more students having their tuition paid out of the Literary Fund or other public money were taken into the new public school system. By June 30, 1871, Accomack County had thirty-two tuition-free schools and Northampton had four.

In 1873 the "Free School Land" bequeathed by Samuel Sandford in 1710 was surveyed and offered for sale to individuals. The survey showed 1660 acres of upland and more than 1700 acres of marsh. A two and one-half acre tract near Jenkins Bridge was reserved for a school and public wharf. The other land was sold to sixteen different people. The

CHAPTER XIV — 1870-1900

largest purchaser got some upland and the marsh, which was converted into a muskrat ranch. The village of Sanford is on part of the "Free School Land." The funds received from the land were made available to the part of Accomack County above Guilford Creek for building purposes. Atlantic District got three-fifths while the Islands and Metompkin districts got one-fifth each.

When James C. Weaver made his final report as superintendent of Accomack County schools in 1885, there were 82 public schools. Of these 18 were graded with more than one teacher. However, private tutors or neighborhood private schools were still used to educate many children.

In 1885 Northampton County had 26 public schools and several excellent and flourishing private schools. John S. Parker had been succeeded as superintendent by John B. Dalby in 1882. John R. Mapp became the third superintendent in 1885 and served until 1888 and was followed by Robert B. Handy. S. S. Wilkins succeeded him in 1893 and remained in office until 1903.

John E. Mapp, M.D. was the second superintendent of Accomack County Schools.

He was born on February 1, 1846, in Accomack County and received his early education in private schools. He was graduated from the College of Physicians and Surgeons in Baltimore. He married Margaret B. LeCato of Accomack County. (Their children and grandchildren have taught in the county school system and a grandson is now chairman of the Accomack County School Board.) After sixteen years in office, Dr. Mapp terminated his work as superintendent in 1901 and devoted his time to his medical practice until his death on April 20, 1927.

One college and at least nine academies served the Eastern Shore during the last half of the nineteenth century. In 1893 Margaret Academy was moved from near Pungoteague to Onancock. The trustees purchased the frame buildings on the site of the present Onancock High School for its use. These buildings had been erected in 1860 for the Atlantic Female College which was established by the Baptist church and closed within a decade. Locustville Academy was also a Baptist school. Other academies on the records were: Craddock and Occohannock Academy, Eastern Shore Academy, Eastville Academy, Jenkins Bridge Academy (a day school only), Machipongo Academy, Onancock Academy and Pungoteague Academy. The last ones closed thirty-one years after the modern public school system was established.

In June 1874 the Federal government established Life-Saving Stations on the Eastern Shore. This was only three years after Congress provided for Life-Saving Service in the United States. It was under the supervision of the Treasury Department. Numerous sea disasters near the Atlantic coast from Maine to Florida had molded public sentiment for something to aid seamen and save the cargoes of damaged ships. Prior to 1874 volunteers rendered valuable service whenever they found a ship in distress. The creation of a life-saving service meant that trained men with the proper equipment would always be near the scenes of possible disaster. Two-story frame houses were built with living quarters for a crew of men and rooms for lifeboats which could be launched on a moment's notice. The length of time on duty was a week or more and time off was the same. This new service attracted young men as a vocation. The stations authorized in 1874 were:

Assateague Beach Station, located on Fishing Point of Assateague Anchorage, $3\frac{1}{8}$ miles southwest of Assateague Light.

Wachapreague Beach Station, located on the south end of Cedar Island, on the north side of Wachapreague Inlet.

Hog Island Station, located near the south end of Hog Island, $1\frac{1}{2}$ miles southwest of Hog Island Light.

Cobbs Island Station, located near the south end of Cobbs Island, $7\frac{7}{8}$ miles southwest of Hog Island Light.

Smiths Island Station, on Smiths Island, $\frac{1}{8}$ mile west of Cape Charles Light.

In the next few years four additional Life-Saving Stations were authorized for the Shore by Acts of Congress on

CHAPTER XIV — 1870-1900

June 18, 1878, and May 4, 1882. The additional stations were:

Popes Island Station, on Popes Island on the Maryland line, 9¾ miles northeast of Assateague Light.

Wallops Beach Station, on Wallops Island, 5½ miles southwest of Assateague Light.

Metompkin Inlet Station, located on south end of Metompkin Island on the north side of Metompkin Inlet.

Parramores Beach Station, located on Parramores Island 2 miles south of Wachapreague Inlet and 11⅝ miles northeast of Hog Island Light.

The keeper had the status of a commissioned officer. He trained and drilled the men at regular intervals and directed their rescue tasks when disaster befell a ship in their area.

The shores from Delaware Bay to the mouth of Chesapeake Bay were designated as Life-Saving District No. 6 and Captain Benjamin W. Rich was appointed as its first superintendent. He was a seaman until he moved to Accomack County in 1857 to engage in farming. He was apppointed Superintendent of the Sixth Life-Saving District in 1875, and served until his death in 1901. During that time the men under his supervision helped in more than 800 sea disasters involving 6300 people and $12 million worth of property of which more than $8 million worth was saved. Only 45 lives were lost in the shipwrecks.

In the year 1884 a railroad was built through the Eastern Shore of Virginia to connect with the line in southern Maryland. The stations originally established took the names of nearby towns and villages although most of them were a mile or so away. When towns and villages were built around the stations, new names became necessary for establishing post offices near the stations. The original stations were: New Church, Messongo, Metompkin, Accomac, Pungoteague, Exmore, Bridgetown, Eastville and Cape Charles.

A harbor was built at the present town of Cape Charles along with the railroad. It was deep enough for large steamships and the station and wharf facilities were spacious and substantial. A steamship met each train to take passengers and mail to Old Point Comfort and Norfolk. When the first trains arrived from New York, passengers transferred to the steamer for a four-hour voyage to Norfolk in good weather. On November 22, 1884, a Shore newspaper contained this item:

> The first through fast express train was run over the N.Y.P. & N.R.R. on Monday night. The steamer *Jane Mosley* left Norfolk at 6:30 P.M. with fifteen through passengers for the North. She made good time to Cape Charles City and the train left immediately. The speed to Wilmington, Delaware, averaged forty miles per hour and the train arrived there at 3:00 A.M., Tuesday.

The *Jane Mosley* apparently was a chartered boat for use while the *Cape Charles*, a steamer equipped with tracks for Pullman cars, was being completed. This luxury liner, which enabled passengers to remain in their seats or berths from New York to Norfolk, was short lived and the practice of having passengers walk aboard the ships was resumed before 1890. The *Cape Charles* was a side-wheeler steamboat with two smoke stacks. It was launched in 1885 and was superseded by the *Old Point Comfort*, another side-wheeler, two years later. The *New York*, a screw-propelled steamer, joined the *Old Point Comfort* in 1890.

William T. Scott owned the land on which Cape Charles Station was built. He had the area west of the station laid out in blocks for a town. The building of homes and churches as well as business houses began immediately. By the end of the year 1885, the town of Cape Charles had a volunteer fire department with some equipment on push carts. This was the beginning of town and village building around the railroad stations.

In less than a year after the railroad was built, a move was made to relocate the Accomack County Courthouse near it. By an Act of the General Assembly approved February 1885, a referendum was held. The proposed new site was north of the present village of Greenbush on the land of the

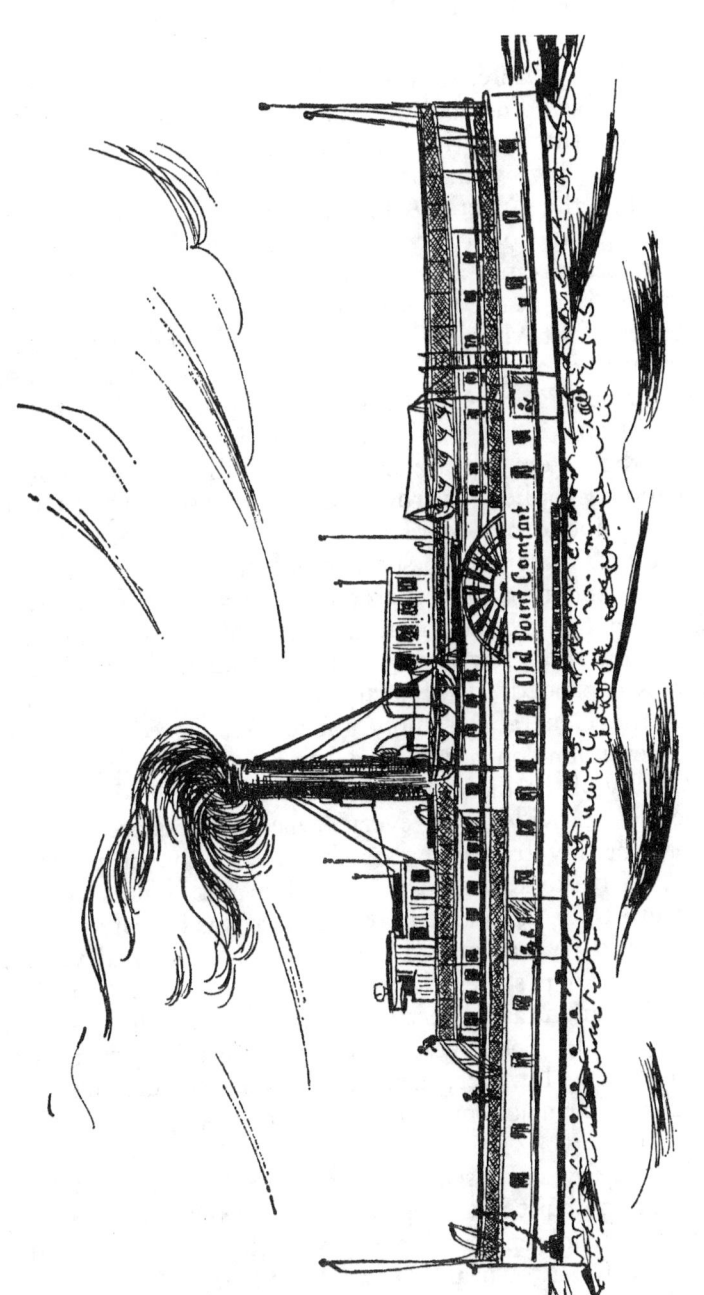

OLD POINT COMFORT
P.R.R. Steamer 1887

heirs of Harry White, deceased, three miles from the location of Accomac. The vote was taken on the fourth Thursday in May and the majority favored leaving the Courthouse where it was. Two years later a Clerk's Office was built.

In 1890 the General Assembly provided for the citizens of Northampton County to vote on the question of moving the county seat from Eastville to Cape Charles. The voting was to take place at the time of the general election on Tuesday after the first Monday in November. The bill designated the wording of the ballots: "For removal of the Courthouse to Cape Charles," or "Against the removal of the Courthouse to Cape Charles." If the removal was favored by the majority of the voters the property at Eastville was to be sold and the money applied toward a new Courthouse and jail. The county was not to pay more than $5000. The town was to pay $5000. The removal issue was defeated.

The problem of protecting crops and gardens from livestock, which had existed from the days of the first private ownership of land, grew worse as the production of commercial vegetables expanded. In January 1896 Northampton Delegates to the General Assembly got an Act passed providing for a referendum on a no-fence law. It was to be county wide but any of the three districts could accept or reject it. A no-fence law provided that every owner of livestock was responsible for any trespassing or damage on the property of another. Livestock was to be fenced in and fences around fields were to be abandoned. If the Act was defeated every farmer would be required to have his fields enclosed with a lawful fence "of posts and boards or posts and wire 44 inches high or of mauled rails 4 feet high." Apparently the no-fence law was passed. Some years later Accomack County passed a similar law. However, incidents between citizens over the livestock of their neighbors continued to occupy space in county court records.

Parksley was the second town to be laid out around a railroad station built in the open country. Henry R. Bennett, a paint salesman representing a Philadelphia firm, saw the opportunity for a town at Metompkin Station, and he inter-

CHAPTER XIV — 1870-1900

ested enough capitalists to form the Parksley Land Improvement Company in 1885. A 160-acre tract of land was purchased from Benjamin F. Parks and surveyed. A business section on both sides of the railroad and residential blocks with broad streets and service alleys for each block were laid out. Lots sold rapidly.

All went well for Metompkin Town until the officials of the corporation filed an application for a post office. They were informed that there was already a post office by that name some three miles to the east of the station. Negotiations were undertaken to get the patrons of that little post office to give up the name in favor of the potential city of Metompkin. When negotiations failed, the officers of the Land Improvement Company chose the name Parksley, in honor of Benjamin F. Parks. In order to guard against the sale of lots adjoining the town, the corporation reserved a strip four feet wide around the town. Every deed contained a clause to the effect that if alcoholic beverage was sold on the lot the land reverted back to the Parksley Land Improvement Company or its successor. Businessmen from Lee Mont, west of this new town, built stores and eventually built homes in Parksley. Some retired people associated with the railroad also built homes.

The experience of settlers around other stations in making applications for post offices duplicated that of Metompkin, so new names were given the stations. Messongo became Hallstown and eventually Hallwood. Accomac Station became Tasley, and Pungoteague Station became Keller. Exmore apparently was a new name and tradition says it was so named because it was the tenth station south of Delaware. Bridgetown Station became Birdsnest, and Eastville Station got a post office although it was a mile from Eastville Courthouse. Oak Hall Station was opened before the post office dilemma arose and the village around it took the name Horsey. At least ten additional stations were opened before the end of the nineteenth century. The early stations, except in Cape Charles, were two-story buildings and the agent's family lived on the second floor.

The railroad with fast trains to New York and connections with other cities hastened the conversion of the Shore crops to sweet and Irish potatoes, strawberries and other perishable foods. Grain was limited mostly to food and feed for the individual farms. Most of the potatoes were shipped in barrels and a barrel factory was among the first industries to start around the railroad stations. The legal weight of a bushel of Irish potatoes was 60 pounds and a barrel held three bushels. A bushel of sweet potatoes had a legal weight of 56 pounds and a barrel held three bushels.

The trains also brought salesmen, called drummers, with large trunks of sample shoes, yard goods, the latest fashions in men's clothing and women's coats, and other items for comfortable living. Hotels were built at the railroad villages and livery stables were maintained to transport the drummers and their samples to stores in the surrounding area. The hotels also were patronized by produce buyers, fertilizer salesmen and bachelors who worked in the community. Near the end of the century at least one dentist spent one week each month as an itinerant practitioner in a hotel room with his portable equipment to serve the surrounding area. Some patients came from a distance by train.

The seafood industry was second only to sweet and Irish potatoes as a source of income near the end of the nineteenth century. In addition to the edible seafoods, menhaden, locally called "old wives," were caught for the manufacture of oil and fertilizer. There were at least three fish factories on the Shore in the late 1800's. Oysters were sent to canning factories in the shell or opened and iced for market in northern cities. Clams, crabs and some turtles were likewise marketed.

By 1891 the oyster rocks were rapidly becoming depleted and the General Assembly strengthened legislation to protect them and to increase the business of leasing oyster grounds to individuals. This practice was already in use but no boundaries of leased grounds were recorded. The Governor recommended a survey of all oyster grounds in the state and that holders of leases be protected by law. This led to the employment of Lieutenant James B. Baylor, of the United States Coast and

Geodetic Survey. All areas that had oysters in them were designated as public grounds, or rocks, and any citizen of Virginia could harvest oysters upon paying a nominal fee for a license. This was recorded as the Baylor Survey and is still in effect. By the end of the century much of the oyster harvest from the Eastern Shore was made from leased grounds where the lessees had brought in shells or rocks as a foundation, then spread seed oysters over them. Oyster farming helped save the oyster industry for the Shore.

The demand for good roads to railroad stations was so great that each magisterial district had a road superintendent who was employed and paid by the Board of Supervisors. He was given the authority to employ the necessary workmen to build roads and bridges at a wage not to exceed 30 cents per hour for actual working time. On the second Monday in January of each year the supervisors estimated the cost of the roads for each district and levied a tax to pay for it. Each county was required to own eight mules to work on the roads, two road scrapers, one stump puller, the necessary plows, hoes, axes and one or more road machines. The supervisors had the authority to buy any other necessary implements. This method of building roads was far different from a century earlier when every man was required to donate a designated number of days, either in person or by a workman he sent, each year to road work. One set of equipment was enough for Northampton but the size of Accomack County necessitated a set for each parish, as the upper and lower parts of the county were still designated.

The vehicles used on the roads near the end of the nineteenth century and some years later have strange sounding names. Among these were tumbril carts, double wagons, single wagons, buggies, hacks, surreys, speed carts and bicycles. The latter was the only vehicle not drawn by an animal. Instances are on record in which horses became frightened by bicycles and got out of control of the driver.

The Shore was widely known for its recreational facilities. Resort hotels were operated on Cobbs Island on the seaside and in Occohannock Neck on the bayside of Northampton County. The former featured surf bathing, croquet and billiards as well as gunning and fishing. The latter was for recreation and health and one of the offerings was "hot salt water baths for rheumatism." The commercial inns which survived from the previous century and new hotels also catered to sports fishermen and those who came in season to shoot wild ducks and geese and marsh hens. The limit per hunter was restricted only by his skill with a gun.

In 1896 an Act of the General Assembly was amended further to protect wildlife on the Shore. It was unlawful to kill rabbits or quail between January 15 and November 15, or to destroy quail eggs at any time. The season for shooting marsh hens was from September 15 to January 15 and no marsh hen eggs were to be taken after June 1. No gulls were to be killed and it was unlawful to take their eggs after July 4.

At this time people went "egging" on seaside islands in the spring in the same sporting spirit as they went gunning in winter. A gallon or a bushel of eggs might be collected in a half day. Some were frequently boiled and eaten on the island along with a packed lunch. The greater part of the harvest was brought home to be eaten by the family and shared with friends and neighbors after a real successful trip. In time the sport of egging was prohibited at all times to help prevent the extinction of certain species of wildlife.

The outstanding public social and recreational event in the last two decades of the nineteenth century and for many years after was the Keller Agricultural Fair. This institution had its beginning in 1878, three years after the Eastern Shore Grange Society was organized. Farm products were exhibited by Grange members at the Turlington Camp Meeting Grounds northeast of the present village of Keller. The next year the fair was held for two days and some colts and other livestock were paraded before the audience. The event met with such success that in 1880 the Grange acquired land for a fair. It included a race track. A Grange Hall was built with living quarters upstairs for the keeper and his family. After the Grange ceased to exist the Eastern Shore Agricultural Fair Association was formed and stock was sold to buy the Grange property and additional land. A large grandstand with an agricultural exhibit hall beneath was built, and in time special buildings for poultry and livestock and stables for race horses were added. Horse racing was a sport in the seventeenth century and the breeding and training of race horses has been a vocation through the years. The Keller Fair attracted race horses from the mainland of Virginia and from neighboring states.

By the end of the century former citizens of the Shore made annual visits to coincide with the Keller Fair. Thursday was designated as homecoming day. Some families brought packed lunches for themselves and friends while others got meals at the "boarding tent" which was a restaurant with a sawdust floor and some of the best cooks on the Shore to prepare the food which was served for a nominal charge. Cape Charles and Tasley held fairs for some years but they never reached the importance of the "Grange Fair" as some people always called it. Keller Fair was also handshaking time for aspirants to political offices from justices of the peace to United States Senators and Congressmen.

Two Eastern Shore men were elected to Congress after 1870. George Tankard Garrison whose home was across Folly Creek from The Folly, and the site of the first Accomack Country Club, represented the First Congressional District from 1881 to 1885. Thomas H. Bayly Browne, one time owner of Bowmans Folly, served from 1887 to 1891.

Every community with a name either had one or more churches or the people attended services of their denomination in a nearby community. Methodist, Baptist, Presbyterian and Episcopal were the denominations with churches on the Shore. A successor to the seventeenth century church at Assawoman had been built at Temperanceville in 1860. This was Emmanuel Episcopal Church, a Gothic style frame building, and it was not used by the Union Army. But in 1887 it was torn down and moved to Jenkins Bridge. The Baptists and Methodists were anticipating the erection of brick churches to replace their early frame ones. Throughout the nineteenth century the Methodist camp meetings were annual events. The camp grounds at Pungoteague were mentioned in 1804 and those at Tangier which featured in the War of 1812 continued in use. The best known one in the 1890's was The Turlington Camp Meeting near the Keller Fair Grounds.

Court days were important social events for the men. Public issues were discussed among friends who, in turn, led discussions back at the country stores which were crossroad seminars from colonial times.

In 1898 a move was made to locate the courthouse in Parksley and the question was to be settled by the Board of Supervisors. At that time people from Chincoteague came to the head of Folly Creek by boat and walked to the Courthouse. One of the points brought out against removing the courthouse to a railroad town was that Chincoteague people would be inconvenienced and exempt from jury duty just as those on Tangier were. The supervisors voted to build a new courthouse in Accomac, where the court had been meeting since 1693. The present courthouse was completed in 1899. Northampton County also built a new courthouse in 1899.

In 1899 the Eastern Shore had 105 post offices, but some of these were on their way out. Marsh Market, at the mouth of Messongo Creek, lost much of its business when a harbor was dredged to Sykes Island which was called Saxis by 1897. Before that time steamboats landed at the Hummock near Marsh Market and small boats ferried the mail and merchandise to Sykes Island. Many of the communities on the Shore had telephone service supplied by a number of small companies. Steamboats held their own against the competition of the railroad. And, telegraph service was available at the railroad stations.

But all of the means of communication and transportation did not spoil the leisurely way of life which characterized the Eastern Shore. People not only knew how to earn a good living but they knew how to enjoy leisure time and the diversions the Shore had to offer.

Chapter XV

1900-1920

In the year 1900 the Eastern Shore was as far advanced in the production of commercial vegetables as any part of the nation and seafood from adjoining waters found markets throughout the East. The population was 46,340, with 32,570 people in Accomack County and 13,770 in Northampton. Their distribution in Accomack County by magisterial districts from the Maryland line was: Atlantic, 7320; Islands District, 2743; Metompkin, 6133; Lee, 9247; and Pungoteague, 7127. In Northampton, from the Accomack County line, the distribution was: Franktown, 5086; Eastville, 4958; and Capeville, 6628. The latter included Cape Charles with a population of 1948. Other incorporated towns were Eastville, Onancock and Belle Haven.

Census figures for 1900 show the agricultural records for the previous year when 11,500 acres of Irish potatoes and 9300 acres of sweet potatoes were grown on the Shore. Although these crops covered less than ten per cent of the 140,500 cultivated acres, Irish and sweet potatoes were the principal money crops. Irish potatoes had a strong appeal because of the short time between planting and harvesting, a good income per acre, and the opportunity for planting another crop on the same land. This second crop was usually corn, and known locally as "tater corn." The greatest need was a marketing system.

The Eastern Shore of Virginia Produce Exchange was chartered by the General Assembly on January 20, 1900. A group of farmers and some professional men met on September 10 of the previous year to consider the possibility of forming a marketing organization. They framed a constitu-

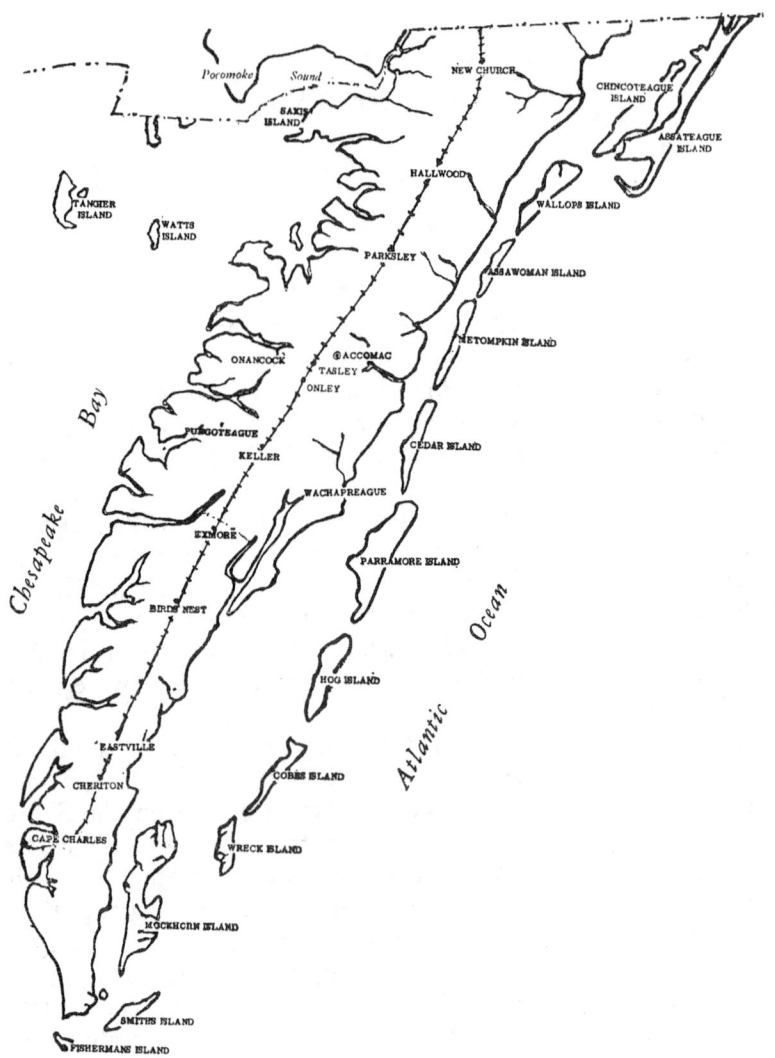

RAILROAD AND MAIN STATIONS 1900

CHAPTER XV — 1900-1920

tion which was approved at a mass-meeting on September 30. The charter stated the object of the organization as follows:

To buy and sell produce as the agent of the producer; to consign produce as agent of the producer; to inspect all produce it may handle; to own and operate storage warehouses and packing houses; and to engage in all other lawful things customarily connected with the trade known as the produce business.

The incorporators were Benjamin T. Gunter, John E. Nottingham, Thomas B. Quinby, L. Thomas LeCato, John W. Bowdoin, John H. Ayres, Albert J. McMath, Thomas B. James, Levin J. Hyslop, Hezekiah A. Wescott, William Elzey, John H. Roberts, William B. Pitts, George Walter Mapp, John T. Williams, Jr., and William E. Thomas.

The incorporators and John H. Wise made up the first board of directors. Benjamin T. Gunter was elected president and Thomas B. Quinby was the first secretary. William A. Burton was employed as general manager, sales manager and treasurer for the first shipping season and L. Thomas LeCato was general inspector. Thomas B. Quinby resigned in September of 1900 and Albert J. McMath was elected secretary-treasurer.

Two grades of potatoes were packed for sale through the Produce Exchange. The first-quality package was the "Red Star Brand" while the second was the "Gear Wheel Brand." Getting quality packages and uniform barrels was one of the difficult tasks in the early days. Small barrels and large barrels had been in general use for Irish potatoes, and one historian stated that early inspectors sometimes found a pumpkin near the bottom of a barrel of sweet potatoes. With the grading system in effect and daily contact with markets in the United States, Canada and Cuba, the Eastern Shore potato market was greatly expanded. The profit per barrel was increased through systematic marketing.

The stockholders of the Exchange got substantial dividends and they built an imposing brick administration building in Onley. The personnel was increased to handle the expanding business and a representative was employed at each railroad station.

The increase in potato acreage in 1901 was phenomenal, and it marked only the beginning of the transition to a one-crop system of farming and a large cash income for the Shore. The demand for more merchandise such as clothes, furniture, imported food, building materials and new vehicles for transportation followed. One of the luxury items purchased in 1901 by three Accomac men was a gasoline launch to be used as a "pleasure boat" in seaside waters.

The hotel business was good and competition was keen for the patronage of the salesmen. During the week of January 18, 1902, one railroad town had forty traveling salesmen among its guests. Livery stables with carriages to transport large trunks of samples also did a thriving business. The most up-to-date of the hotels had running water from large elevated tanks into which the water was pumped by windmills above the tanks. The Wachapreague Hotel, one of the largest ever built on the Shore, opened for business in 1902. It was designed for commercial trade and sports fishermen and gunners. A steamer from New York to Norfolk stopped near Wachapreague, and livery stable managers at Keller stood ready to transport passengers who arrived by train.

Commercial ice plants were among the new industries which were established. Railroad cars carried blocks of ice along with crates of strawberries, and they were also equipped with ice chambers to cool the entire cars. Commercial ice was in demand for home use as fast as people could get refrigerators, and the ice wagons made house-to-house deliveries.

Vegetable canning was started on the Shore in 1900. John W. Taylor of Wharton Place, near Mappsville, opened a factory for the canning of tomatoes in the fall of that year. Other factories opened and closed until 1917 when H. E. Kelley of New Church began canning vegetables for sale during World War I. John W. Taylor Packing Company and H. E. Kelley and Co., Inc. are still in business.

The Victorian style of architecture made its appearance on the Shore when the new towns of Cape Charles and Parks-

CHAPTER XV — 1900-1920

ley were built. At first the houses were two-story rectangular buildings with four gables, but as time went on, the fad for more ornate roof lines with cupolas grew. Bulging rooms with six or more windows and spacious porches on three sides of the houses characterized the houses built in the first two decades of the twentieth century. Many early colonial and Georgian houses were remodelled and Victorian porches added to give them a fashionable look. Fortunately, people appreciated their good furniture enough to refrain from trading it for the golden oak of the times. Phonographs were new and so few people had them in 1902 that "a graphaphone party" was a newsworthy social gathering.

When the report reached the Shore that the Wright Brothers had actually flown a flying machine at Kitty Hawk, North Carolina, on December 17, 1903, the few people who paid any attention to the report in a Norfolk newspaper were skeptical. Only birds, kites and balloons were supposed to fly.

Some people had seen horseless carriages, called automobiles, on visits to the city and a few were aspiring to own one early in the century. The first one was owned by Claude Nottingham of Onancock about 1906. It has been said that ladies would not go out in their carriages until the said Nottingham was consulted to see if he expected to use that horse-frightening machine that day. W. P. Bell of Accomac owned the second automobile on the Shore, and it is described as a one-cylinder affair with the motor under the seat, the crank-starter on one side and a top like a buggy with front and side curtains to snap in place in case of rain. Through the year 1910 the purchase of an automobile, usually made in Baltimore and brought home by steamboat, was news for the papers.

On March 17, 1906, the General Assembly approved an Act for operating automobiles. Every owner was required to apply to the Secretary of the Commonwealth for a certificate of registration. The registration certificate contained a number assigned to the automobile, the owner's name and address and the registration date. One license plate bearing the registration number was supplied for the rear of the automobile. The registration fee was $2.00 and the license was good for the life of the car unless it was sold. Then the new owner applied for a new registration. The rate of speed was fixed at fifteen miles per hour in the open country and eight miles per hour for going around curves, up and down hills, and in villages, towns, or cities.

The driver was to watch for the approach of horseback riders and vehicles drawn by animals. If the driver or rider found his animal frightened, he was to signal the driver of the horseless carriage to stop until the frightened animal passed. If such driver were a man, he could be asked to lead the frightened animal past his horseless carriage. If the horseless carriage driver wished to pass an animal-drawn vehicle, he was to give the signal by a bell, gong or horn and passing speed was not to exceed four miles per hour. If the animal became frightened, the driver was to get out and hold it until it became quiet, then drive his automobile past it. Fines of from $10 to $100 were imposed for failure to obey these rules.

Interest in road improvement on a state-wide basis had been growing for some years before the advent of the automobile. Benjamin T. Gunter represented the Eastern Shore at the Governor's Good Road Conference in Richmond in 1902. Road building was a business of the Board of Supervisors on a district basis.

Public schools gained in favor and replaced private academies early in the century. The first graduating class in a high school on the Shore was at Cape Charles in 1901 with three members. Elmore Dickinson was the principal and the four-room building was on Monroe Avenue.

The first graduates in Accomack County were two girls in 1903. Edgar Sydenstricker was principal. He had succeeded G. Goodwyn Joynes who became superintendent:

> G. Goodwyn Joynes was born near Onancock on September 6, 1865. After his graduation from Dickinson College, Carlisle, Pennsylvania, he taught for two years at Finneys Gate School near Onancock, and then became principal of the Onancock Graded Public School.

CHAPTER XV — 1900-1920

In 1880 he married Sallie Wright Northam. They sent their children to the public school when their friends were ardent supporters of private schools and academies. In July 1901 he became Superintendent of Accomack County Schools and served in that capacity until his retirement in 1924. He died at his home on Market Street, Onancock, in 1932.

The first public schoolhouse in Onancock was in a building located in what is now a field two blocks east of Kerr Place. The high school was established in a building erected for a garment factory on Kerr Street. It remained there until 1918 when the site of the present building was purchased. A former Margaret Academy building was used until the brick building was completed in 1921.

Margaret Academy was operated during the term 1901-1902 with C. W. Mason as principal. On November 30, 1901, he submitted a list of twenty-six names of students with "distinguished standing" for the first quarter. This century old institution of learning was closed in the spring of 1902.

Pungoteague Academy closed when a public high school was established in 1902 for the Pungoteague-Harborton area. A notice appeared in the county paper in August advising parents to send their children to the public school.

The year 1902 brought the establishment of high schools in a number of places in Accomack County and the number of small schools increased. Superintendent Joynes' report in July 1908 showed 153 schools.

Northampton County also established high schools and increased the number of elementary schools. Luther Nottingham became county superintendent in 1903 and held the office for six years. A. Preston Scott succeeded him in 1909. He had a B.A. degree from Hampden-Sydney College and was on the faculty of The Presbyterian College, Fredericksburg, when he returned to his home county as superintendent. After two years he entered private business there. Edward G. Tankard was superintendent from 1911 to 1921. He was born near Hadlock, Northampton County, in 1862 and died in 1946.

He was recognized as one of the Shore's outstanding business men.

A teacher training department was established in the Onancock High School in 1908 and continued until 1915. Students from the Maryland line to Cape Charles boarded in private homes in Onancock to take this course in the tenth and eleventh grades, or after they graduated from high school. Upon completion of the "Normal School Course," as it was called, and reaching the age of eighteen years a student was issued a teacher's certificate. This provided a supply of teachers for the smaller schools when graduates from colleges or institutions of higher learning were not available.

The first children on the Shore to have transportation to school at public expense were from Lee Mont and Bayside to Hunting Creek in 1902. Benches were built on the sides of the platform of a farm wagon and a step was lowered at the back for children to get in or out. In clear warm weather the wagon had no cover, but an oval frame with canvas over it provided protection from rain or chilly weather.

Interest in local history antedated the twentieth century. It reached a visible form in historical markers in the first twenty years of this century. In 1899 the Confederate Monument was dedicated at Parksley. It was erected by the Harmanson-West Camp Confederate Volunteers in memory of their dead comrades from Accomack and Northampton Counties. Then in 1913 a Confederate monument was dedicated in Eastville. It was erected by the Harmanson-West Camp Confederate Veterans, the Daughters of the Confederacy and the citizens of the Eastern Shore in memory of the soldiers from Accomack and Northampton who lost their lives in Confederate service.

On May 14, 1908, a monument was dedicated to Francis Makemie at his former home and burial place on Holden Creek not far from its junction with Pocomoke Sound. This life size monument on a high pedestal is dedicated to:

The chief founder of organized Presbytery in America,
A. D. 1706, and the First Moderator of the
General Presbytery.

CHAPTER XV — 1900-1920

This monument and a brick pyramid with a marble tablet bearing an inscription about Makemie's wife's family and his children, including Madam Holden for whom the creek is named, were placed in a small park. This park and the monument were gifts of the American Presbyterian Historical Society, with headquarters in Philadelphia. Bloomtown Railroad Station was changed to Makemie Park. A local Makemie Memorial Association was organized to care for the park and to further interest in Francis Makemie. The association is still active. A memorial service was held at the little park in 1958, the 300th anniversary of Makemie's birth.

Speeches made at the dedication services of the Accomack and Northampton courthouses preserved some of the Shore's history and created a new interest in the Shore's rich heritage, including court records which are continuous from 1632.

The most dedicated student of local history in the last quarter of the nineteenth and first decade of the twentieth century was Thomas Teackle Upshur:

Thomas Teackle Upshur was born at Brownsville, Northampton County, December 22, 1844. He entered Virginia Military Institute in 1859 and volunteered for Confederate service in 1861. He was appointed drill master for a company under Captain Spencer Fletcher of Jenkins Bridge. He left the Shore before it was occupied by Union soldiers and spent the rest of the war years in a company of scouts and couriers.

After the war he became associated with a Baltimore business firm and was sent to a branch in Sumter, South Carolina. There he married Caroline deSaussure Blanding. Before 1880 he returned to Brownsville and engaged in farming and delving in the ancient Court Records of Northampton County. He mastered the skill of reading the handwriting of the early clerks and did extensive research on his family back to Sir George Yeardley. He wrote articles for historical magazines which brought him well deserved recognition.

In 1892 Thomas Teackle Upshur was commissioned by the Virginia State Library to transcribe the first and second books of the Accomack-Northampton Court Records. He completed the assignment in 1896, with two books in handwriting as even as engraving and more intricately indexed than the originals.

He was then commissioned to transcribe other records for Northampton County. In his later years he worked in a rocking chair at home with a board across the arms. His handwriting continued to resemble engraving to the last word.

Thomas Teackle Upshur died on January 14, 1910, leaving his local history work unfinished. His children shared his records with others interested in Shore history.

The establishment of the "McMaster Old Home Essay Award" by John Stevenson McMaster for a Maryland school in 1908, and extending it to include Accomac, Onancock and Chincoteague high schools by 1911, did much to keep alive the interest in Shore history. A trust fund provides medals for essay winners in the senior classes of the high schools designated by the founder.

In 1911 *The Early History of the Eastern Shore of Virginia* by Jennings Cropper Wise, was published. This followed several other excellent books by members of Governor Wise's family which deal with certain phases of the Shore—principally biographies. These writings did little to make the rest of the state and nation aware of the progressive segment of Virginia between the Chesapeake and the Atlantic. State and national office seekers however did not neglect it. Post offices were secured through the chairman of the Democratic or Republican party in a county, and there were 105 new jobs each time the political affiliation of the President of the United States changed. The Shore got its first Rural Free Delivery mail service on June 1, 1905, with a route on Chincoteague Island.

The census of 1910 shows that Accomack County had a population of 36,650, the highest on record, and there were

CHAPTER XV — 1900-1920

2977 farms. Northampton's population was 16,672, but it was not to reach its maximum until two decades later. Northampton had 1298 farms. Accomack planted 14,519 acres of Irish potatoes the year before the census, and Northampton planted 16,109 acres. The yield for the two counties was 3,-019,000 bushels. Accomack planted 14,811 acres of sweet potatoes while Northampton planted 4121 acres. The total yield was 3,123,129 bushels. Accomack planted 993 acres in strawberries and Northampton planted only 21 acres. The total yield was 1,703,079 quarts. Other vegetables, including cabbage, onions and tomatoes were planted on 2725 acres in the two counties. Strawberries had been listed in the past two censuses but the acreage did not increase as did that of Irish and sweet potatoes. These figures, which represent a total of more than 53,000 acres in vegetables and strawberries, show that the Eastern Shore was a truck farming area. Grain was still being grown for corn meal and to feed the livestock, including 9380 horses and 1721 mules.

The railroad company furnished freight and express cars for its share of the produce transportation business. Passenger service from New York to Norfolk required less time after the *Pennsylvania*, a large screw-propelled steamship, replaced the side-wheeler *Old Point Comfort*. In 1907 the *Maryland*, another screw-propelled ship with as much speed as the *Pennsylvania* and *New York*, made two round trips daily between Cape Charles, Old Point Comfort and Norfolk.

Steamboats which had served the Shore for more than half a century got their share of the produce business as the acreage increased. Freight and passenger service was available from most of the bayside creeks during the growing season and at the height of the oyster season. Between these seasons the boats ran less frequently. The business increased to the extent that service was expanded in 1910. Many farmers took a leisurely trip to Baltimore at the end of the harvest season for the sociability on the boat and to visit friends. The fare was reasonable and the food was just right for a hungry man. In some instances the captain of a boat took good patrons without charge near the end of the potato season. Steamboat captains worked hard to hold their customers when railroad competition was keen.

Life Saving Service, which had been a valuable institution on the ocean side of the Eastern Shore and elsewhere for almost half a century, was combined with the Revenue Cutter Service and organized as the United States Coast Guard by an Act of Congress on January 28, 1915. Although the Coast Guard remained under the Treasury Department, the men became naval reserve units for use in time of war. They were eligible for retirement pensions after long and faithful service. The Revenue Cutter Service predated Life Saving Service and its principal business was to see that goods of an illegal nature or regular imports were not smuggled in through ports that had no custom houses.

The Shore became a part of the Fifth Coast Guard District. From the beginning of this century the stations from Popes Island to Smiths Island were connected by a telephone relay system so facilities from two or more stations could be combined in case of a major sea disaster. After the formation of the Coast Guard, two-story buildings were erected with living quarters for the crew, boat houses with slanting platforms and storage space for other equipment. Earlier quarters were in one-story buildings with watch towers on top and boat houses attached to the sides. The invention of wireless telegraphy which most ships used removed the necessity for keeping the look-out towers manned.

During World War I the Coast Guard was the sole armed protection of the Eastern Shore from European enemies. Beaches were patrolled with diligence to prevent the landing of Axis spies in small boats from submarines. Constant watch was maintained at the Cape Charles Station at the mouth of Chesapeake Bay for enemy ships for the protruding periscopes of enemy submarines. Some Coast Guard men were sent for navy duty in other places and others were trained for duty on the coast which had the natural protection of 3000 miles of ocean between it and the European enemies.

When Congress declared war against Germany on April 6, 1917, most of the men under forty years of age who had

CHAPTER XV — 1900-1920

attended military schools applied for commissions and many others enlisted. In time others were drafted after the National Draft Act was passed and each county was assigned a quota of men to be supplied each month. A Selective Service Board was appointed in each Shore county to choose from among the registered men those who were to supply each month's quota. The memorial plaques list 31 in Accomack and 21 in Northampton who lost their lives defending the principles on which the United States were founded.

The imprint made by World War I on the Eastern Shore dinner tables is part of the Shore's history. When sugar was rationed, people were astounded. They were epicures and only the ability to pay for sugar and other food items not produced at home had governed purchases. Then a national appeal was made for families to observe "wheatless days and meatless days" to permit more of those items to be shipped to the American Army in Europe and civilians in England and France. Corn meal molded in transit, and the supply of livestock in the United States was not sufficient to meet the demands of World War I.

The number of automobiles increased so fast on the Shore during World War I that the General Assembly approved an Act to regulate the operation of motor vehicles in Accomack and Northampton counties as follows:

> It shall be unlawful for the owner of an automobile to permit it to be operated by any person under twelve years of age; to fail to keep to the extreme right side of the road when meeting a horse or horse drawn vehicle; and to use lights without apparatus for shading or dimming them when approaching other users of the highway.

When the men returned from training camps or overseas, jobs were plentiful and there was a place in college for those who chose to continue their education. Many of them did. Potato growing was attractive enough to cause many of the young men to engage in farming. A few were lured to cities for some good jobs in the rapidly expanding automobile industry.

In 1919 almost every returning steamboat brought

new automobiles from Baltimore and trains brought some on flat cars. Filling stations sprang up and garages followed. Brick churches were built in many communities to replace frame ones and a new boom was in the making for home building. People invested their money in stocks and bonds or made loans to those who wanted to buy more land on which to grow more Irish potatoes. Land prices spiralled week by week. "Horse and buggy" days were rapidly fading away and the hitching post was being replaced by parking space wherever Shore people assembled in business areas, at church and at the Keller Fair.

Chapter XVI

1920-1940

The year 1920 began the "Rubber Tire Era" into which the Shore had been moving for a decade. The census showed that 53,267 acres of Irish potatoes were grown the previous year and the acreage was increased. This quick money crop brought the highest prices on record in 1920. New automobiles and small trucks exceeded those in previous years. Automobile dealers were in business and garages were available for service. Filling stations sprang up on the roadsides and there was competition to see who could be the closest to the road. An Act of the General Assembly prohibited a gasoline tank from being filled while on a public road. Filling stations then were built farther back with circular drives to the pumps.

Some of the islands were not interested in automobiles for they had no room for them. Among these were Hog Island, with the post office called Broadwater, on the seaside of Northampton, and Assateague and Tangier in Accomack County. Saxis was connected with the mainland by a "corduroy road" after 1888. This type of road was covered with small logs split in half lengthways and placed side by side across the road. Chincoteague did have automobiles and was looking forward to driving them to the mainland. The boyhood dream of a native son showed signs of being realized upon the organization of the Chincoteague Toll Road and Bridge Company in 1919.

John B. Whealton was born April 3, 1860, on Chincoteague Island. After getting a limited education in a public school, he went to sea. By his sixteenth birthday he had been on trading expeditions to South America, Europe, Africa and Asia, including one voyage to China.

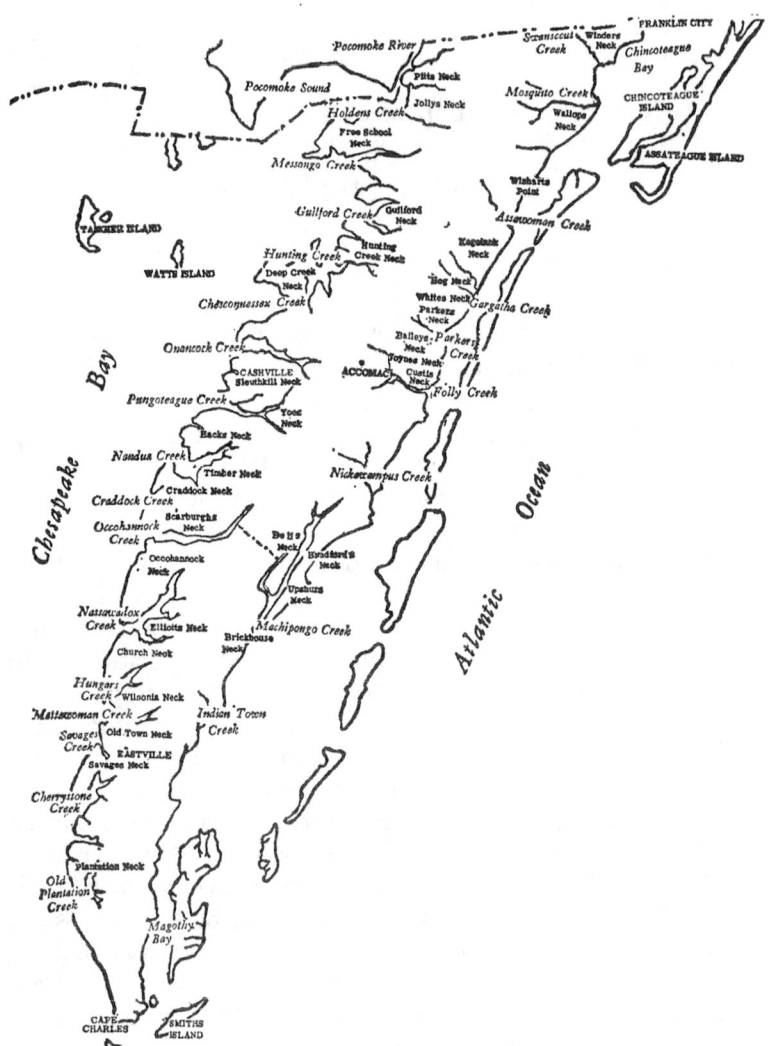

CREEKS AND NECKS 1920

CHAPTER XVI — 1920-1940

He had seen roads and bridges over short stretches of marsh and he began to plan for a land connection for Chincoteague. He was a thrifty seaman and owned a four-masted schooner before 1890. With a well-trained crew he made his trading expeditions profitable.

An illness, which would have deactivated a weaker man, made it necessary for him to give up his life as a merchant seaman, but led John into a new vocation which helped him realize his dream. He went to Norfolk and got a job with a firm which made excavations for basements and built roads. From there he went to Tampa, Florida, and set up his own construction company which got contracts for building roads with a mixture of oyster shells and dirt. He returned to Chincoteague in the summer of 1918 and began work toward organizing a stock company to build a road and bridge system from Chincoteague to the mainland. As soon as enough stock was subscribed to pay an engineer he hastened to Accomac and engaged one. Before Christmas the application for a charter for the Chincoteague Toll Road and Bridge Company was in the hands of the State Corporation Commission.

The Charter was granted on January 21, 1919. The incorporators were: LeRoy Jester, E. J. Bowden, H. J. Jester, John W. Winder, John Leonard, D. J. Whealton, T. P. Selby, E. W. Watson, E. E. Adams, W. J. Adams, J. T. Mears and John B. Whealton. D. J. Whealton was president and LeRoy Jester was secretary.

John B. Whealton, whose dream was taking on visible form, was known as "Captain Jack." He studied the route previously surveyed from the south end of the island to Wallops Neck on the mainland and convinced the directors that it should be changed to a site in the business section of town. A new survey was made and the Federal government granted permission for a drawbridge to span Chincoteague Channel. The Governor had called a special session of the General Assembly for September 1919 and an application for a permit to cross the marshes and salt water creeks was made. Bids for the contract were advertised in August.

The General Assembly approved the bill on September 4, 1919, for:

> A road to be built from A. F. Jester's dock, next to the Atlantic Hotel Dock, leading across Chincoteague Channel to the marsh and then across Black Narrows Channel and marsh, then in a southwestern direction across Wide Narrows to Queen Sound at the mouth of Shell Bay, then in a westerly direction to W. H. Hickman's Farm in Wallops Neck.

The bill became effective on the day it was passed and the bids were opened when the telegram arrived at Chincoteague. John B. Whealton was awarded the contract for $144,000. No guarantee for a completion date was required. Stockholders on the island, on the mainland and in other states watched the progress of the work and they sometimes grew impatient.

On November 15, 1922, the long-awaited opening of the Chincoteague Toll Road and Bridge system took place. Some 4000 visitors were on the island to hear the Governor speak and to witness the cutting of the ribbon which was placed after the many automobiles from the mainland and adjoining states had crossed. The Governor commended the builder and all others who had worked diligently as directors without remuneration and those who had bought the stock. He not only proclaimed a new era for the island, but he prophesied that some people in the audience would ride over a hard-surfaced road from the Maryland line to Cape Charles. Before the ceremony was completed rain began to fall, but everyone stayed until it was over.

The causeways had not been tested in such a rain and they failed to stand up under the automobile traffic. The section adjoining the mainland was the last to give up and ninety-six cars were stuck on the causeways. People with small boats spent the night evacuating people from the causeways. Since the hotel was already filled with visitors who had come to spend the night, the evacuees who were taken to the island were made comfortable in private homes. The next

CHAPTER XVI — 1920-1940

morning Captain Jack Whealton, the hero of the previous day, was on the causeway with his hip boots on to help rescue the automobiles. For two days cars were ferried on barges to Wisharts Point or Franklin City.

The causeways had been built with soil pumped from the creeks and marshes and mixed with some shell. When the visitors were safely home Captain Whealton began the task of rebuilding the causeway. Oyster shells from packing houses far and near were added and covered with soil. Before Christmas 1922 the Chincoteague Bridge and Toll Road Company was in business and the shell and dirt were firm enough to hold up in heavy traffic in wet or dry weather.

Captain Jack Whealton returned to Tampa with other ideas. He was dreaming of a road from Chincoteague to Assateague and a resort on that island to rival Atlantic City. And he was dreaming of toll-free passage to Chincoteague when the investors got their money back with a fair rate of interest. He died in Tampa in 1928. The State Highway Department paid for the stock and the crossing to Chincoteague became toll free on July 1, 1930.

The prophecy of the Governor about a paved road through the Shore was within the realm of possibility at the time. On March 24, 1922, the General Assembly approved an Act to create a State Highway Commission of five members to be appointed by the Governor. This commission had the authority to accept roads for the State Highway System and to establish routes. A survey had already been made through the Shore and the present U. S. 13 was to be in the state system.

The big issue to be settled was whether to build roads on a pay-as-you-go basis from automobile license fees, now sold annually, and gasoline taxes, or to borrow money and build roads immediately on a state-wide basis. A referendum in 1923 showed that the voters of the state favored the pay-as-you-go road building plan.

The route of the proposed highway from the Maryland line to Cape Charles was a controversial issue from 1922 until 1927. The first concrete was poured south of the Maryland line and from Cape Charles to a point six miles northward in 1923. There was no objection to the location of these strips. The controversy localized on the road from Tasley to Exmore. One group insisted on its following the old stage route which went through Onancock, Pungoteague and Belle Haven. The other group favored a new roadbed parallel to the railroad. The latter was the choice of the State Highway Commission and the new road was built as fast as funds were available.

The towns that were bypassed took steps to build hard surface roads to the paved road. Public roads not in the state highway system continued to be financed by local taxes until the state took over all public roads.

The opening of the Accomac Hotel in the spring of 1922 was one of the spectacular events of the decade. It was built as a community project after fire destroyed the colonial tavern which had served those attending court and had the distinction of being the birthplace of Governor Henry A. Wise. The handsome brick building with seventeen bedrooms, a men's lobby, a women's parlor, writing room and a spacious dining room, was second to none outside of a city. Automobile taxi service was maintained from Tasley for the benefit of the traveling public.

The manager of this hotel came from Norfolk and his only complaint was the tremendous cost of bringing his Nash automobile across the bay. The gasoline had to be drained from the car at Norfolk dock where it was pushed onto the steamer by deck hands. Likewise it was pushed off at Cape Charles where the gasoline tank was replenished at his expense. The express charge for transporting the car was $18 in addition to the sacrifice of the gasoline in Norfolk. Fire regulations did not permit the presence of gasoline on the steamer. On August 24, 1925, the Pennsylvania Railroad put into effect a refund system for the benefit of travelers who had to drain their tanks.

Women began to take more interest in public affairs after they were given the right to vote on August 26, 1920. One early project was to prohibit the keeping of hogs in one of the

CHAPTER XVI — 1920-1940

towns. Enough voters signed a petition to cause the town council to hold a referendum along with a regular election. The amendment was printed and blocks were provided "for" or "against" it. The amendment was defeated. The women admitted that they thought they were voting against the hogs.

On February 11, 1921, a National Guard unit was created on the Shore when Archibald E. Tanner, then principal of Onancock High School, who had previously formed a cadet corps of students, received orders from the Adjutant General of Virginia to organize a National Guard Unit. The Governor appointed Archibald E. Tanner as commanding officer with the rank of Major. The temporary armory was on the third floor of the Matthews Building, now the shirt factory, in Parksley.

On July 27, 1921, the Shore National Guard was officially mustered in and designated as the 7th Company, 2nd Provisional Infantry with the First Platoon at Parksley and the Second at Chincoteague. A few weeks later the Chincoteague Platoon was transferred to Coast Artillery. In February 1922 the Parksley Platoon was divided and one platoon drilled in Onancock. These platoons were Company K of the 183rd Infantry Division. The present armory in Onancock was completed in 1955 and the National Guard Unit is Anti-Aircraft Artillery.

The public school system underwent a change in March 1922 when an Act of the General Assembly abolished the district school boards, which had their own clerks and treasurers and the responsibility of keeping up the buildings and employing teachers. The same Act created the "County Unit System" in which one school board member is chosen from each magisterial district, and one from each town consisting of a separate district. These members compose the county school board and a chairman is chosen from the members. This paved the way for needed consolidation. School buildings remained the responsibility of the magisterial districts.

For the school term 1924-1925 Accomack County had seventy-one schools. Sixteen of these were four-year high schools and two others taught eighth and ninth grade subjects, including algebra and Latin. School buses replaced school wagons. The first hot soup served at a school in Accomack County to supplement the home-packed lunches was in Atlantic District in 1923.

There were 29 schools in Northampton in the 1924-1925 term. Of these, 6 were four-year high schools, and 2 others offered some high school subjects. William H. Wilkins was superintendent from 1921 to 1927.

Two highway troopers for the Shore were appointed in 1927. They wore gray uniforms and traveled on motorcycles. Prior to that time district inspectors, in unmarked cars, made periodic visits to the Shore to check on violations such as counterfeit license plates and improper registration of vehicles.

In 1927 the Shore had twenty-four banks. Some of them had branches in nearby towns. Their assets were $10,490,359. Some were National, others were State, and Thomas H. Blackstone had a private bank in Accomac. The assets of the banks did not register the wealth on the Shore because many people had large investments in stocks and bonds. Others were private money lenders with mortgages on real estate. The ambition of a thrifty small businessman or farmer was to own a home with a sizeable garden in one of the towns and have $10,000 loaned on interest at 6 per cent. If a man that well fixed chose to retire, he and his wife could live comfortably on $600 in cash, and be reasonably certain of having debt-free real estate to leave to their children. Many people attained this goal in the prosperous 1920's and refrained from speculation for quick gain, while others took risky ventures to make more money.

The railroad was prosperous and willing to invest in a new ferry. The *Virginia Lee,* the finest steamboat that ever plied the waters between Cape Charles, Old Point and Norfolk, was put into service in 1928. It was 300 feet long and had an automobile deck capable of carrying up to eighty cars. The task of driving them around deck posts and parking them on the designated inch of space, as uniformed crew men directed the activity, was an exacting one. When all cars were on, a deck hand turned a huge screw resembling the steering

VIRGINIA LEE
P.R.R. Steamer 1928

wheel of a car until the rounded stern of the steamer was enclosed.

The elegant dining room was on the lower deck. The crisp linens, pretty dishes and uniformed waiters equalled the luxuries enjoyed in Pullman diners, and the food was delicious. The large main deck was furnished with comfortable chairs and the ladies' lounge was as elegant as one in a good hotel. There were comfortable staterooms for passengers who chose to spend the night on the boat in readiness for an early sailing in the morning. This boat was as handsome as an ocean liner and it was as seaworthy.

Train passengers to and from New York and other points north transferred to the steamer or left it at Cape Charles. The *Virginia Lee* and the *Maryland* each made three round trips daily between Cape Charles, Old Point and Norfolk. The latter had an improvised automobile deck. The fares for ferrying cars were high enough to encourage people to travel by train rather than private automobile. When holiday traffic required it, the *Pennsylvania* was used and extra coaches were added to the trains at Cape Charles.

The Northampton-Accomack Memorial Hospital, which had been one doctor's dream for twenty-five years and the working ambition of many people since 1921, was opened for service in 1928. Dr. W. J. Sturgis of Nassawadox had been thinking in terms of a hospital for the Shore from the day he took his first surgery patient to a Baltimore hospital in 1903, the year he began the practice of medicine. (He had tried to form a stock company to build a hospital, but did not get enough support to incorporate.)

In 1920 there was enough interest in a hospital as a memorial to the men who had lost their lives in World War I to justify a fund-raising campaign. This was completed in November. Dr. W. J. Sturgis and B. D. Holland, Sr. were appointed to purchase land on which to erect the building. In January a two-acre tract in Nassawadox was bought for $3000 and a set of ready-made plans and specifications for a fifty-bed hospital was purchased from an architect's firm for $1000. The specifications called for 150,000 brick and a car load of

CHAPTER XVI — 1920-1940

patented windows. They were bought for $8000. The brick were put on the building site and the windows were stored in Dr. Sturgis' barn. All the money had been spent.

A Bi-County Ladies' Auxiliary was organized by Mrs. Bessie B. Anderson whose husband had died after delayed surgery following a trip by train to Baltimore. The ladies held bazaars, served a luncheon at Kiptopeke each year and conducted annual membership campaigns. They also helped impress the need for a hospital on the minds of the public.

In 1922 the General Assembly enacted a law permitting boards of supervisors to contribute funds toward World War I memorials. All requests for more than $500 had to be accompanied by the signatures of at least one-fourth of the qualified voters. The ladies got the signatures requesting $15,000 from each county. Dr. John W. Bowdoin who served on the Accomack Board of Supervisors for more than thirty years and whose ancestors lived at Bowdoin Hungars, near Eastville, favored the plan for a bi-county hospital and helped dispel the idea that each county could have its own. Each county appropriated $15,000.

A new hospital required the sponsorship of one already in operation. Finding one to sponsor a community hospital on the Eastern Shore required more than one trial. Johnston-Willis Hospital, Richmond, signed a five-year contract with the Northampton-Accomack Memorial Hospital and agreed to send two surgeons and an internal medicine specialist when the building was completed and equipped.

Northampton-Accomack Memorial Hospital was opened with appropriate ceremonies on August 17, 1928. General Hugh S. Cumming, Surgeon General, United States Public Health Service, was the principal speaker. John E. Nottingham (later Circuit Court Judge), president of the Board of Trustees, made the presentation speech. Hon. G. Walter Mapp made the acceptance speech in which he said, "Generations yet to come will voice their gratitude for this labor of love and service." The Pennsylvania Railroad Band furnished the music.

The original staff consisted of Dr. Don Daniel and Dr.

William Carey Henderson, surgeons, and Dr. John R. Hamilton, internal medicine specialist. These doctors had rooms in the hospital and got their meals from the kitchen which was under their supervision. Dr. Daniel was recalled to head the surgery department of Johnston-Willis, and Dr. Harry Lee Denoon came in his place. The first superintendent of nurses was Miss Margaret Walkley.

The first Board of Trustees was: Mrs. Bessie B. Anderson, F. B. Bell, Dr. J. W. Bowdoin, Mrs. Elizabeth P. Costin, Mrs. G. W. Curtis, E. V. Downes, Dr. E. W. P. Downing, W. P. Godwin, Ben T. Gunter, Dr. G. W. Holland, Dr. S. S. Kellam, Mrs. G. Walter Mapp, J. Brooks Mapp, Mrs. J. S. Mills, John E. Nottingham, Dr. John W. Robertson, James S. Rogers, Dr. W. J. Sturgis, Mrs. Jane Ames Taylor, J. C. Walker, Judge N. B. Wescott, M. Smith Wilson and Mrs. Henry A. Wise.

Physicians on the Shore were given the privilege of using the hospital for maternity cases. Dr. W. J. Sturgis not only saw his dream of a hospital on the Shore come true but he enjoyed its benefits for more than thirty years. He practiced as a family physician until his death in 1959. One of his sons joined the surgical staff of the hospital after World War II.

Interest in local history was encouraged by the women's patriotic societies. The Daughters of the American Revolution took the initiative in getting government markers for the graves of Revolutionary soldiers and sailors. In 1928 a tablet was placed on the grave of the commander of the Battle of the Barges at Scott Hall in Onancock. The inscription is:

In memory of
Commodore Whaley
U. S. Navy, Revolutionary War

The same organization helped get the early court records restored and indexed. This project is still under way.

The United Daughters of the Confederacy helped get markers for the graves of Confederate soldiers. A collection of Civil War relics was assembled by this organization for

CHAPTER XVI — 1920-1940

display in a room in the Debtors Prison building in Accomac.

The late 1920's were profitable years for Shore farmers and watermen as well as business and professional men who served them. Irish potato growing was so profitable that many families abandoned the custom of growing and storing food.

The price of farm land increased with the income and many people bought more land on which to grow more Irish potatoes on credit. Some even mortgaged their inherited farms and homes to buy more land. Federal Land Bank loans were popular because of the lower rate of interest than at local banks.

New homes were built and old ones were modernized. Windmills, which had been used to pump water for a limited number of homes, were replaced with gasoline or electric pumps. Bathrooms were installed as fast as plumbers could get the supplies and mechanical refrigerators, which became a threat to the ice man in this decade, were in great demand. The roads were filled with late model cars and a few families even had two cars.

Thrifty people who already had stocks and bonds bought more, and additional people invested in securities. Others made loans to business firms or individuals through local banks. A few had diversified investments, including Government bonds.

The Shore was widely known for its recreational facilities. The hotels were patronized by sportsmen from northern cities during fishing seasons and at wildfowl shooting time. Local people enjoyed these phases of recreation and horse racing at Keller Fair time. Many people owned pleasure boats that would have been acceptable in a yacht race.

The Shore had three country clubs and each had a nine-hole golf course. The Maplewood Golf Course was between Exmore and Nassawadox on a tract of land which was leased. The Accomack Country Club leased part of the Garrison Farm and the colonial house on the north side of Folly Creek. The Maplewood club disbanded when its lease expired. The Accomack Club was discontinued at the beginning of World War

II and the farm containing the golf course was sold to a dairyman. The Cape Charles Country Club bought a tract of land on the south side of Kings Creek and built a clubhouse and it is still active.

The stock market crash in October 1929 brought immediate loss to some people and the economic depression that followed affected everybody on the Shore in time. Irish potato prices went low and there was not enough income to pay the bills. In turn the creditors were unable to pay the wholesale firms. Many small merchants were forced to go out of business while others could only get credit for a short time. Some grocery salesmen covering the area became collecting agents. They got pay for the previous order before taking another. Professional people could not collect enough to pay expenses. Schools were closed early when the county had no funds for the ninth month and county officials did without their salaries for months at a time.

The State Highway Department took over the primary roads in 1928 and allotted funds from the gasoline tax and automobile licenses to the counties. On June 30, 1930, the state took over the assets of the Chincoteague Toll Road and Bridge Company. The stockholders were paid par value for their stock, and the state allotted $100,000 to repair the bridges and causeways, and to build a road from Wattsville to Oak Hall Farm, now T's Corner. (The road was not given a hard surface at that time.)

The "Stone Road," now U. S. Route 13, was completed between Cape Charles and the Maryland line and opened with a colorful ceremony, with all members of the State Highway Commission present, on July 1, 1931. The strip of concrete was sixty-two miles long and nine years were required for building it. Early in this decade all public roads on the Shore were made a part of the State Highway System and classified as primary and secondary roads. Automobile drivers' licenses were issued in 1934. An Act of the General Assembly of that year made a license a requirement for driving.

A ferry franchise was granted to the Peninsula Ferry Company in 1930 and a ferry began operation between the north side of Cape Charles and Pine Beach, near Ocean View. The big open steamer had the capacity for one hundred cars and the fares were lower than those of the Pennsylvania Railroad steamers. Although the latter lowered its fares, the new ferry was a success.

Before the "Stone Road" was finished, Charles F. Russell, a contractor in the county, visualized the tourist business which would be forthcoming. He built a dining room and twelve tourist cabins in the spring of 1931. He offered a prize for a name, and "Whispering Pines" was chosen. Facilities were expanded to take care of the volume of business which increased year by year. The original cabins were sold to give space for motel buildings.

In 1933 the Virginia Ferry Company superseded the Peninsula Ferry Company. A streamlined steamer, the *Delmarva*, especially designed for automobiles and trucks was built and the Shore terminal was moved to the Pennsylvania Railroad Terminal and the southern terminal was at Little Creek where the Pennsylvania had built tracks for its box car barges. Presumably the Pennsylvania Railroad owned a large amount of the stock in the new ferry company. Other steamers were added as time went on.

"Home and Garden Tours" began on the Shore in June 1934 under the sponsorship of St. James Episcopal Church, Accomac. Nine places in Accomac and Onancock were included in a block ticket for seventy-five cents which included afternoon tea. Proceeds from the tour went for improvements for the historic church.

The following year the Hospital Auxiliary conducted a two-day tour. The beautiful estate, Kiptopeke, which had been open for hospital benefits during the struggling years before the building was completed, was included in the tour. Such tours were held annually until the Eastern Shore became a part of the "Virginia Garden Week Tours" in 1941.

The year 1934 brought the full force of the economic depression which had been spreading like a dread disease from the time of the stock market crash in 1929. The demand for Irish potatoes had decreased in northern cities, and other sections of the country were producing both early and late crops. The late potatoes could be stored and Irish potatoes were available every month in the year. Eastern Shore potatoes had become infected with a pest called the tuber moth which destroyed them while in storage. In 1934 potato prices fell below production cost and the Shore was engulfed in the nation-wide depression.

During the years the Irish potato was the money crop many people became accustomed to buying food, clothes and other necessities, as well as luxuries, on credit. When potatoes were sold, the bills were paid and the process was repeated for the next twelve months. Merchants, fertilizer salesmen, insecticide salesmen and almost everybody associated with the potato industry did business on credit. When the Irish potato crop did not pay out, everybody was penalized. By 1935 firms which formerly had commendable credit ratings could buy only on a cash basis. Country storekeepers were among the hardest hit of small businessmen. Unemployment, which had hardly been known on the Shore in the past, became widespread.

Home gardening and canning took on a new meaning and housewives began to use their time and skills to provide balanced meals from homegrown food, when there was but little money to buy the luxuries which had been taken for granted during the prosperous years. The home demonstration agent helped the women learn new homemaking thrift methods. The courage with which people met the disaster was their salvation. This, with thrift and industry, enabled many families to send their children through college. Some families lost their homes through circumstances beyond their control and paid rent until they could buy them back.

Works Progress Administration projects in which government funds were allotted to counties were developed. Roads, water systems, mosquito control, sewing rooms for women, in which clothes were made for needy people, were among the relief projects on the Shore. The most unusual of these was the revival of making linen. Flax was grown, processed, spun and woven into beautiful curtains for schools and other public buildings, including the library at Hyde Park, New York. The unfortunate thing about this project was that it was so time-consuming that products could never have been sold to yield forty cents an hour for the workers. That was the minimum wage after 1936 for people making items to be sold in interstate commerce.

In 1937 the first horseless farm was operated on the Shore. This was on the west side of U. S. Route 13 at Tasley and various kinds of tractors were supplied and the demonstration was financed by a farm implement manufacturer. The undertaking was a spectacular success and tractors began to replace horses and mules up and down the Shore. Also, trucks replaced farm wagons during this decade.

When Germany started World War II on September 1, 1939, farmers on the Shore were harvesting crops other than potatoes. Soybeans were among the new crops and the list of vegetables for canning had expanded to include pumpkins. A plant for processing quick-frozen foods had been opened at Exmore and a number of people were finding employment there. By the spring of 1940 many men had gone to ship yards and war material plants to work. As in World War I, the United States began helping friendly countries against a ruthless enemy and preparing to defend her own rights on the high seas and at home if necessary.

Chapter XVII

1940-1960

In 1940 the Shore was a peaceful farming area with its 50,627 people emerging from the depression years with hope and courage. Many families had adopted the practices of their ancestors by growing and storing food for year-round use. Diversified farming had replaced the one-crop system of the early part of the century and many acres of farm land were in the "soil bank." The United States government paid a nominal rent for part of each participating farm to keep certain crops from glutting the market. Such land was planted with grain or beans to be plowed under to enrich the land. The W.P.A. program was providing jobs on school buildings, sidewalks, drainage projects and public water systems. Some women were employed in the linen weaving project.

There was but little concern about the war in Europe until France fell and friendly England was in danger. When Congress passed the Selective Service Act and the Shore counties were given their first quotas for draftees there was some uneasiness but no widespread concern. The 3000 miles of ocean provided a natural barrier. But this state of mind was short lived.

In August 1940 the Government acquired land for a fort at the mouth of Chesapeake Bay. Kiptopeke estate and adjacent farm land were acquired for Fort John Custis. This defense area at the tip of the peninsula and Fishermans Island covered 798 acres. This fort was the first of many visible signs of war.

The year 1941 was a prosperous one. New model automobiles replaced those used during the depression years. Tractors and other farm machinery sold fast and savings ac-

CHAPTER XVII — 1940-1960

counts were started by new customers. The price of Irish potatoes, however, did not climb to its pre-depression level.

On Sunday afternoon, December 7, 1941, some people were listening to radios in their new cars, others were listening to radios at home and still others were not in touch with what was going on, when the announcement came that the Japanese had bombed Pearl Harbor. Everyone on the Shore who kept up with affairs of the Government knew that Congress would declare war on Germany and Japan.

Civilian Defense organizations and the Red Cross chapters went into immediate action. Volunteers were secured in every locality for educational purposes and to drill people in self-preservation in the event of any enemy attack. By the end of January 1942 classes were under way in home nursing and nutrition, with registered nurses and home economists as instructors. First Aid classes were taught by physicians, and volunteer firemen went to school at defense centers to qualify as instructors in air-raid defense, poison gas countermeasures and coping with expected sabotage. All these people served without pay. In addition to the educational work, the Red Cross chapters opened home service departments to aid service men and their families with various problems which the government assigned to this agency. Stewart K. Powell was Chairman of the Accomack County Red Cross Chapter and A. F. Dize was chairman from Northampton.

The air raid wardens were organized so that a message received by the Civilian Defense coordinator in Accomac or Eastville could be relayed to every locality in less than ten minutes. Telephones were attended at all times and a number of blackout drills were held. Wardens checked their town streets or rural areas to see that no lights could be seen and they had the authority to report for prosecution those who did not conform to rules. Apparently the only person fined during the entire time was a newcomer who refused to stop a car and turn off the lights. Nobody was supposed to have a light in a house after dark unless somebody was at home.

Fire sirens were used for air-raid warning signals and

for the "all clear signal" somewhat like a fire-drill signal in a public school. Only people with civilian defense identification cards, and physicians who had identification tags on their cars, were permitted outside during an air-raid drill. Fortunately, Tangier had radio telephone communication established in 1940 so the entire Shore could be reached.

The Shore was in a continuous dim-out region until the end of the European phase of the war. Street lights were hooded so no light could shine upward and the upper parts of automobile headlights were painted black. All outside activities which usually had bright lights limited their operating time to daylight hours. Even Keller Fair omitted night events.

Food rationing was inevitable and government officials set up an educational program to prepare the public for it. Civilian mobilization was a unit of the County Civilian Defense organization. Women in the various towns and villages accepted the responsibility of chairmen of block leaders. These chairmen recommended a woman to cover each block. A community chairman was secured for each magisterial district with neighborhood leaders to represent twenty families or less. These people were given training by the volunteer home economists. A pamphlet entitled "Share the Meat" was issued. This publication explained that government purchases of meat for men in uniform, and some for allies, would reduce the amount available for civilians to 117 pounds per person in 1943. The amount purchased during 1941 was approximately 200 pounds per person. When several bales of the booklets arrived in Accomac they were divided for towns and magisterial districts by a formula worked out from the 1940 census figures so there would be one for each family.

This program forewarned the people of the Shore of the drastic changes that were coming to their dinner tables. When the dates were set for getting ration books, every family was represented at the schoolhouse or other building where teachers and other volunteers made records of applicants and handed out the books with names written on them. Coupons for sugar, coffee and canned goods were in one kind of book.

CHAPTER XVII — 1940-1960

Those who wanted extra sugar for canning could get permits only by standing in line at the Ration Board Office in Accomac or a specially arranged center in a magisterial district and then finding a store which had sugar. Butter, lard, salad oil, cooking oil and soap were in another book. Gasoline, kerosene and fuel oil coupons were in still another type of coupon book. It was a strange experience for people to be prohibited from purchasing food as they wished so long as they had the money to pay for it. The loyal people on the Shore understood that these methods were necessary for victory and the preservation of private enterprise and the freedom which had been taken for granted in America for so many years.

Community canneries were established in the schools. People took their food to process it in large boilers or steam pressure cookers. The few family-size pressure cookers on the market were rationed.

Shoes were rationed and a shoe coupon was a cherished Christmas or birthday present. Clothes were scarce in stores and silk and nylon hose disappeared and rayon ones were hard to find. Manufacturers were prohibited from putting pockets in women's coats or furnishing a second pair of trousers for men's suits.

In February 1942 the papers carried a grim headline, "Axis Submarines Mine Virginia Waters." The little airport near Parksley was taken over by the Civil Air Patrol in April. The social hall of the firehouse was rented for living quarters for seventy-five men. They watched the coastlines from bomb-laden planes during the day. Small army posts were established at Chincoteague and Accomac. With the aid of trained dogs they patrolled the shores from dusk to dawn.

This patrol work was to prevent saboteurs from landing and to locate submarines. The number of submarines destroyed by Civil Air Patrol planes was never made public. Ten ships were officially listed as having been torpedoed off the Virginia coast. One of these was laden with laundry soap for the use of service men. This ship got to a beach and an Accomack County man bought the soap and sold it by the case.

Each cake was 4 x 4 x 24 inches. After the salt sediment was scraped off it was quite usable for family laundry. Explosions could be heard on the Shore and sometimes pictures and plaster fell. It is assumed that the explosions on the ocean side were from ships being torpedoed or planes bombing enemy submarines.

In April 1942 the Government bought a site in Wallops Neck, west of Chincoteague Island, for a naval air station. The land was cleared and a landing strip was built over the road that had led to the bridge and causeway system. The Civil Air Patrol began using it in January 1943. Frame buildings were erected for offices and for some members of the unit and work proceeded on other landing strips. The Chincoteague Naval Air Station was commissioned on March 5, 1943, as an auxiliary to the Norfolk Naval Air Station. Additional land was purchased. The personnel was 2038 when World War II ended in August 1945.

The Agricultural Census of 1945 shows what Shore farmers were doing to help feed armed forces around the world and civilians in defense plants in this country. There were 12,090 acres planted in tomatoes, 26,563 acres of Irish potatoes, 11,038 acres of sweet potatoes and 33,881 acres of corn. Peas, string beans, lima beans, turnip greens, broccoli, spinach and strawberries were other crops of significance. The number of tractors had increased to 1073 and many farmers were awaiting their turn on the order lists.

Labor for harvesting the crops became acute in 1943 and the Government arranged to bring workers from the Bahama Islands. The first detachment arrived in Accomack County the first week in June. A camp had been built somewhat like the small army posts on the Shore. A chef was provided and a supply of army rations was on hand. While civilians were hungry for meat, these people refused to eat it as it was cooked. Some of the people actually became ill. Then a cook was chosen from the group and food was prepared as they liked it. Chicken was fried in deep fat without flour and then dusted with pepper. Most of the vegetables were a mixture of some kind and highly seasoned with onion and

CHAPTER XVII — 1940-1960

pepper. When the food was adjusted, the Bahama laborers fared well.

The poultry industry which had been started on a large scale in the middle 1930's was expanded to help meet the constantly increasing demand. The census showed that 5,745,-420 chickens were grown in Accomack County and 233,083 in Northampton in 1944.

Among the unusual wartime industries was the dressing of kosher turkeys. A rabbi was at the dressing plant to examine the turkey and cut its throat if it looked healthy. One that did not look just right was rejected. Most of the turkey pickers were local women and they lined up with the bird in their hands to await their turn before the rabbi. He expressed regret when a bird was rejected for the pickers were paid by the number they dressed.

The Northampton-Accomack Memorial Hospital got a new wing through a small local fund and $116,000 as a Government grant during World War II. This was secured through Congressman S. Otis Bland, a college roommate of Dr. W. J. Sturgis. The use of the hospital by the Chincoteague Naval Air Station, Fort John Custis and the Coast Guard justified the government grant for the two-story wing. After the war a nurses' home was built and appropriately named the Bessie B. Anderson Memorial Nurses' Home. A Government grant and a local fund drive made this possible. Local funds helped remodel the original building for needed extra space. The imposing porch with high steps and large dormic columns was converted into sun porches for patients, and the space beneath was utilized to good advantage. The hospital is a living memorial to those who lost their lives in both World Wars.

When the announcement of the Japanese surrender ending World War II was made on August 14, 1945, there was great rejoicing, even by families who were in grief over the loss of loved ones. *The Gold Star Honor Roll in Virginia,* published by the World War II History Commission, listed seventy-two for Accomack and thirty-seven for Northampton —a total of 109 Shore men who lost their lives.

Before the first atomic bomb was dropped over Japan, the Langley Field Research Center of the National Advisory Committee for Aeronautics had an operating base on Wallops Island. A survey of the island was made on May 3, 1945. With the exception of the site of the Coast Guard Station at the north end, the island was owned by a group of northern sportsmen who had used it for fishing and shooting wildfowl before World War II. After the survey the Government purchased 80 acres at the south end and leased 1000 acres. Construction of facilities for firing rockets was started on May 10 and the first test rocket was fired on June 27. A dummy missile was launched on July 4 and the first research vehicle was sent up on July 8, 1945. On November 7, 1949, the Government purchased the remainder of the island and expanded its research work.

Everything associated with research was on the island but there were no living quarters. The employees lived in various towns on the Shore and went to Wallops by boat from the south side of Assawoman Creek. Some of the scientists came by plane from Langley Field at intervals.

The Chincoteague Naval Air Station was converted into a training and research center with a personnel larger than during World War II. Living quarters were so hard to find that a group of apartment houses were built near the entrance to the Naval Air Station to supplement the houses which had been built by the navy. The village was called Toms Cove Apartments. A large number of local people were employed by the navy also.

Farm products brought good prices and canning factories continued to work to full capacity. The demand for civilian goods which had been restricted, and in some cases disappeared from the market during the war years, was high. Electric refrigerators, stoves, toasters, vacuum cleaners and other household appliances were sold as fast as dealers could stock them. Home freezers, which appeared on the market just before World War II, were in demand by farm families who were growing and storing their own food and others who bought food to store. Rental lockers at frozen food plants were used for a while but the travel involved in going for the food soon made them unprofitable.

New automobiles were most in demand. The few that dealers secured during the war years were rationed and sold to people who most needed them to carry on necessary work. Some dealers went out of business during that time and new ones opened firms as the supply increased. Young men who had gone into the armed forces before they owned a car were among the most impatient customers.

Television sets became available to people on the Shore for the first time in the late 1940's and for some years the supply did not come in fast enough to meet the demand. Home television replaced radio more rapidly than the radio outmoded the record player in the 1920's. Home television also reduced the attendance at motion picture theaters to the extent that some of those on the Shore were closed within ten years after this new form of entertainment came on the market.

Home building flourished when materials were back on the market after the war years. Contractors and carpenters were engaged for months in advance and plumbers, electricians and painters had long waiting lists of customers. The ranch house made its appearance on the Shore at this time. This type of architecture resembles the bungalow of the 1920's with a breezeway and garage added. Most homes that were in need of paint at the end of the depression did not get it until after World War II because of the shortage of both paint and workmen during the war years. By 1950 old houses were reconditioned and many new ones were built.

Military installations and other uses for the coastal area were threatening the survival of waterfowl and other wildlife by the end of World War II. Both the State and Federal governments took steps to prevent their becoming extinct. In 1945 the United States government bought the Virginia part of Assateague Island and established the Chincoteague National Wildlife Refuge, covering 8809 acres. The Government purchase included some 250 acres of the Shore's best oyster grounds. Watermen who had been leasing these grounds from private owners got new leases from the government. Wild ponies owned by the Chincoteague Volunteer Fire Department were permitted to remain in the wildlife area and firemen were given permission to round them up for the annual swim to Chincoteague for "Pony Penning," one of the best known events on the Delmarva Peninsula. The Wildlife Refuge is used for biological studies, feeding, and banding wild ducks and geese during their flights to the South for winter and back to the North for nesting in the summer. This refuge serves as a motel, especially for snow geese which were almost extinct in 1945.

 The Virginia Department of Conservation and Development bought three tracts of land for wildlife refuges. The Saxis Marsh Wildlife Refuge, in Accomack County, was started in 1957. Part of the area has an interesting history as public land and later as a unique private enterprise. It was in the "Free School" bequest of Samuel Sandford in 1710 and was sold in 1873, after the public school system was established in Accomack County. The purchaser established a muskrat ranch on the marsh land. Windmills were installed to operate pumps to provide fresh water during dry weather. The ranch had ceased to be profitable and all but one of the picturesque windmills had disappeared when the state bought the land in 1957. Additional purchases of adjoining marsh land have been made and the refuge contains approximately 5000 acres. A hard surface state road through the marsh connects Saxis Island with the mainland of the Eastern Shore.

 Sound Beach was bought for a wildlife refuge in 1960. This is a 759 acre tract of marsh, sandy beach and woodland, between the north bank of Onancock Creek and Chesapeake Bay. Additional acreage including Robertsons Point will eventually be added to the refuge.

 Mockhorn Island, on the seaside in Northampton County, was purchased by the state in 1959 for a wildlife refuge. It contains 6000 acres. The island was used for various commercial purposes until 1933 when it was left to revert to a semi-tropical wilderness. It had been patented for a cattle range in the seventeenth century. At one time clay-lined

CHAPTER XVII — 1940-1960

vats were constructed to use in making salt by the evaporation of sea water by the sun. In time some private homes were built. After a tropical hurricane with high tides destroyed the buildings in 1933 the owners continued to pay taxes but made no use of it. The Mockhorn Island Wildlife Refuge contains both marsh and woodland.

The railroad through the Shore, with separate tracks for north- and south-bound trains, was used to capacity during the war years. Mile-long trains with flat cars carrying landing boats, iced cars for produce, open cars for coal or oil and passenger trains for civilians and troops were passing day and night. The freight cars were put on barges with tracks at Cape Charles and pulled to Little Creek by tug boats as they still are. Passengers transferred to the steamer *Maryland* at Cape Charles. Changes came rapidly after World War II.

Cargo trucks got much of the produce business, oil was brought in by boat, and two bus lines got most of the passengers who did not travel in private cars. The steam engines on the trains were replaced with streamlined Diesel engines with faint whistles, in comparison with the whistles of the steam locomotives. But the new ones could be operated more economically.

A ferry terminal was built at Kiptopeke Beach, seven miles below the town of Cape Charles. Two lines of concrete Liberty ships bought as war surplus formed jetties for a new harbor. A waiting room, ticket office and restaurant were built. This new harbor was completed in May 1950 and became the terminal for the Virginia Ferry Company's boats to Little Creek. The *Maryland* had been replaced by an old boat the *Elisha Lee* when the former failed to pass inspection. In February 1953 it was discontinued. The following year all passenger and mail trains were discontinued. Most of the railroad stations were closed and express was brought to the remaining ones by truck. The railroad offices and shop at Cape Charles were closed and the station at the wharf was torn down.

In 1954 the General Assembly authorized the formation of the Chesapeake Bay Ferry Commission through a bill introduced by Wrendo M. Godwin, Delegate from Accomack County. Judge Jeff F. Walter, Circuit Court Judge of Accomack and Northampton counties, appointed two members of the Commission. Judges in the Hampton Roads area appointed five other members. Lucius J. Kellam of Accomack County was chairman. George R. Mapp, Jr. from Northampton was the other Shore member. In July 1957 the Commission was enlarged to include eleven members. Milton T. Hickman was added to represent the Shore at large. The Commission took over the ferry system after bonds were sold to pay the stockholders in the Virginia Ferry Company. The fleet had five ships. They were the *Delmarva, Princess Anne, Pocahontas, Northampton* and *Accomack*. The *Accomack* has its own story:

> The *Virginia Lee* which was built with an automobile deck in 1928 was taken over by the government in 1942. It was considered suitable for a troop transport ship so it underwent some conversion for that purpose, but it was later rejected. Then the coal burning steam engines were replaced with Diesel engines and large fuel oil tanks which drastically reduced its cargo tonnage and hampered its usefulness as a transport ship.
>
> In March 1943 the ship was sent to Para, Brazil, for use in the rubber industry in the Amazon River area. After World War II the ship was sold to a steamship line and made into an excursion boat. As the excursion boat *Holiday* it began to operate between Boston and Provincetown in 1949. It had 7500 square feet of wooden dance floor, a children's playroom, a snack bar and an attractive dining room. On February 3, 1951, this excursion boat encountered a storm off the coast of North Carolina while it was being taken to Miami for the winter season. In a damaged condition it was towed to Morehead City and offered for sale.
>
> The Virginia Ferry Company purchased the *Holiday,* formerly the floating palace *Virginia Lee,* and had it converted again. It became a member of the ferry fleet under the name *Accomack* in the summer

CHAPTER XVII — 1940-1960

of 1951.

The Chesapeake Bay Ferry Commission had the first three ships of the fleet enlarged and added the *Virginia Beach* and the *Old Point Comfort*. Immediately after its formation, the Commission began exploring possibilities for a bridge and tunnel system across the Chesapeake Bay.

Radio Station WESR, founded by Brooks Russell, was opened on January 23, 1958, as a daytime station with world news coverage. It carries a variety of sponsored programs and public service features.

The Chincoteague Naval Air Station was closed on June 30, 1959. The announcement six months earlier was a shock to the business people who had customers among the military and civilian employees, and to local people who had been employed there for almost seventeen years. However, the closing of this military installation proved to be a blessing in disguise. Preliminary steps had been taken for the National Aeronautics and Space Administration to acquire 1000 acres of land west of Wallops Island. This would have meant the relocation of some people whose ancestors had lived on the land since patent days. But it would not have included the village of Assawoman and the site of the seventeenth century brick church. Instead of taking over the proposed tract, which was a half mile wide and more than two and a half miles along the marsh, the NASA expansion was made on the Naval Air Station site.

On July 1, 1959, the administrative and technical service support facilities of Wallops Island were moved to the mainland. When the National Aeronautics and Space Administration superseded the National Advisory Committee for Aeronautics in October 1958, Wallops Island was separated from the Langley Field Research Center which started the operations at Wallops in 1945. The Chincoteague branch post office which had served the Naval Air Station became independent with the name Wallops Island, Virginia. The Air Station site covers 2400 acres. Some of the houses were made available to NASA personnel and office buildings, along with one hangar, were converted into quarters for the administrative and support facilities. The land outside of the enclosed area was leased for agricultural purposes in 1960.

The decade of the 1950's ended with a smaller population on the Shore than at any other time in the twentieth century. But the economy was rapidly adjusted to the changed conditions and the gradual increase in the NASA personnel put more money in circulation. Plans that had been made for expanding religious and recreational facilities were being carried out. Agricultural products continued to be the principal sources of income. The number of farms declined each year while the acreage of most of the remaining ones was increased. With improved seed and fertilizer used with mechanized equipment, and with irrigation in some cases, the yield was increased. The Shore lost a cherished institution with the closing of the Keller Agricultural Fair in 1957. For almost a century this had been an annual event the last week in August.

Chapter XVIII

1960-1964

The Shore had a population of 47,601 in April 1960 and the number of families was 12,131. One- and two-horse farms had disappeared along with the animals that once pulled the plows. The average size of farms had increased and the number decreased more than 50 per cent from the 1945 census. Then there were 2402 and only 1175 in 1960. Less farm labor is required for mechanized farming than was necessary for horse-drawn plows but the harvesting of vegetables must be done by human hands. Approximately 10,000 migratory laborers come to the Shore at the height of the harvest season.

Land that has been in use for three hundred years is highly productive even when it is dependent on rain for its moisture. The 11,413 irrigated acres have even a higher yield. The Eastern Shore Branch of the Virginia Truck Experiment Station, which was located on a new site near Painter in 1958, has tested seed, fertilizer, types of soil, cultural methods and pest control measures since 1913 to help increase production of commercial vegetables. The acreage of the principal crops grown in 1959 was: 36,326 in soybeans; 19,061 in Irish potatoes; 14,682 in sweet potatoes; 11,708 in tomatoes; 6744 in snap beans; 30,075 in other vegetables; and 990 in strawberries. Land in the soil bank was 2100 acres.

The growing of ornamental shrubs and plants is profitable on the Shore. There are seven nurseries and some of these do wholesale business only. Gulf Stream Nursery, Inc. is widely known for roses it has patented as well as for evergreen shrubs which are sold to retail firms throughout the East.

Woodland covers 102,000 acres with loblolly pine as the principal forest crop. Almost every farm has some woodland which serves as a windbreak, source of income and variety for the landscape. Timber is sold for lumber and pulpwood.

The Virginia Division of Forestry has maintained a department on the Shore since 1946. Preservation of woodlands, reseeding cut-over land, keeping a check on insects and diseases of forest trees and fire prevention are among the services rendered.

The broiler industry is important although a million fewer broilers were marketed in 1959 than in 1945. The 1959 total was 4,886,870. This business is as much a game of chance and luck as any agricultural product. In three months a grower can make a good profit or lose several thousand dollars. In winter the houses must be heated with stoves and in hot weather they must be cooled with ice and fans. In extreme weather sometimes the mortality is high regardless of the care. When broilers reach the right weight for market, they must be sold. There is no such thing as holding them for higher prices since they will soon grow beyond the broiler stage.

A Poultry Diagnostic Laboratory was established in 1949 to help the broiler growers find the causes of sickness and death in flocks of chickens in time to avoid the loss of entire flocks. The works of this laboratory was expanded to check on diseases of cattle and other farm animals. It is now called the Regional Regulatory Laboratory.

Food packing and processing are thriving industries. Eight canning factories fill orders for millions of cases of tomatoes, peas, lima beans, snap beans, pumpkin, spinach, Irish potatoes and sweet potatoes. Dulany Foods, Incorporated, at Exmore is one of the large frozen food plants on the East Coast. It was opened in May 1938 and has furnished employment for many people in the past twenty-five years. Packing green tomatoes to be sold and ripened under controlled temperature in warehouses as stores need them, is quite a business before tomato canning begins.

The seafood business is important although it has di-

CHAPTER XVIII — 1960-1964

minished during the twentieth century. Oysters, clams and crabs are sold in large quantities and some firms operate deep-sea fishing fleets. There are forty-two wholesale seafood dealers on the Shore. The Virginia Institute of Marine Science at Wachapreague does research on diseases and pests that kill shell fish and make the information available to watermen throughout the state.

Each county has its own department of health, department of welfare, soil conservation department and farm and home demonstration agents. The State Police Department with fifteen troopers, including the sergeant in charge, and the State Highway Department with a resident engineer, serve both Accomack and Northampton counties.

The Shore has some industries that are not related to agriculture or seafoods. A garment plant now known as the R and G Shirt Corporation in Parksley was opened in 1937. The Bayshore Concrete Company in Cape Charles is among the new industries. Book publishing by The Eastern Shore News, Inc., Onancock, is a new business on the Shore.

The public schools on the Shore have continued to follow the earlier trend toward consolidation. Northampton has two county high schools, a high school with an elementary section in Cape Charles and seven elementary schools. Accomack has seven high schools; five of these have elementary sections. When the present building program is completed, the elementary schools will be reduced to ten. Transportation is furnished for all people of school age who live outside of towns where the schools are located.

The Eastern Shore Public Library, which was opened in 1957, serves all communities with bookmobile visits once a month. The central library in Accomac has an excellent collection of general reference books and more than fifty titles dealing with Accomack and Northampton counties. It also has historical indexes seldom found in a rural library.

The Shore has 153 churches representing fourteen denominations. Methodists, Baptists, Episcopalians and Presbyterians are the most widely known of the denominations.

Some new churches have been built in recent years and educational buildings have been built for existing ones. Hungars and St. George are the only colonial churches still in use. Each has acquired a brick parish house. Emmanuel at Jenkins Bridge, the successor to the brick church at Assawoman in the 1690's, is of historical and architectural interest. The vertical, or board-and-batten weatherboarding was matched for the parish house with such precision that the entire building appears to have been erected at one time. And some of the brick from the foundation of the church at Assawoman were used in the floor of the entrance. The church at Jenkins Bridge is one of four with communion silver dating from colonial times. Its large chalice bears the London date line 1749-50. St. George has the oldest communion service with the dates 1734-1735. Christ Church in Eastville has the silver from the Magothy Bay Church with the dates 1736-37. Hungars communion service has the date 1742. The historic silver is used on special occasions.

There are three weekly newspapers on the Eastern Shore and at least one of these gets an annual award in the Virginia Press Association entries. The first paper of which any record was found was the *National Recorder,* started in Accomac in 1860. It was a Civil War casualty and its presses were used for printing a Union Army paper. Another early paper was *The Eastern Shore Herald,* established in Eastville on April 8, 1881, by Thomas M. Scott and Julius W. Borum. From 1912 to 1947 it was edited by Benjamin T. Fisher. In 1885 *The Pioneer* was established and published in Cape Charles by William Bullitt Fitzhugh until 1901. *The Farmer and Fisherman* was established by Nathaniel B. Rich, Wachapreague, in 1890, with John H. Johnson as his associate. In 1891 it was moved to Belle Haven. In 1901 John H. Johnson left the Shore and the paper was discontinued. *The Eastern Virginian,* Onancock, was established in the early 1870's and James C. Weaver, first superintendent of Accomack County schools, was associated with it in 1888.

The Peninsula Enterprise, Accomac, was established on June 30, 1881, by John W. Edmonds. After his death in

CHAPTER XVIII — 1960-1964

1914 his sons, John W. Edmonds, Jr. and Alfred B. Edmonds became the owners. After the death of Alfred B. in 1962 John W. Jr., and his sons, John W. III and Franklin Spicer Edmonds, bought the part owned by the estate of the deceased partner. John W. Edmonds, Jr. has been editor since 1914. Historical features are "From Our Files" and "Know the Eastern Shore."

The Northampton Times was founded in Cape Charles before 1903 with John T. Daniel as editor. It remained in the Daniel family until 1959 when The Eastern Shore News, Inc. bought it. Marion C. Daniel is the editor.

The Eastern Shore News, Onancock, was established as *The Accomack News* in 1896 and edited by James C. Rowles. The next owner was Nehemiah Nock who sold it to L. D. Teackle Quinby in 1907. Spencer F. Rogers became the owner and publisher in 1910. John T. Borum, and associates in the Eastern Shore Publishing Company, purchased *The Accomack News* in 1920. In 1924 this company purchased *The Eastern Shore News* which had been published in Cape Charles from 1920. *The Eastern Shore News* has been published in Onancock since the consolidation. John T. Borum was editor from 1920 to 1957. In 1944 he and his wife Thelma Borum became owners of the Eastern Shore Publishing Company. In 1946 they published a daily evening paper along with the weekly. In 1957 George N. McMath and Ben D. Byrd bought the assets of the Eastern Shore Publishing Company and incorporated as The Eastern Shore News, Inc. George N. McMath is editor. Among the historical features are: "The Shoreline," started by Calvin Robinson in April 1928 and edited by James E. Mears since 1933; and "Through the Years" and "Where Were You?" columns edited by A. Parker Barnes.

Organizations are numerous and a member of a service club visiting on the Shore has a good chance of finding a place to keep his attendance record intact at a Rotary, Kiwanis, Lions or Ruritan club. The Elks have a spacious home near Accomac. Masonic lodges and other secret organizations are found in several communities. The Chamber of Commerce

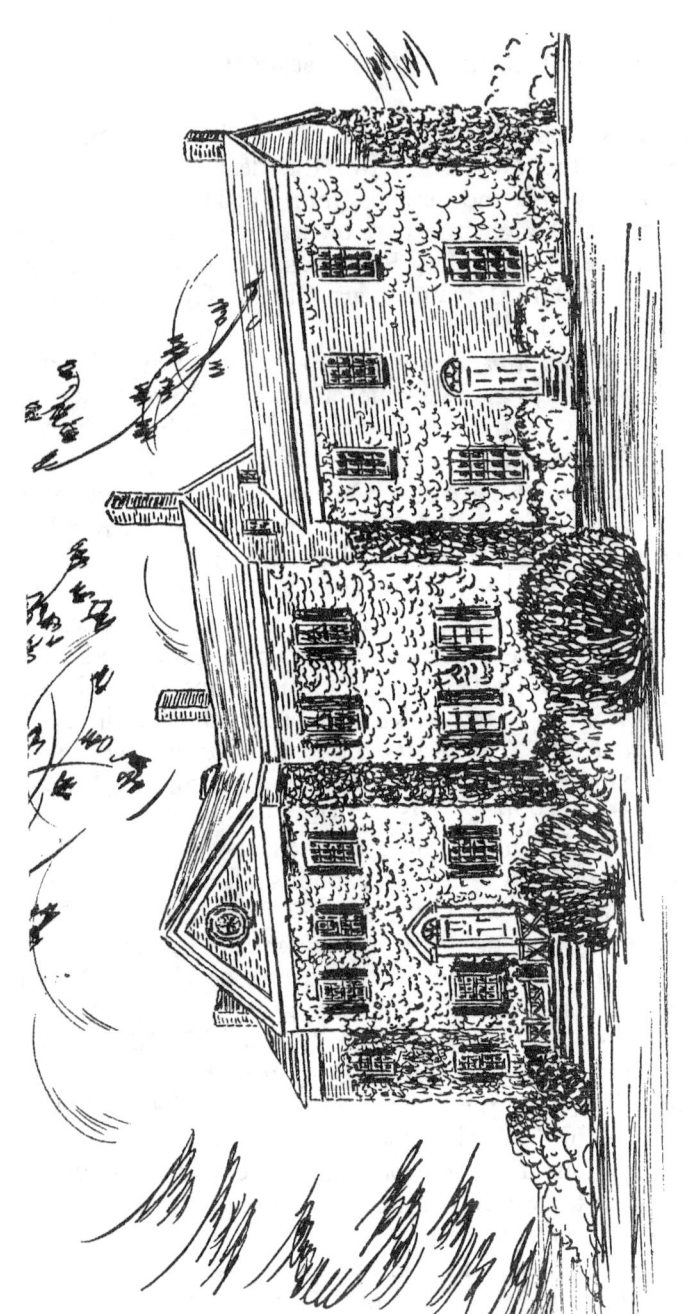

MANOR HOUSE Kerr Place 1797

EASTERN SHORE OF VIRGINIA HISTORICAL SOCIETY, Inc. 1960

CHAPTER XVIII — 1960-1964   259

of the Eastern Shore has headquarters with an executive secretary in Accomac. The Jaycee organization (Junior Chamber of Commerce) is made up of young business and professional men of both counties.

Both counties have Women's Clubs which are affiliated with the General Federation of Women's Clubs. The Accomack County Woman's Club built a clubhouse in 1963 with the help of a generous gift from Herman C. Watson as a memorial to his wife, Carrie Whealton Watson. A Business and Professional Women's Club serves both counties and Accomack has a Soroptimist Club with a junior club.

The Eastern Shore of Virginia Historical Society, organized in 1957, bought Kerr Place in Onancock in 1960 for its headquarters. The APVA (Association for the Preservation of Virginia Antiquities) has a chapter in each county. The patriotic societies with chapters are the DAR (Daughters of the American Revolution), CAR (Children of the American Revolution) and the UDC (United Daughters of the Confederacy). Garden clubs hold flower shows and sponsor other activities. The oldest social club on the Shore is the Parksley Three Arts Club organized in 1920 to locate and train the talent of its members in music, literature and drama. It has a membership of both men and women.

The Eastern Shore Yacht and Country Club has a nine-hole golf course, swimming pool and an air-conditioned clubhouse on historic Pungoteague Creek. This club held its first meeting in August 1959 and the following January it purchased a 126-acre tract of land. The swimming pool was opened in 1960 and the other facilities were ready for use in 1961. This club is a member of the Delmarva Golf Association.

The Cape Charles Country Club which was organized in 1928 has been continuous. Its golf course rivals that of the new club for water hazards and sand traps. The clubhouse faces historic Kings Creek near Chesapeake Bay.

In September 1962 Chincoteague Ocean Beach on the southeast end of Assateague Island was opened. Wyle Maddox and associates had made one of the dreams of John B.

Whealton come true. In 1956 the General Assembly authorized the formation of the Chincoteague-Assateague Bridge and Beach Authority. The Federal government granted permission for a bridge to be built to the Wildlife Refuge and for a road to cross it to the beach. A steel bridge that was being replaced in New York was purchased by the Authority. It was partly dismantled and placed on a barge for the voyage to Assateague Inlet where it was reassembled. The task was long drawn-out but the stockholders were patient and the workmen were diligent. The town of Chincoteague built an approach street to the bridge and named it Maddox Boulevard. The road through the Wildlife Preserve is fenced on both sides and wild ponies graze leisurely among the odd-shaped trees and marsh grass. A first drive to Chincoteague Ocean Beach is a memorable experience for anyone.

During the last week in July the ponies are rounded up for a swim to Chincoteague for Pony Penning, the most widely publicized carnival in the East. On Tuesday experienced horsemen enter the Wildlife Refuge on their saddle horses and round up the ponies. On Wednesday the ponies swim to Chincoteague and spend the night in a pound in the center of the carnival grounds. On Thursday some of the ponies are put on the block and sold to the highest bidder by a well-trained auctioneer. The proceeds help finance the activities of the Chincoteague Volunteer Fire Department, which owns all the ponies in the Wildlife Preserve. Then on Friday of Pony Penning Week the old stock and ponies that have not been sold are returned to Assateague to graze undisturbed, except by high tides, until Pony Penning Week of the following year.

Pony Penning had its origin in Colonial times when livestock owners were required to mark the young in the presence of the neighbors. Sheep Penning was also an annual event in various communities but not for entertainment. The roundup on Chincoteague was called "Horse Penning" in 1924, and the entertainment was a baseball game between the Chincoteague and Cape Charles teams. At that time the ponies were privately owned.

CHAPTER XVIII — 1960-1964

Ponies have featured in the economy of Chincoteague for three centuries and the annual Pony Penning brings tourists to the entire Eastern Shore. In the year 1900 ponies on Chincoteague and Assateague were owned by a great many people. Each owner had his own brand mark registered in the Clerk's Office at Accomac. One way of starting a savings account for a baby was to give him a mare colt and deposit the proceeds from sales of the offsprings to his account until he was grown. The ponies on Chincoteague Island are still privately owned. Those at the Beebe Ranch and the Clarence Burton Barns are the most widely known. Children's books by Marguerite Henry, especially *Misty of Chincoteague* published in 1947 and *Stormy, Misty's Foal*, published in 1963, helped publicize the Eastern Shore. The former was made into a motion picture with professional actors and local people taking part in 1960. Tourists come to see ponies the year round and every hotel, motel and private home with rooms to rent on the Eastern Shore is filled during Pony Penning Week.

The Eastern Shore was first included in the Virginia Garden Week tours in 1941 but tours were already well known in both Accomack and Northampton counties. Kiptopeke Day was started in 1927 when Major and Mrs. Henry A. Wise opened their palatial home and gardens to the public for the benefit of the Northampton-Accomack Memorial Hospital which was nearing completion. Incidentally, that house was in the area on which Fort John Custis was built, and it was in the right-of-way acquired from the government for the approach road to the Bridge-Tunnel and it was torn down in 1963. A church sponsored a tour including nine homes in 1934, and from 1935 to 1941 the Hospital Auxiliary sponsored a well organized tour including houses in both counties. Other organizations have also held tours. A total of sixty-six homes and ten public buildings have been open for tours. This annual tour on Thursday and Friday of the last week in April attracts visitors from many states to see the historic places and hear their stories told by charming hostesses.

Cedar Island promises recreational facilities for local people and those from other areas. Lots have been sold for cottages in the future Ocean City, Virginia. Some cottages have been built and owners and their friends go to them in private boats from Folly Creek. Steps have been taken to connect the island with the mainland by a bridge and causeways resembling the road between Chincoteague and Assateague islands.

Seven of Virginia's ocean islands have lifeboat stations. They are Smiths Island at the mouth of Chesapeake Bay, Cobbs Island, Hog Island, Little Machipongo Island, Parramore Island, Metompkin Island, Assateague Island, and Popes Island near the Maryland line. Each station has living quarters for the men while they are on duty and the necessary rescue equipment for boats or ships in distress. The employees have their homes on the mainland of the Eastern Shore or on Chincoteague Island and they work in shifts. But in case of disaster all are subject to around-the-clock duty. These lifeboat stations are in the Fifth Coast Guard District with headquarters in Norfolk.

The Cape Charles Air Force Station at the mouth of Chesapeake Bay is the only military installation on the Shore. It superseded Fort John Custis which was established as a coast artillery station during World War II. It covers an area of 798 acres less the right of way for the access road and administration buildings of the Chesapeake Bay Bridge-Tunnel.

Wallops Station, National Aeronautics and Space Administration, had brought worldwide publicity to the Eastern Shore by the end of the year 1963. More than 5000 rockets had been launched since activities began there in 1945. They included weather vehicles which caused a salmon colored sky glow that was visible for miles; capsules carrying Monkey Sam and Miss Sam, two of the experimental animals sent aloft in preparation for putting the first man into space; earth satellites which were put into orbit and numerous other experimental vehicles. Space scientists from friendly countries around the world had been to Wallops to learn to fire rockets

CHAPTER XVIII — 1960-1964

made in their countries as well as to study the methods of firing those made in the United States. Robert L. Krieger, one of the first space engineers at Langley Field and a member of the first task force at Wallops in 1945, is Director. He had the title of "Engineer in Charge" from 1948 until the National Aeronautics and Space Administration replaced the National Committee for Civil Aeronautics in 1958, and Wallops became an independent unit of NASA. At that time his title was changed to Director.

Wallops Island was patented by John Wallop in 1672. He had previously patented Wallops Neck where the Chincoteague Naval Air Station was located until the site was transferred to NASA in 1959. In 1960 Wallops Island was connected with the mainland at Assawoman by a bridge and causeway system over Cat Creek and through the marsh. A wide road was built from Assawoman to Wallops Station. One weekend in October the island and station are open to visitors for self-guided automobile tours. This event attracts visitors from many states and the principal Eastern cities.

The Eastern Shore of Virginia Branch of the University of Virginia, a community college at Wallops Station NASA, was authorized for liberal arts and technical courses by an Act of the General Assembly in February 1964, and provisions were made for opening it in September. The Eastern Shore Chamber of Commerce led the promotional program, Wallops Station offered one of the barracks of the former naval air station for the college building, and the Boards of Supervisors in Accomack and Northampton counties passed Resolutions urging the General Assembly to authorize the establishment of the college. Senator E. Almer Ames, Jr., Delegates Howard H. Adams and George N. McMath sponsored the necessary legislation in the General Assembly.

On August 1, 1960, The Chesapeake Bay Ferry Commission, which had been operating the ferries since 1954, adopted plans for a road to be built over and under Chesapeake Bay from the southern tip of the Eastern Shore to a point five miles west of Cape Henry, now in the city of Virginia Beach. The route which the engineers had chosen for this

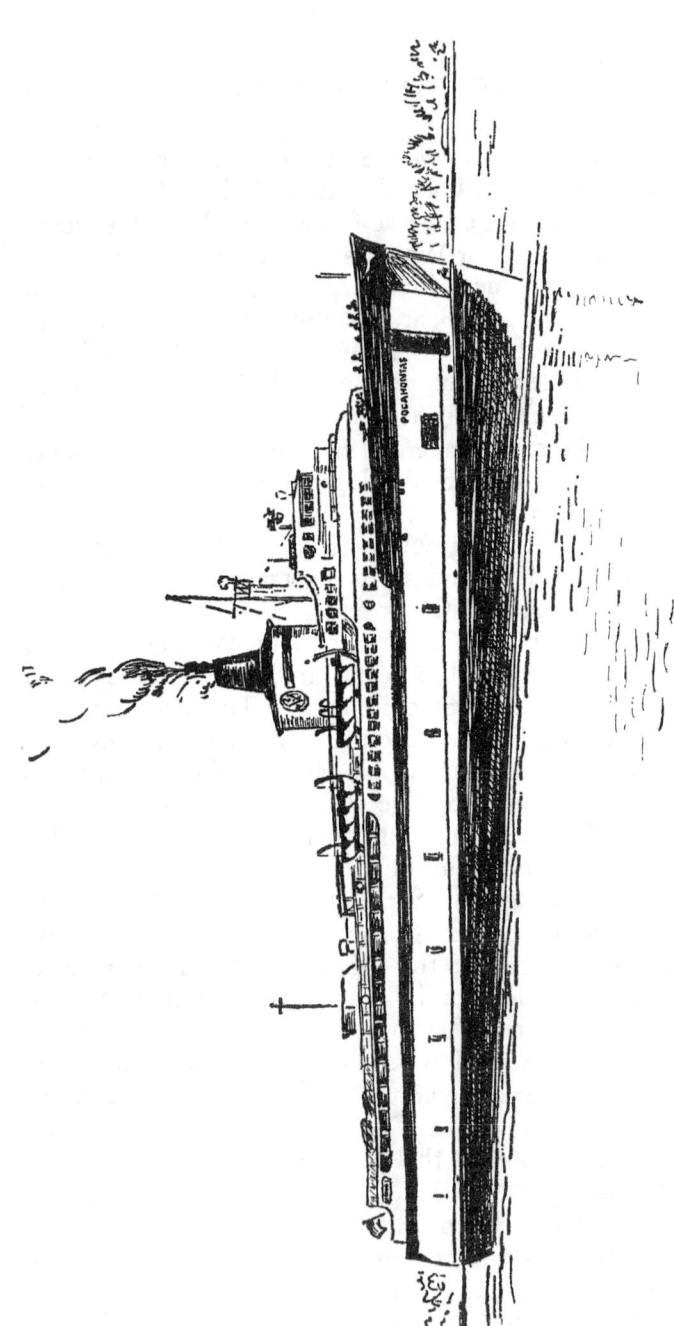

POCAHONTAS
Flagship of Last Ferry Fleet 1964

CHAPTER XVIII — 1960-1964

road was near the path of the three ton boat used by Captain John Smith and his party to cross the bay and explore the Eastern Shore in the summer of 1608, a few months after the Virginia Capes had been named for Henry and Charles, the sons of King James I.

When the plans for the road were adopted, the name of the governing body was changed to The Chesapeake Bay Bridge and Tunnel Commission. Bonds were sold to raise the $200 million needed for the project and the first pile was driven in an impressive ceremony on October 26, 1960. By the spring of 1962 parts of the causeway were visible from the ferries which the road was to replace.

The road over and under Chesapeake Bay is 17.6 miles long. There are four man-made islands with 8 acres of land in each; 12.2 miles of trestle; two tunnels under the ship channels 5738 feet and 5450 feet in length; and two bridges across North Channel and Fisherman Inlet. The principal materials that went into this road sound more like a tall tale than a reality. Among these were "110 million pounds of steel, 34 thousand carloads of rock, 550 thousand cubic yards of concrete and 4 million cubic yards of sand." The land connection was near enough complete for two of the engineers to walk the 17.6 miles the last week in October 1963, and the opening date was set for April 15, 1964 by the Chesapeake Bay Bridge and Tunnel Commission. The ferries were sold to be delivered when the road was opened, and a white sea gull in flight on a blue background was adopted as the Bridge-Tunnel Emblem.

The highway from the toll gates at the north end of the Bridge-Tunnel to the Maryland line goes through almost level country but the scenery is varied and picturesque. The tender green foliage against a background of pine in early spring is accented with dogwood and other blooming trees. The white blooms of the Irish potatoes the last of May make a setting for a gala festival, and the crape myrtle in August outdoes both for roadside beauty. The autumn leaves rival a mountain scene, and the bare brown fields in winter are broken here and there by a patch of turnip greens which turn to a golden yellow in March. But all this scenery fails to give a true picture of the Eastern Shore. Most of the historic homes are on by-roads or winding creeks and the most scenic drives are over roads across the marshes which U. S. Route 13 by-passes. But all the driving which one can do throughout Accomack and Northampton counties, without encountering a traffic stop-light, will not give a true picture of the Eastern Shore.

It has been said by many who have traveled far and wide that the Eastern Shore is a state of mind as well as a highly developed geographical area with almost half a hundred thousand people. All the changes, in war and in peace, which have altered the methods of earning a living, have not changed the "way of life." The Bridge-Tunnel will bring some changes but it is to be hoped that the people will still take time to live by the philosophy expressed in the slogan of the Eastern Shore of Virginia Chamber of Commerce: Living—Like you like it!

The End

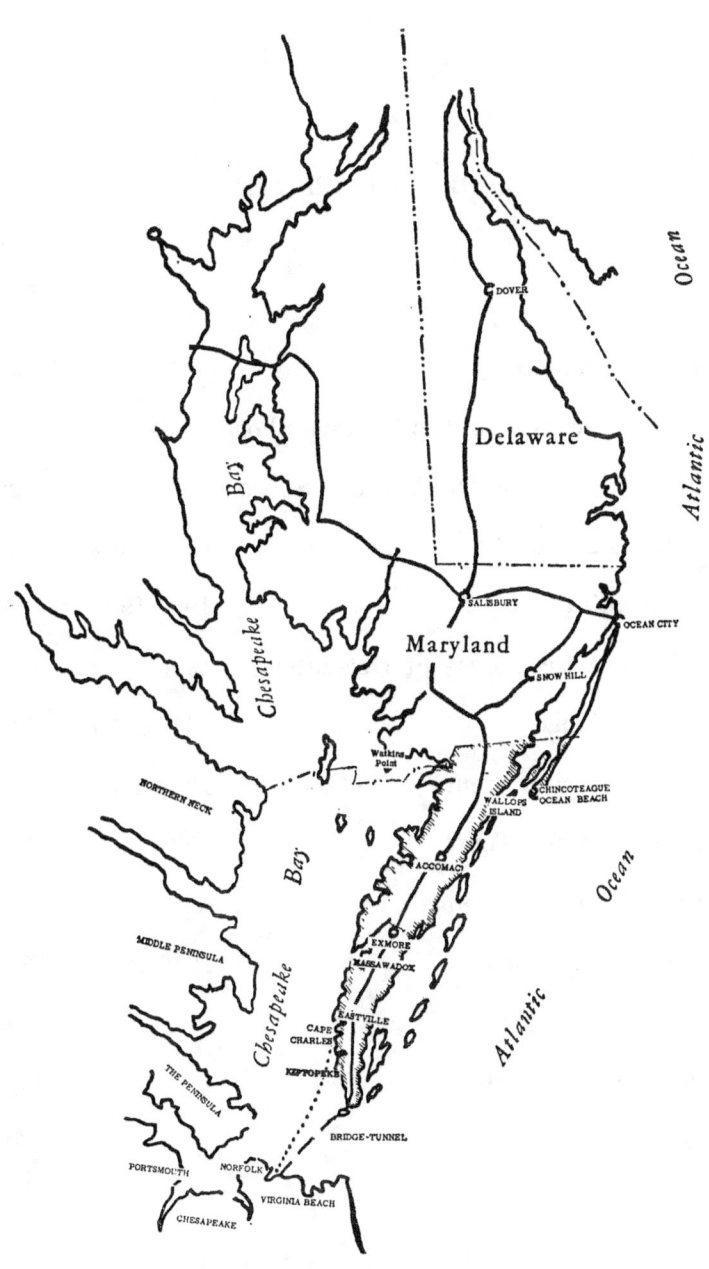

THE DELMARVA PENINSULA 1964

INDEX TO APPENDIX

		Page
Acknowledgments		269-70
Federal Officers from the Eastern Shore	1900-1964	272
State Officers from the Eastern Shore	1900-1964	272
Circuit Court Judges	1831-1964	272
State Senators	1900-1964	272-3
Members of the House of Delegates	1900-1964	273
Clerks of Court	1632-1964	273-4
County Superintendents of Schools	1924-1964	274
Homes Open for Tours	1934-1964	275-7
Historic Public Buildings		277
Eastern Shore Authors	1940-1964	278-80
Notes by Chapters and Pages		281-9
Selected Bibliography		290-3
Index		294

Appendix

ACKNOWLEDGMENTS

The author acknowledges with sincere thanks all the help that has been given in the preparation of this volume. But those who assisted are in no way responsible for the subject matter, interpretations and conclusions. General thanks are extended to everyone who assisted or encouraged the writer, and special thanks are given those who carried out definite assignments.

The greater part of the research was done on the Eastern Shore where court records are continuous from 1632. Thomas H. James, clerk of the Northampton County Court, and Virginia Williams, deputy clerk; J. Fulton Ayres, clerk of the Accomack County Court, and Mildred Grant Melson (Mrs. J. Revell) and Beulah Lowe Mason (Mrs. J. Milton), deputies, rendered courteous service over a period of years. William H. Savedge, Jr., librarian, Catherine Spicer Edmonds (Mrs. John W., Jr.), assistant, and other staff members of the Eastern Shore Public Library were helpful.

The Virginia State Library helped in more ways than can be listed. Milton C. Russell and Bertie Craig Smith (Mrs. Pinkney A.) of the Research and Circulation Department; and John W. Dudley of the Archives, deserve special mention. The Library of Congress, the John Carter Brown Library, Colonial Williamsburg, and the College of William and Mary helped. John L. Lockhead, librarian at the Mariners Museum, helped with the information about the ferries.

The Virginia Historical Society was both inspirational and helpful. John Melville Jennings, director, helped in the selection of the title; James A. Fleming and Virginius C. Hall, Jr. rendered personal service in the library. The

Maryland Historical Society supplied photostatic copies of material which helped clarify some incidents in the narrative.

Judge Jefferson F. Walter and attorneys in Accomack and Northampton counties helped locate material by finding books in the clerks' offices, making suggestions for searching other sources, and permitting the use of their professional libraries. These attorneys were: Howard H. Adams, B. Drummond Ayres, E. Almer Ames, Jr., Benjamin T. Gunter, Jr. and J. Brooks Mapp.

Levin Nock Davis, secretary of the State Board of Elections, the Reverend Samuel F. Gouldthorpe, rector of St. James and St. George Episcopal churches, and Mark C. Lewis, Eastern Shore genealogist, rendered valuable assistance.

Colleagues in the Accomack County school system who assisted with specific phases of the manuscript are: Henry L. Derby, Arthur King Fisher, Oliver C. Greenwood, Leonard W. Johnson, W. Avery Lewis, J. D. Pennewell, Jr., Lucy Lingo Phillips (Mrs. William) and John W. Waterfield, Jr. Those who helped in other ways are: Avalon Drummond Bodley (Mrs. Milton D.), Earl G. Hoppes, Charles T. Huckstep, John C. Justis, Elizabeth Payne Miles (Mrs. Vernon W.), Melvin G. Nuckols, Thomas Phillips, and Nina Glyer Tarr (Mrs. Daniel, Jr.). Those in the Northampton County school system who helped with specific phases of the manuscript or by personal interview are: William F. Lawson, Jr., Margaret C. Scott and B. Gordon Wescott.

Other Eastern Shore people who assisted in tracking down needed information or supplied documents in their libraries are: Byron O. Bonniwell, Bernice FitzGerald Broughton (Mrs. Max C.), Johna H. Davis, Elidie Jones Fletcher (Mrs. Donald F., Sr.), Lois Chandler Hearne (Mrs. H. Roland), Bessie Trevvett Lewis (Mrs. Edward C.), L. Floyd Nock, Jr., Sarah N. N. Parker, Annie Rippon Parks (Mrs. Stephen T.), Burton H. R. Randall, John W. Robertson, M.D., Nell C. Scott, Anne Floyd Upshur, Evelyn Watts (Mrs. Paul F.), and Fairy Mapp White (Mrs. Rooker J.).

The owners of homes and public buildings used to illustrate the architecture of the Eastern Shore are: John R. Ham-

ACKNOWLEDGMENTS

iton, M.D., and Gladys Lee Hamilton of End View; Henry J. and Fredonia Rowland Richardson of Hills Farm; Kathryn Custis Ross (Mrs. Samuel T.) of Seymour House; John Andrews Upshur, Commander USN (ret.), and Eleanor Walton Upshur of Drummonds Mill Farm; The Accomack County Chapter of the Association for the Preservation of Virginia Antiquities, custodians of the Debtors Prison; the Eastern Shore of Virginia Historical Society, Inc., owner of Kerr Place; and the Vestry of St. James Episcopal Church, owner of the Rectory.

Dudley B. Miller, assistant professor of Industrial Education, East Texas State College, and a nephew of the author, made the floor plans; Katherine Roberts Wescott (Mrs. Joseph Vernes) made the pen-and-ink sketches; A. Parker Barnes assisted the author with the maps; and Billie Woods Fletcher (Mrs. W. Beverly) typed the manuscript.

Royce W. Chesser, associate professor, School of Education, College of William and Mary, checked the notes by chapters; J. Paul Hudson, curator of the National Park Service Museum, Jamestown Island, read the seventeenth century chapters of the manuscript and offered helpful suggestions; and Robert L. Krieger, director of Wallops Station NASA, helped in many ways, including furnishing the information about the operations at Wallops and checking the page proofs of the chapters including it.

Margaret Denny Dixon (Mrs. John W.), historical writer and friend, offered advice and inspiration and read the material from the third draft through the page proofs.

George N. McMath and Ben D. Byrd gave editorial advice and assistance in many other ways in the final stages of the preparation of the manuscript. They, and all other members of the staff at *The Eastern Shore News, Inc.,* have had a tremendously important part in the completion and publication of this book in 1964, the 350th Anniversary of the first English settlement on the Eastern Shore, and the year of the opening of the Chesapeake Bay Bridge-Tunnel.

Parksley, Virginia
April 15, 1964   Nora Miller Turman

FEDERAL, STATE AND COUNTY OFFICIALS

FEDERAL OFFICIALS FROM THE EASTERN SHORE 1900-1964

Robert L. Ailworth, United States Marshal	1933-1954
William Andrew Dickinson, Collector of Customs for the State of Virginia	1953-1961
Walkley E. Johnson, Clerk of the United States Court for Eastern District of Virginia	1947-
Assistant District Attorney	1940-1947
Clarence G. Smithers, United States Marshal	1921-1930

STATE OFFICIALS FROM THE EASTERN SHORE 1900-1964
(Only chairmen and secretaries of appointed offices)

Levin Nock Davis, Secretary of State Board of Elections	1947-
Associate Counsel, State Corporation Commission	1942-1944
Director of Motion Picture Censorship Board	1944-1947
William Bullitt Fitzhugh, Sergeant-at-Arms of the House of Delegates	1926-1944
John Henry Johnson, Chief Pension Clerk for Confederate veterans and their widows	1912-1961
Assistant in office of State Auditor	1901-1912
Other public service	1883-1901

Commission of Fisheries
(Board of Fisheries until 1908)

John W. Bowdoin, M.D., Chairman	1902-1906
Milton T. Hickman, Chairman	1958-
Charles M. Lankford, Jr., Chairman	1942-1958
G. Walter Mapp, Chairman	1938-1941
J. Brooks Mapp, Chairman	1941-1942
S. Wilkins Matthews, Secretary	1906-1912
Shellfish Commissioner	1927-1928
Quinton G. Nottingham, Secretary	1918-1922
Thomas Henry Nottingham, Shellfish Commissioner	1924-1927
John S. Parsons, Chairman	1916-1920

CIRCUIT COURT JUDGES
1831-1964

Abel Parker Upshur	1831-1841
Thomas H. Bayly	1842-1843
George P. Scarburgh	1844-1852
Edward P. Pitts	1852-1869
George T. Garrison	1870-1881
Benjamin T. Gunter	1881-1897
John W. G. Blackstone	1898-1908
Clarence W. Robinson	1908-1910
James H. Fletcher	1910-1922
Nathaniel B. Wescott	1922-1930
John E. Nottingham	1930-1942
Jefferson F. Walter	1942-

STATE SENATORS 1900-1964
(Accomack, Northampton and Princess Anne Counties)

E. Almer Ames, Jr.	1956-
Warner Ames	1923-1927
George L. Doughty	1928-1932

FEDERAL, STATE AND COUNTY OFFICIALS 273

Jack Etheridge (Princess Anne County)   1952-1955
Ben T. Gunter, Sr.   1903-1910
Ben T. Gunter, Jr.   1944-1950
G. Walter Mapp   1911-1923
Jefferson F. Walter   1932-1942

MEMBERS OF THE HOUSE OF DELEGATES
Accomack County

B. Drummond Ayres		1928-
Peter D. Copes		1944-1947
Levin Nock Davis	1930-1933,	1940-1942
Wrendo M. Godwin	1938,	1948-1955
George N. McMath		1963-
S. Wilkins Matthews		1900-1902
J. Harry Rew		1912-1927
John R. Rew		1904-1910
Melvin L. Shreves		1956-1962
Roy D. White		1934-1937

Northampton County
(Floater Delegate for Accomack and Northampton)

Howard H. Adams		1934-
William Bullitt Fitzhugh	1910-1912,	1918-1919
J. Fred Floyd, M.D.		1916-1918
John E. Nottingham	1900-1904,	1920-1924
Thomas B. Robertson		1914-1916
Charles Smith		1904-1906
Warren J. Topping		1926-1933
John T. Wilkins, III		1906-1908

CLERKS OF COURT
Accomack County (entire Shore 1634-1642)

Henry Bagwell   1632-1634
(Accomack Plantation)
Henry Bagwell   1632-1638
George Dawe   1637-1639
Henry Bagwell   1639-1640
George Dawe   1640-1642

Northampton County (entire Shore 1642-1663)

Edwin Conway   1642-1648
Edmond Matthews   1648-1658
John Boys   1658-1659
Robert Hutchinson   1659-1663

Northampton County (after the Shore was divided)

Robert Hutchinson   1663-1665
William Melling   1665-1670
John Culpepper   1670-1674

(Accomack County was temporarily reunited with Northampton)

Daniel Neech   1674-1703
Hancock Custis   1703-1705
Robert Howson   1705-1720
Hilary Stringer   1720-1721
Godfrey Poole   1721-1729
Thomas Cable   1729-1743

FEDERAL, STATE AND COUNTY OFFICIALS

Griffin Stith	1743-1783
William Stith	1783-1791
Thomas L. Savage	1791-1813
Caleb B. Upshur	1813-1821
Nathaniel J. Winder	1821-1844
Lewis O. Rogers	1844-1852
LaFayette Harmanson	1852-1869
James M. Brickhouse	1869-1884
Gilmor S. Kendall	1884-1891
T. Sanford Spady	1891-1899
Rodney W. Nottingham	1899-1912
George T. Tyson	1912-1954
Thomas H. James	1954-

CLERKS OF COURT
Accomack County (upper part of the peninsula)

Robert Hutchinson	1663-1670
John Culpepper (clerk of the entire Shore)	1670-1674
Daniel Neech, Deputy for Accomack	1671-1674
Francis Lord	1674-1675
John Washbourne	1675-1703
Robert Snead	1703-1712
Charles Snead	1712-1717
John Jackson	1717-1737
George Holden	1737-1774
Littleton Savage	1774-1805
Edmund Bayly	1805-1805
John Wise	1805-1812
Richard Bayly	1812-1828
Thomas R. Joynes	1828-1845
James J. Ailworth	1845-1850
John W. Gillett	1850-1862
John B. Ailworth	1862-1865
John W. Gillett	1865-1869
William H. B. Custis	1869-1887
Montcalm Oldham, Jr.	1887-1900
Robert H. Oldham	1900-1904
John D. Grant, Sr.	1904-1910
John D. Grant, Jr.	1910-1941
Robert H. Oldham, Jr.	1941-1956
Robert M. Oldham	1956-1960
J. Fulton Ayres	1960-

SUPERINTENDENTS OF SCHOOLS 1925-1964
Accomack County

J. Milton Shue	1925-1929
Henry A. Wise	1929-1954
Roscoe M. Doub	1953-1957
Royce W. Chesser	1957-1962
Oliver C. Greenwood	1962-

Northampton County

W. D. Peters	1921-1928
George J. Oliver	1928-1938
A. S. DeHaven	1938-1950
W. F. Lawson, Jr.	1950-

HOMES OPENED FOR TOURS 1934-1964

Name	Location	Owners January 1, 1964
Bayford	Bayford	Miss Florence Walker Miss Vena Walker
Bowmans Folly	Accomac	Gen. and Mrs. Beverly Browne (USA Ret.)
Brownsville	Nassawadox	Miss Anne Floyd Upshur Mrs. Florence Upshur Dick and nieces
Cedar Grove	Bridgetown	Mrs. Helen Wilkins Mapp Mrs. Julia Wilkins Nottingham
Cessford	Eastville	Mrs. Ellen Ailworth Scott
Chatham	Bridgetown	J. Holland Scott Estate
Cokesbury	Onancock	Mr. and Mrs. Germain S. Brown
Colonial Hall	Belle Haven	Dr. and Mrs. Milton Kellam
Concord	Exmore	Mr. and Mrs. Joseph E. Mears
Corbin Hall	Horntown	Mrs. Frances C. Rogers
Coventon	Eastville	Mrs. Margaret Wilkins Wescoat Mrs. Ann Wilkins Holland
Cropperville Farm	Accomac	Mr. and Mrs. Eugene A. Smith
Crystal Palace	Franktown	Mr. and Mrs. Charles M. Lankford, Jr.
Drummond Place	Accomac	Mr. and Mrs. Roland F. Marshall
Drummonds Mill Farm	Accomac	Com. and Mrs. John A. Upshur
Elkington	Eastville	Mr. Quinton G. Nottingham
End View	Hadlock	Dr. and Mrs. John R. Hamilton
Eyre Hall	Eastville	Mr. H. Furlong Baldwin and Miss Mary Eyre Baldwin
Eyreville	Eastville	Mr. and Mrs. G. L. Webster
Finneys Wharf	Onancock	Mr. and Mrs. Hugh P. McKay
Green Farm	Hallwood	Mr. and Mrs. R. LeCato Conquest
Gulf Stream House and Gardens	Wachapreague	Mr. Jacques Legendre and Mr. Robert Talley

HOMES OPENED FOR TOURS 1934-1964

Hedra Cottage	Craddockville	Dr. John Ames
Hills Farm	Greenbush	Mr. and Mrs. Henry J. Richardson
Ingleside	Eastville	Mrs. Addison Jarvis
Kelso Place	Savageville	Mr. and Mrs. C. L. Belote
Kendall Grove	Kendall Grove	Benjamin W. Mears' Estate
Kerr Place	Onancock	Eastern Shore of Virginia Historical Society, Inc.
Kirwanton	Eastville	Mr. and Mrs. Kirwan C. Forrest
Matthews House	Parksley	Mr. and Mrs. Carroll G. Matthews
Meadville	Onancock	Mr. G. Goodwyn Joynes, Jr.
Milford	Sea View	Mr. and Mrs. Kemper Goffigon, III
Mount Custis	Accomac	Mr. and Mrs. H. Watson Twyford
Mount Pleasant	Belle Haven	Mr. and Mrs. Lucius J. Kellam
Nickawampus Creek Farm	Wachapreague	Mr. and Mrs. John M. Durbin
Oak Grove	Eastville	Mr. and Mrs. J. Edward Johnston
Oatlands	Onancock	Mr. and Mrs. John Van Kesteren, Jr.
Park Hall	Eastville	Mr. and Mrs. Edward M. T. Addison
Pine View	Accomac	Mrs. Warner Ames Mrs. L. C. M. Smythe Mrs. J. Fred Edmonds
Prospect Hill	Birdsnest	Mr. and Mrs. Alex G. Dunton
Roseland	Accomac	Mr. and Mrs. Hal G. Browne
Ross House	Gargatha	Mr. and Mrs. Bransford M. Ross
Rural Hill	Accomac	Mr. and Mrs. William P. Bell, III
Seven Gables	Accomac	Mr. and Mrs. E. Almer Ames, Jr.
Seymour House	Accomac	Mrs. Samuel T. Ross and Mrs. George T. Buck, Jr.
Shirley	Harborton	Mr. and Mrs. George D. Besler
Solitude	Machipongo	Mr. and Mrs. Wendell K. Webber
Stockley	Eastville	Mr. and Mrs. Julian N. Holland

HOMES OPENED FOR TOURS 1934-1964

Taylor House	Temperanceville	Mr. and Mrs. Emmett G. Taylor, Jr.
The Cottage	Accomac	Mr. and Mrs. Robert E. Cooney
The Folly	Accomac	Mr. and Mrs. L. Floyd Nock, Jr.
The Haven	Accomac	Mr. and Mrs. George Walter Mapp, Jr.
The Hermitage	Craddockville	Mrs. Charles B. Mountcastle
The Rectory	Accomac	St. James Episcopal Church
Vaucluse	Bridgetown	Mrs. Verne Minich
Wainhouse	Exmore	Dr. and Mrs. A. W. D. Mears
Warwick	Quinby	Mr. and Mrs. Richard Hollerith
Wesley	Onancock	Mr. and Mrs. Edward M. Treanor
West View	Accomac	Mr. and Mrs. B. Drummond Ayres
Wharton	Mappsville	Mr. and Mrs. Charles R. Busch
White Cliff	Eastville	Mr. and Mrs. Edward T. Smith
Windingdale	Belle Haven	Mr. and Mrs. Lucius J. Kellam
Windy Hill Farm	Parksley	Mr. and Mrs. Claude R. Ewell
Winona	Bridgetown	Mr. and Mrs. J. Henry Bell
Woodbourne	Accomac	Mr. and Mrs. David C. Wessels

HISTORIC PUBLIC BUILDINGS

Northampton County Seat, Eastville
    Clerks Office with continuous Court Records from 1632
    Debtors Prison Museum
    Old Jail
    First Brick Courthouse (rebuilt)
    Christ Episcopal Church
    Hungars Episcopal Church (Colonial) - Bridgetown

Accomack County Seat, Accomac
    Clerks Office with continuous Court Records from 1663
    Debtors Prison Museum - hall, parlor and loft type of architecture - built for the jailor and his family.
    Francis Makemie Presbyterian Church
    Kerr Place, Onancock, a manor house now owned by the Eastern Shore of Virginia Historical Society, Inc.
    St. George Episcopal Church (Colonial), Pungoteague
    St. James Episcopal Church, Accomac

EASTERN SHORE AUTHORS 1940-1964

SUSIE MAY AMES, Ph.D., daughter of Samuel W. and Annie Mears Ames, was born in Pungoteague, Accomack County, and was graduated from high school there. She received her B.A. degree from Randolph-Macon Woman's College, did summer school work at the University of Chicago and the University of California and received her M.A. and Ph.D. degrees from Columbia University. She taught in high schools in Virginia and Maryland and in the Eastern Kentucky State Normal School before joining the faculty of Randolph-Macon Woman's College where she retired as Professor of History in 1955. She was one of the founders and second president of the Eastern Shore of Virginia Historical Society. Her articles illuminating Eastern Shore history have appeared in many historical publications including the **Journal of Business and Economic History, William and Mary Quarterly** and the **Virginia Magazine of History and Biography.** Her best known books are **Studies of the Virginia Eastern Shore in the Seventeenth Century,** Richmond, 1940; **Some Colonial Foundations of Virginia's Eastern Shore,** in **The Eastern Shore of Maryland and Virginia,** ed. by Charles Clark, 3 volumes, New York, 1950; **County Court Records of Accomack-Northampton, Virginia, 1632-1640.** Edited for the American Historical Association, Washington, D. C., 1954; **Reading, Writing and Arithmetic in Virginia, 1607-1699,** Richmond, 1957; and **A Calendar of the Early History of Virginia's Eastern Shore,** Onancock, 1959.

JAY SHENTON LODGE (1889-1962), son of the Reverend Wilson Wesley and Harriet Estabrook Lodge, was born in Salisbury, New Brunswick, Canada, and was graduated from the University of Mount Allison in that province. He received seminary training for the Methodist ministry at Emory University, Atlanta, Georgia. He married Frances Billups of Norfolk, Virginia, and two sons and two daughters were born to them. He was a gifted writer of both prose and poetry. When failing health required his retirement from the Virginia Methodist Conference he devoted his time to writing and won distinction as a columnist for a daily and a weekly newspaper. More than three hundred poems were published in newspapers and magazines in the United States and Canada. He wrote one book **The Strolling Scribe,** Onancock, (posthumously) 1963.

JAMES EGBERT MEARS (1884-), son of James H. and Rose Wise Mears, was born in Hacks Neck, Accomack County. He married Mrs. Caroline Horner Corcoran of Chicago. He served as administrative assistant to the president of Sullins College, as a chamber of commerce secretary and as operator of a domestic and foreign travel service before his retirement in Hollywood, Florida. Although he left the Eastern Shore early in life he has constantly done research and writing about the Shore. **Hacks Neck and its People,** 1937, with a Supplement in 1963, and "The Eastern Shore of Virginia in the Nineteenth and Twentieth Centuries" in **The Eastern Shore of Maryland and Virginia,** ed. by Charles Clark, 3 volumes, New York, 1950, are his best known writings. He has been editor of "The Shoreline" in **The Eastern Shore News** since 1933 and has written for other Shore newspapers. His clippings in thirteen scrapbooks have been indexed by him and put on microfilm by the Virginia State Library. The Virginia Historical Society Library and the Eastern Shore Public Library own copies of the microfilm.

WILBER JACKSON MILLINER, JR., son of Wilber J. and Iva Martin Milliner, was born in Locustville, Accomack County, and was graduated from Onancock High School in 1947. After two years at Randolph-Macon Academy he entered the business of farming. In 1955 he married Faye Joyce Brown. He began trapping local wild animals with saleable skins in his childhood. The otter was most interesting to him and the most difficult to lure into his traps. From personal experience and extensive research he wrote **Fooling Mister Otter**, Onancock, 1961.

MAHALINDA KELLAM PARKS, daughter of Alfred S. and E. Byrd Kellam, was born in Wachapreague, Accomack County, and was graduated from Onancock High School in the class of 1906. Her special interest was in music and she continued to study under Miss Margaret Groton of Onancock. In 1907 she married Everett P. Parks (1888-1947) and one son and two daughters were born to them. She has been a church organist for thirty-five years and has written poetry for many years. Children's poetry is most interesting to her. Her book which she illustrated with silhouettes is **Little Castles in the Air**, Onancock, 1963.

JOHN WILLIAM ROBERTSON, M.D., son of Dr. Edgar Waples and Bell Britton Robertson, was born in Onancock, Accomack County. He attended Margaret Academy and was graduated from Onancock High School in the class of 1905. After graduation from the University of Maryland Medical School he joined his father in the practice of medicine with the office on North Street, Onancock, where his practice has been continuous except while he was in the armed forces during World War I. In 1921 he installed the first X-ray equipment on the Eastern Shore and combined the specialty as an X-ray practitioner with his general practice. He married Lula Price of Snow Hill, Maryland, and two daughters were born to them. Photography as a hobby began in 1902 and he was recognized as a photographic artist even before he finished high school. **On Land and Sea, A Pictorial Review of the Eastern Shore of Virginia**, Onancock, 1961; and **Land of the Evergreen**, Onancock, 1963, contain selections from the collection of more than three thousand pictures in his files.

NORA MILLER TURMAN, daughter of Milam W. and Pearl Garland Miller, was born near Minden, Louisiana, and was graduated from high school there. She received her B.A. degree from George Peabody College. After receiving her M.A. from Cornell University in the class of 1931, she came to the Eastern Shore as an employee of V.P.I., Blacksburg. She married Charles Franklin Turman, D.D.S. of Parksley in 1938. After his death she became Atlantic High School Librarian. In summer school at Madison and Longwood colleges she got her credits for a library certificate. Writing was a hobby even in her high school years and she became interested in historical research while in college. She has written articles for general, professional and historical magazines, including the **Journal of Home Economics** and the **Virginia Magazine of History and Biography**. Her best known writings are: **George Yeardley: Governor of Virginia and Organizer of the General Assembly in 1619**, Richmond, 1959; **Sir George Yeardley** in the **Encyclopedia Americana**, 1964; **Inventory of the Estate of Argoll Yeardley of Northampton County, Virginia, in 1655** (edited Richmond, 1962); **The Episcopal Church in Accomack County from 1652**, Onancock, 1954; **The Parksley Three Arts Club**, Onancock, 1947; **The Girl in the Rural Family**, Chapel Hill, 1935; and Introduction to **On Land and Sea**, Onancock, 1961.

JOHN ANDREWS UPSHUR, U.S.N. Cmdr. Ret., son of Robert Lee and Julia Andrews Upshur, was born in Norfolk, Virginia. He was graduated from the United States Military Academy in the class of 1921, after having been on active duty as a cadet in World War I. He married Eleanor Walton of Atlanta, Georgia, and a son and a daughter were born to them. He served with the Atlantic, Pacific and Asiatic fleets and as an instructor at the Naval Academy. In 1937 he joined the staff of Colonial Williamsburg where he was in charge of Merchandising Operations. While in that position he developed the organization's Reproduction Program. During World War II he was on leave from his civilian position for active duty with the United States Navy. In 1956 he retired from Colonial Williamsburg but remained on the staff as a consultant. He and his wife restored the house on Drummonds Mill Farm near Accomac. **Upshur Family in Virginia** by John Andrews Upshur, Richmond, 1955, is a history of the family and connections who have lived on the Eastern Shore since 1640. It won the annual award of the National Genealogical Society.

KATHERINE ROBERTS WESCOTT, daughter of William T. and Katherine Joynes Roberts, was born in Nassawadox, Northampton County, and received her B.A. degree from Longwood College in 1939 with a major in art and recognition for her ability as a poet. She was a public school teacher and gave private art lessons. In 1942 she married Joseph V. Wescott, O. D., of Onancock, where they live. A son and a daughter were born to them. Her poems have appeared in a number of periodicals and her illustrated book of Eastern Shore poems, **Salt and Sand**, Onancock, 1963, bespeaks her success as a poet and an artist. She made the sketches for this historical narrative.

RALPH THOMAS WHITELAW (1880-1950), the son of Robert H. and Mary Westgate Whitelaw, was born in St. Louis, Missouri, and attended Smith Academy there. He received his B.A. degree from Amherst in the class of 1902 and became president of Whitelaw Brothers Chemical Company the same year. He held that position until his retirement except while he was on leave for YMCA work with the armed forces in France during World War I. In 1922 he married Paula Oertell of St. Louis. In 1926 they bought Warwick in Accomack County and restored it for a retirement home. He grew peonies for market for some years, then entered the real estate business. He began historical research and writing during his first year on the Shore. After his wife's death he sold Warwick and built a house near Accomac. He devoted more than fifteen years to a study of the land patents on the Shore and related history of those with historic houses. His book, **Virginia's Eastern Shore**, was published in two volumes by the Virginia Historical Society in 1951. This publication received the annual award given by the American Association for State and Local History for 1951.

HENRY ALEXANDER WISE, son of Edgar S. and Elizabeth Jacob Wise, was born in Craddockville, Accomack County, and received his early education there and at Pungoteague. He received his B.S. degree from Virginia Polytechnic Institute in the class of 1898 and M.A. degrees from both Centre College, Kentucky, and the University of South Carolina. He began his teaching career in Accomack County. He was on the faculty of Converse College in South Carolina when he was elected to the position of superintendent of Accomack County schools in 1929. After his retirement in 1954 he taught extension classes in Virginia History for the College of William and Mary. His writings in both poetry and prose have appeared in a number of periodicals. His published books are: **Just Little Things and Other Poems**, Accomac, 1933, and **Over on the Eastern Shore**, Onancock, 1962.

NOTES BY CHAPTERS AND PAGES

These notes were made for the general reader, who may want additional information on some incidents in the narrative, but they should be adequate for a future researcher. The year, month, and day have been used of many incidents so they can be located in the original documents, manuscript copies, microcards, microfilms, microsheets, printed form, photostats, or typescripts. Months and years, but not the days, before 1752 were transcribed to the New Style Calendar. County court records on the Eastern Shore are continuous from 1632. Other source material should be easily located from these notes and the selected bibliography.

Page   Chapter I   1603-25

1   Thomas Canner, "A Relation of the Voyage to Virginia ... in 1603," **Purchas His Pilgrimes**, XVIII, pp. 329-35.

2   Clifford M. Lewis, **The Spanish Jesuit Mission in Virginia 1570-72.**

3-5   John Smith, **Travels and Works of Captain John Smith**, I, pp. 343-6 and II, pp. 412-14.

5   Susan M. Kingsbury, ed., **Records of the Virginia Company**, III, p. 304. Land purchased on the Eastern Shore in 1614.

6-7   Ralph T. Whitelaw, **Virginia's Eastern Shore**, pp. 167-76. Company land.

6-7   Nora Miller Turman, **George Yeardley**, p. 144. Company tenants.

Page   Chapter II   1625-1634

13   Nathaniel C. Hale, **Virginia Venturer**, A Biography of William Claiborne 1600-1677.

13-14   Nell Marion Nugent, **Cavaliers and Pioneers**, Abstracts of Virginia Land Patents, p. 10.

14-16   H. R. McIlwaine, ed., **Minutes of the Council and General Court**, p. 156. Three settlements are named.

16   Turman, **George Yeardley**, pp. 183-86. Will of Sir George Yeardley and its probate.

18-21   Sloan Manuscript No. 3662, British Museum Library. A description of Lord Baltimore's Newfoundland Patent and circumstances surrounding his Virginia Patent.

21   William Macdonald, **Documentary Source Book of American History**, pp. 32-5. Charter of 1632 with Eastern Shore of Virginia reserved for the Crown.

21   McIlwaine, **Minutes of the Council and General Court**, p. 321. Act establishing a monthly court for Accomack Plantation.

24   Susie M. Ames, ed., **Accomack-Northampton Court Records 1632-40**, p. 4. First entry by Henry Bagwell, clerk.

25   Ibid., p. 158. Reference to Thomas Savage and some Indians having been employed to round up cattle for Edmund Scarburgh I.

Page   Chapter III   1634-1642

27   Ames, **Accomack-Northampton Court Records**, p. 17. Sheriff was chosen for Accomack County.

29   Ibid., p. 29. Vestry and specifications for parsonage house.

29   Whitelaw, **Virginia's Eastern Shore**, p. 142. Glebe land is located.

31-34   Turman, **George Yeardley**, pp. 44, index and chapter notes.

	Early life of Thomas Savage and the documents in which details were found.
34	Kingsbury, **Records of the Virginia Company**, IV, p. 319. Land records sent to England in 1625 list Thomas Savage, "his dividents."
34	Ames, **Accomack-Northampton Court Records**, p. 42. Suit against the estate of Thomas Savage was referred to Jamestown.
34	Ibid., p. 101. Estate of John Howe was billed for his funeral and grave in the chancel of the church.
38	Susie M. Ames, **Studies of the Virginia Eastern Shore in the Seventeenth Century**, pp. 179-207. A ducking stool is described on p. 190.
38	Ames, **Accomack-Northampton Court Records** (sentences imposed by the court for various crimes using conventional devices). See index.
	Ibid., p. 143. Inventory of an estate including a silver forge.
Page	Chapter IV 1642-1652
43-45	Northampton County Court Records, Book II. Military districts can be found from the names of their commanders in the index.
45-46	The inventory of the estate of William Burdett was filed on April 24, 1645.
48	A chapel of ease was a house of worship remote from the main church. Divine services were conducted by lay readers when the minister could not be present.
49-50	Henry Norwood, "A Voyage to Virginia in 1649-50," in Peter Force ed., **Tracts and Other Papers**, III, No. 10, p. 49, and in Francis Coleman Rosenberger, Virginia Reader, pp. 116-171.
Page	Chapter V 1652-1663
54	Whitelaw, Virginia's Eastern Shore, I, p. 129. A copy of the "Northampton Protest" with the names of the signers.
57	Northampton County Court Record Book IV, p. 197. A deed of gift from Nathaniel Littleton to his daughter. His estate must have been settled at Jamestown since no record was found of his will mentioned in the deed of gift, inventory, or certification of his wife as executrix. She was serving in that capacity at the time of her death. Her will was probated in Northampton County on November 6, 1656.
58	Turman, "Inventory of the Estate of Argoll Yeardley," **The Virginia Magazine of History and Biography**, October 1962, pp. 410-19. Inventory was taken on October 29, 1655. Original is in Northampton Court Record Book V.
Note	Naturalization papers of some Dutch citizens, including John Custis II and Ann Yeardley, are among the Northampton County Loose Papers in the Clerk's Office, Eastville.
Page	Chapter VI 1663-1674
64	The law required the owner of a servant child to register his name and age. If the age was unknown, the child was presented to the court and his age was estimated and recorded. When he reached the age of 16 years, the master began paying a head tax, or tithe, on him.
65	An ordinary was an inn, or licensed place for keeping paying guests. The keeper was required to furnish beds and

NOTES BY CHAPTERS AND PAGES 283

	meals for the guests, and stables and feed for their horses.
65	Whitelaw, **Virginia's Eastern Shore**, pp. 1386-89. The account of the controversy over the Virginia-Maryland line is given and documented.
66	Susie M. Ames, "The Bear and the Cub," **The Peninsula Enterprise**, January 18, 1958. Account of the play and a list of references in the Accomack County court records, prepared for the Eastern Shore of Virginia Historical Society when it made the application for the Historical Marker which is on U. S. Route 13, east of Pungoteague, where the play was given.
68	William Walter Hening, Statutes at Large, 11, p. 244. Land Reform Act.
68	Richard L. Morton, **Colonial Virginia**, II, p. 420. Undesirable practices and abuses of the headright system and the Reform Act are explained.
71	Whitelaw, **Virginia's Eastern Shore**. Information about Ann Toft and Daniel Jenifer.
74	Augustin Herrman, **Map of Virginia and Maryland in 1670**.
Page	Chapter VII 1674-1700
75	Court records in the Clerk's Office in Accomac are continuous from 1663 but they are entered as the Upper Court of Northampton County for the time the entire Eastern Shore was reunited as one county, 1670-74.
76-7	Morton, **Colonial Virginia**, I, pp. 208, 303 and 309. The proprietary grant of the Eastern Shore and the mainland of Virginia to two noblemen.
78	Ibid., pp. 258-72. Bacon's Rebellion.
81	Whitelaw, **Virginia's Eastern Shore**, pp. 218-21. John Savage, 1625-1678.
81-2	Ibid., pp. 677-79. Biographical material about Southy Littleton. The Inventory of his estate was filed in Accomack County on January 10, 1680.
86	Jennings Cropper Wise. **The Early History of the Eastern Shore of Virginia**, pp. 184-7. Information about pirates on the Shore.
86	Lloyd Haynes Williams, **Pirates of Colonial Virginia**. An explanation of the pirate menace with copies of documents in the appendix.
87-8	Whitelaw, **Virginia's Eastern Shore**, I, pp. 108-9. Biographical information about General John Custis. His will was probated in Northampton County on February 10, 1696.
89-90	Richard Pratt, Ladies' Home Journal, April 1963, pp. 74-5. Color pictures of Hills Farm.
Page	Chapter VIII 1700-1714
92	Census figures quoted were found in the court records. Whitelaw, **Virginia's Eastern Shore**, I, pp. 563 and II, pp. 1385. The total number of acres of land patented on the Eastern Shore was 360,250 by the end of patent times.
94	**Acts of the General Assembly** for 1705 contain the only records found for the ferries of 1705-24.
95	Water mills with ponds were eventually supplemented by tidemills. Mason's Mill, near Parksley, was the last of its kind on the Shore. It was destroyed in a storm in 1943.
99	Whitelaw, **Virginia's Eastern Shore**, I, pp. 248-62. North-

ampton courthouses.

	Ibid., pp. 1027-33. Accomack Courthouses.
100	Littleton Purnell Bowen, **The Days of Makemie**, Francis Makemie.
100	I. Marshall Page, **The Story of Francis Makemie**. Appendix contains a copy of every item in the Accomack County Court Records pertaining to Makemie.
100-1	Whitelaw, **Virginia's Eastern Shore**, II, pp. 1282-5. Makemie.
101	Colonial Manuscripts. Fulham Palace Library, London. Reports of the Reverend William Black.
103	William S. Perry, **Historical Collections Relating to the American Colonial Church**, I, pp. 300-2. A copy of the answers to a questionnaire sent to the Bishop of London in 1724. The name of the schoolmaster is given.

Page	Chapter IX 1714-1752
107	Hening, **Statutes at Large**. Pay for soldiers throughout the Colonial Period.
109-10	Ibid., pp. 349-54 and IV, pp. 94-101. Ballast laws. Appointments of overseers are recorded in the county court order books.
111	Accomack County Order Book 1737-44, p. 99. "An assignment of all tobacco and casks to be levied for the building of Pungoteague Church." In 1959 Burton H. R. Randall and William H. Guy uncovered the foundations of the east and west sections of the church and Finlay F. Ferguson, architect for the Parish House, made an archaeological floor plan. It is a Greek Cross with a semicircular extension at the east end. This drawing and a sketch made in 1819 show that this end resembled a wing of the restored Capitol in Colonial Williamsburg. The present St. George Church was the north-south transept of the original brick church.
113	Gambrel roof house. See illustration, p. 140.
114	Whitelaw, **Virginia's Eastern Shore**, I, pp. 320-24. John Custis III of Custis Hungars and inscription on his tomb.
114-15	Ibid., pp. 108-17. John Custis IV of Arlington and Williamsburg.
114-15	Douglas Southall Freeman, **George Washington**, II, p. 291. John Custis IV and descendants associated with the Eastern Shore.
115	Whitelaw, **Virginia's Eastern Shore**, I, p. 110. Love letter to Lucy Parke.
115	Earl G. Swem, **Brothers of the Spade**, pp. 9-20. Sketch of life of John Custis IV, and explanation of his will. His will was proved in James City County on April 9, 1750 . . . The records of that county have been destroyed. Owing to some of his property being in England, the will was filed in the Prerogative Court of Canterbury, England, and was proved on November 19, 1753. An abstract is in printed form in the Virginia State Library.
115-16	The inscription on the tomb is given with spelling, punctuation and capitalization as it appears with two exceptions. The is spelled out and the letter h is left out of Williamsburg(h).
116-17	Hening, **Statutes at Large**, I, p. 393. Note explains the Calendar Reform Act of 1751.

NOTES BY CHAPTERS AND PAGES 285

Page	
	Chapter X 1752-1790
118	William Edwin Hemphill, and others, **Cavalier Commonwealth,** pp. 104-15. Dates and details of French and Indian War.
122	Accomack-St. George Parish line (See map p. 192 same as Lee-Metompkin District line.)
126	Macdonald, **Documentary Source Book of American History,** Import duties imposed on the colonies, pp. 86-92.
127	Whitelaw, **Virginia's Eastern Shore,** I, pp. 189-91. Littleton Eyre.
130	Ibid., I, p. 42.
130-31	Barton Haxall Wise, **A Memoir of General John Cropper.** Also "Cropper Papers" in the Virginia Historical Society Library.
130-31	John H. Gwathmey, **Historical Register of Virginians in the Revolution,** p. 194. War records and later military commissions of John Cropper.
132	**Maryland Historical Society Magazine,** IV, p. 115 and XIV, pp. 269-70. Commodore or Captain Zedekiah Walley or Whaley who was killed in the "Battle of the Barges."

Page	
	Chapter XI 1790-1800
139	Whitelaw, **Virginia's Eastern Shore,** I, p. 490, origin of the name T B.
139 and 142	Ibid., End View and its builders.
140-41	End View. Illustrations.
143-45	Map on page 157 shows locations of the places named.
146-49	Illustrations of sections, completed house and floor plan shows how the typical Eastern Shore style of architecture was developed for economic and utilitarian purposes. The kitchen ends of Seven Gables and the Ailworth Cottage are among other surviving sections of houses built to secure the deeds.
150-52	"The William Young Account Book" is owned by Nell C. Scott, a descendant.
	Accounts were kept in English money. Note that $40 paid on an account was recorded in pounds, shillings and pence. At least two decades passed before there was enough United States money in circulation for general use.

Page	
	Chapter XII 1800-1840
156	Samuel Waples was the official for the district including Accomack and Northampton counties for the Second Census of the United States in 1800. The Accomack rolls were located in 1948, among papers which had been stored since 1887. No other complete Virginia county lists have been found for this census.
160-61	G. MacLaren Brydon, **Virginia's Mother Church,** II. See index. Separation of Church and State.
162	Adam Wallace, **The Parson of the Islands.** Joshua Thomas persuaded the British soldiers to spare the trees on the Camp Meeting grounds.
162-3	Whitelaw, **Virginia's Eastern Shore,** I, pp. 815-17. Battle of Pungoteague.
163-5	Ibid., General John Cropper.
163-5	Barton Haxall Wise, **A Memoir of General John Cropper.**
163-5	"Cropper Papers," Virginia Historical Society.

165	Whitelaw, **Virginia's Eastern Shore**, I, p. 174. Floyd's Ferry Franchise.
166-7	Joseph Martin, **A Comprehensive Gazetteer of Virginia**, pp. 249-50. The castor oil industry is reported. Relics of one factory are at Brownsville, near Nassawadox.
167-9	Ibid., pp. 111-12 Accomack County, and pp. 249-51 Northampton County.
170	The ice house illustrated is at the Folly. Among the others which have survived are those at the Seymour House, Accomac; Nock's Pasture, Accomac; Woodbourne, Accomac; Poplar Hill, near Eastville; and Kendall Grove, north of Eastville.
171-2	Robert Hamilton, "Lighthouses of the East Coast."

Page   Chapter XIII   1840-1870

173	The U. S. Census of 1840 was the first to include agricultural products.
174-75	Claude H. Hall, **Abel Parker Upshur 1790-1844.** John Andrews Upshur, Upshur Family in Virginia, pp. 416-20. Whitelaw, **Virginia's Eastern Shore**, I, pp. 416-20. As a member of the General Court, Judge Upshur presided over Circuit Courts which included those in Accomack and Northampton counties. The General Court was the State Supreme Court for criminal cases until 1852.
175	Mears, in Clark, **The Eastern Shore of Maryland and Virginia**, II, p. 588. Steamboat ferries. A painting of the Joseph E. Coffee is at the Mariners' Museum, Newport News.
176	Turman and Others, "A Brief History of Education in Accomack County."
177	Northampton County Order Book 1851-1857, pp. 64. Magisterial districts into which the county was divided in 1852. Areas and boundaries were retained in 1870 but the districts, or townships, were given names instead of numbers. Originally the present Capeville District was Number 1. Accomack County Order Book 1851-1854, pp. 194-7. In 1852 Accomack County was divided into 6 districts. Numbers 1, 2 and 3 were below the Parish line established in 1763. Numbers 4, 5 and 6 were above this line. Number 6 extended from Holdens Creek to the ocean and included the present Islands Magisterial District and all the mainland to the Maryland line.
178	Barton Haxall Wise, **The Life of Henry A. Wise 1806-1876.** John S. Wise, The End of An Era.
180-81	"The Account Book of Spencer D. Finney" is owned by Byron O. Bonniwell.
183	Robert Hamilton, "Lighthouses of the East Coast."
184	Assateague Light is at 37 degrees 54 minutes and 42 seconds north latitude, and 75 degrees 21 minutes and 23 seconds west longitude.
185-6	Mears, in Clark, **The Eastern Shore of Maryland and Virginia**, II, pp. 603-12. Susie M. Ames, "Federal Policy Toward the Eastern Shore of Virginia in 1861." The Virginia Magazine of History and Biography, October 1961, pp. 432-459.
189	Henry H. Lockwood, General Order No. 18. Margaret Scarburgh Smith (Mrs. Eugene A.) owns a signed copy.

NOTES BY CHAPTERS AND PAGES

Page	Chapter XIV 1870-1900
191	Northampton County Deed Book No. 37, 1867-71, p. 435.
192	Map - Districts and Boundary Creeks in 1870.
193-5	Accomack County Deed Book No. 46, 1869-71, pp. 348-51. Report of commissioners appointed by the Governor.
195	Emory Lewis, Pioneers of Public Education in Accomack County from 1870 to 1925. McMaster Essay from Chincoteague High School in 1935. A grandson and namesake of the first superintendent was principal.
196-7	James C. Weaver, "An Epitomized History of Education in Accomack County," in **Report of the State Superintendent of Public Instruction for 1885.**
196	The Accomack County Surveyor's Book for 1873 contains a plat map of the Free School land as it was divided for sale.
198-9	**The Peninsula Enterprise,** August 8, 1936, lists the Life-saving Stations.
199-200	Whitelaw, Virginia's Eastern Shore, I, pp. 144-5 gives an account of the building of the town of Cape Charles.
199 and 203	Henry R. Bennett, founder of the town of Parksley, told the story of the first railroad stations and the post office conflicts to the author in 1939.
199-200	Mears, in Clark, **The Eastern Shore of Maryland and Virginia,** pp. 590-92 describes the coming of the railroad and town building.
208	Fairy Mapp White, "Turlington Camp Meeting."
Page	Chapter XV 1900-1920
212	Clark, **The Eastern Shore of Maryland and Virginia,** III, p. 285 and p. 254-6. Pioneers in vegetable canning on the Shore.
214	The Cape Charles High School files contain the names of the members of the first graduating class which was in 1901.
215-16	**Annual Report of the State Superintendent of Instruction** showed the amount of money appropriated for the Normal Department of Onancock High School. Graduates and other students were interviewed. Practice teaching was done with individual students who were called from their regular classes at scheduled times.
216	Wise, "A Brief History of Education on the Eastern Shore" contains the information regarding early transportation of students. It was secured in an interview with G. Goodwyn Joynes in 1928.
216	Turman and Others, "A Brief History of Education in Accomack County," pp. 10-14. Wise, **Over on the Eastern Shore,** pp. 49-52.
216-17	Whitelaw, Virginia's Eastern Shore, II, pp. 1283-85. Makemie Monument.
218	"Accomack-Northampton Court Records," Book I and Book II, manuscript copies in the Virginia State Library give the dates on which Thomas Teackle Upshur was commissioned to do the work and the dates on which the volumes were received by the librarian.
220	The Accomack County Memorial Plaque for World War I is on the front of the Courthouse. The Northampton County Memorial Plaque is at the Memorial Library, Cape Charles.

288   NOTES BY CHAPTERS AND PAGES

Page	
223 and	Chapter XVI 1920-1940
225	Thalia Virginia Jones. "Benefactors of Chincoteague: William J. Matthews, John Leonard and John B. Whealton."
224	U. S. Department of Agriculture Soil Maps of Accomack and Northampton counties, 1920.
225	State Corporation Commission, Richmond. Names of the incorporators of the Chincoteague Toll Road and Bridge Company.
226-7	J. Brooks Mapp, attorney for the Corporation and its president when the road was opened, described the opening day and related incidents to the author.
229-30	Annual Reports of the State Superintendent of Public Instruction and reports of principals and head teachers.
231-2	Mears, in Clark, The Eastern Shore. Railroad steamers are named. Photographs are in the Mariners' Museum.
232-4	W. J. Sturgis, Sr., M.D., "The Northampton-Accomack Memorial Hospital from Its Beginning," The Eastern Shore News, November 26, 1953.
238-9	Dicton Wector, The Age of the Great Depression 1929-1941, pp. 76-78. W.P.A.
239	Turman, "Hand Loomed American Linen," The Weaver, July-August 1941, pp. 28-30.
Page	
240-45	Chapter XVII 1940-1960
	"The War Years" was given weekly coverage by The Eastern Shore News and The Peninsula Enterprise.
	Thelma Borum, "A Chronology of the Eastern Shore in World War II," The Eastern Shore News, August 16, 1945.
243	Edward Rowe Snow, Famous Lighthouses of North America, pp. 165-67. Ships destroyed off the Virginia Coast during World War II.
244	Sonja Lewis Holloway, "The Chincoteague Naval Air Station," McMaster Essay, Chincoteague High School, 1956.
245	W. Edwin Hemphill, Editor, Gold Star Honor Roll of Virginians in World War II, pp. 1-3 and p. 288.
246	Robert L. Krieger, "Wallops."
247-8	"Chincoteague Wildlife Refuge Strategic for American Waterfowl," Virginia Wildlife, September 1947, reprinted in The Peninsula Enterprise, September 19, 1947.
248	Whitelaw, Virginia's Eastern Shore, I, p. 90. Early use of Mockhorn Island.
250	Mariners Museum Library Clipping Book No. 110 and No. 113. The story of the Virginia Lee from 1928 until it became a part of the Chesapeake Bay Ferry fleet in 1951.
251	Krieger, "Wallops."
Page	
255	Chapter XVIII 1960-1964
	Wise, Over on the Eastern Shore, pp. 56-7. Biography of Mary Nottingham Smith (Mrs. Robert L.), the supervisor of schools for whom Mary Nottingham Smith High School was named.
255-6	The number of churches was secured from the Eastern Shore newspapers through the announcements of services over a period of six weeks.
255-6	George Carrington Mason, Colonial Churches in Tidewater Virginia.
	Sarah Ann Steele, A History of Holy Trinity Episcopal

Church.
Turman, **The Episcopal Church in Accomack County from 1652.**
Blanche Sydnor White, **History of the Baptists on the Eastern Shore 1776-1959.**
Whitelaw, Virginia's Eastern Shore, II, pp. 1390-1405.

256 Mears, in Clark, The Eastern Shore of Maryland and Virginia, II, pp. 598-9. Newspapers. Editors and former editors were also interviewed.

258 Kerr Place, built in 1797 with a later addition, has an overall length of 108 feet and a maximum depth of 38 feet. It is one of the most cherished architectural gems on the Eastern Shore.

261 **Historic Garden Week in Virginia,** 1941-1964, the annual guidebook, and newspaper announcements of local tours were used to identify the 66 homes which have been open for tours.

262 "Sam Got Down," Time, December 14, 1959, p. 52.
262-3 Krieger, "Wallops," NASA.
265 **Over and Under the Sea,** Chesapeake Bay Bridge-Tunnel publication, p. 4, lists the principal materials used.
265-6 Robertson, **On Land and Sea,** Introduction, pp. 6-7.

SELECTED BIBLIOGRAPHY

BIBLIOGRAPHIES AND INDEXES

Ames, Susie M. An Itemized List of Accomack and Northampton Court Records Books, 1632-1783, in **Studies of the Virginia Eastern Shore in the Seventeenth Century**, Richmond, 1940, pp. 250-51.

Swem, Earl G. **A Selected Bibliography of Virginia, 1607-1699** by Earl G. Swem, John M. Jennings and James A. Servies, Richmond, 1957.

Swem, Earl G. **Virginia Historical Index**, Roanoke, 1934-36. 2v.

DOCUMENTS - Manuscripts

Accomack County Court Records, 1663, Accomac.
"Cropper Papers." The Virginia Historical Society.
"Custis Papers." The Virginia Historical Society.
Muster Roll (census) of the Virginia Colony in 1624, in the Public Records Office, London. Photostatic copy in the Virginia State Library.
Northampton County Court Records, 1632, Eastville.
Sloan Manuscripts. British Museum Library, London. Photostatic copy of items used in the Eastern Shore Public Library, Accomac.
Second Census of the United States, Schedule for Accomack County, Virginia, in 1800. Virginia State Library. Micropage copy in Accomack County Clerks Office.

DOCUMENTS - Printed

Acts of the General Assembly of Virginia (State) from 1776. Richmond.
County Court Records of Accomack-Northampton, Virginia, 1632-1640. Susie M. Ames, ed. Washington, 1954.
Minutes of the Council and General Court of Colonial Virginia, 1622-32, 1670-76. H. R. McIlwaine, ed. Richmond, 1924.
Records of the Virginia Company of London. Susan M. Kingsbury, ed. Washington, 1906-35. 4v.
Statutes at Large; Being a Collection of the Laws of Virginia . . .1619-1792. William W. Hening, ed. Richmond, 1809-23. 13v.
Tracts and Other Papers Relating to the Colonies in North America, to the year 1776. Peter Force, comp. Washington, 1836-46. 4v.
Travels and Works of Captain John Smith, Edward Arber, ed. Edinburgh, 1910. 2v.

BOOKS
(Including printed documents)

Ames, Susie M., ed. **County Court Records of Accomack-Northampton, Virginia, 1632-40.** VII of the American Legal Record Series. Washington, 1954.
Ames, Susie M. **Studies of the Virginia Eastern Shore in the Seventeenth Century**, Richmond, 1940.
Asbury, Francis. 1745-1816. **Journal of the First Methodist Bishop in Virginia**, New York, 1821. 3v.
Bowen, Littleton Purnell. **The Days of Makemie.** New York, 1885.
Brydon, G. McLaren. **Virginia's Mother Church and the Political Conditions Under Which It Grew.** Richmond: Virginia Historical Society, 1947-1952. 2 volumes.

Clark, Charles B. **The Eastern Shore of Maryland and Virginia.** New York, 1950. 3v.
Force, Peter, comp. **Tracts and Other Papers . . . to the year 1776.** Washington, 1836-46. 4v.
Freeman, Douglas Southall. **George Washington.** New York, 1948-57. 7v.
Garden Clubs of Virginia, comp. **Historic Garden Week in Virginia.** Richmond, Annual.
Gwathmey, John H. **Historical Register of Virginians in the Revolution.** Richmond, 1938.
Hale, Nathaniel C. **Virginia Venturer, a Historical Biography of William Claiborne, 1600-1677.** Richmond, 1951.
Hall, Claude H. **Abel Parker Upshur, Conservative Virginian 1790-1844.** Madison, Wisconsin, 1964.
Hemphill, William Edwin, ed. **Gold Star Honor Roll of Virginians in the Second World War.** Charlottesville, 1947.
Hemphill, William Edwin. **Cavalier Commonwealth** by William Edwin Hemphill, Marvin Wilson Schlegel and Sadie Ethel Engelberg. New York, 1957.
Hening, William W., ed. **The Statutes at Large; Being a Collection of All the Laws of Virginia . . . 1619-1792.** Richmond, 1809-1823. 13v.
Hotten, John Camden. **The Original List of Persons . . . Who Went from Great Britain to the American Plantations, 1600-1700.** London, 1874.
Kingsbury, Susan M., ed. **Records of the Virginia Company of London.** Washington, 1906-1935. 4v.
Lewis, Clifford M. **The Spanish Jesuit Mission in Virginia, 1570-1572** by Clifford M. Lewis and Albert J. Loomie. Richmond, 1953.
Macdonald, William, ed. **Documentary Source Book of American History, 1606-1926.** New York, 1937.
Martin, Joseph. **A Comprehensive Gazetteer of Virginia and the District of Columbia.** Charlottesville, 1835.
Mason, George Carrington. **Colonial Churches of Tidewater Virginia.** Richmond, 1945.
McIlwaine, H. R., ed. **Minutes of the Council and General Court of Colonial Virginia 1622-1632, 1670-1676,** with notes and excerpts from original Council and General Court Records into 1683, now lost. Richmond, 1924.
Morton, Richard L. **Colonial Virginia.** Chapel Hill, 1960. 2 vols.
Norwood, Henry. "A Voyage to Virginia", 1649-50, in Peter Force, comp. **Tracts and Other Papers . . . to 1776.** III No. 10.
Nugent, Nell Marion, editor. **Cavaliers and Pioneers, Abstracts of the Virginia Land Patents and Grants 1623-1666.** Richmond, 1934. This book covers the period in which 50 acres of land could be patented for each person brought into the colony. It contains the names of the patentees and their headrights.
Page, I. Marshall. **The Story of Francis Makemie.** Grand Rapids, 1938.
Perry, William S. **Historical Collections Relating to the American Colonial Church.** I, Virginia. Hartford, Conn., 1870.
Purchas, Samuel. **Purchas His Pilgrimes.** Glasgow, 1906. 20v.
Robertson, John William, M.D. **On Land and Sea,** A Pictorial Review of the Virginia Eastern Shore. Onancock, 1961.
Rosenberger, Francis Coleman. **Virginia Reader,** a Treasury of Writings from the First Voyages to the Present. New York, 1948.
Smith, John. **Captain John Smith, Travels and Works,** ed. by Edward

SELECTED BIBLIOGRAPHY

Arber. Edinburgh, 1910. 2v.
Snow, Edward Rowe. **Famous Lighthouses of North America.** New York, 1955.
Steele, Sarah Ann. **A History of Holy Trinity Episcopal Church.** Onancock, 1961.
Swem, Earl G. **Brothers of the Spade, Correspondence of Peter Collinson of London, and John Custis of Williamsburg, 1734-46.** Barre, Mass., 1957.
Swem, Earl G., comp. **Virginia Historical Index.** Roanoke, 1924-36. 2v.
Turman, Nora Miller. **The Episcopal Church in Accomack County from 1652.** Onancock, 1954.
Turman, Nora Miller. **George Yeardley, Governor of Virginia and Organizer of the General Assembly in 1619.** Richmond, 1959.
Turman, Nora Miller, and others. **A History of the Parksley Three Arts Club,** by Nora Miller Turman, Nell C. Drummond (Mrs. C. Lester), John Herbert Hopkins, W. Avery Lewis, Florence W. Rew (Mrs. John R.) and Nell C. Scott. Onancock, 1947.
United States Census, 1790 to 1960. Agriculture included from 1840 and a separate agricultural census from 1925. Washington, Continuous.
United States Postal Guide. Washington, Annual.
Upshur, John Andrews. **Upshur Family in Virginia.** Richmond, 1955.
Wallace, Adam. **The Parson of the Islands, A Biography of the Late Reverend Joshua Thomas.** Philadelphia, 1872.
Wecter, Dicton. **The Age of the Great Depression, 1929-1941.** New York, 1948.
White, Blanche Sydnor. **History of the Baptists on the Eastern Shore of Virginia, 1776-1959.** Baltimore, 1959.
Whitelaw, Ralph T. **Virginia's Eastern Shore.** 2v. Richmond, 1951.
Williams, Lloyd Haynes. **Pirates of Colonial Virginia.** Richmond, 1937. The appendix contains copies of documents pertaining to the punishment of pirates.
Wise, Barton Haxall. **The Life of Henry A. Wise of Virginia, 1806-76.** New York, 1899.
Wise, Barton Haxall. **A Memoir of General John Cropper of Accomack County, Virginia.** Richmond, 1892.
Wise, Henry Alexander. **Over on the Eastern Shore.** Onancock, 1962.
Wise, Jennings Cropper. **Ye Kingdom of Accawmacke or The Eastern Shore of Virginia in the Seventeenth Century.** Richmond, 1911.
Wise, John S. **The End of an Era.** New York, 1902.

MAPS

Augustin Herrman's **Map of Virginia and Maryland.** London, 1673. Made by him from the survey he made in 1670. Facsimile copies in the John Carter Brown Library and the Accomack County Clerk's Office and a positive photostatic copy is in the Eastern Shore Public Library.
Captain John Smith's **Map of Virginia.** London, 1612.
Captain John Smith's **Map of Virginia.** B. C. McCary, ed. Richmond, 1957.
New York and Norfolk Airline Railway Map and Profile, Virginia Section, May 1855. Print in Archives of the Virginia State Library and a photostatic copy is in the Eastern Shore Public Library.
U. S. Department of Agriculture. **Soil Survey Maps of Accomack and Northampton Counties.** Washington, 1920.

SELECTED BIBLIOGRAPHY 293

Virginia Department of Highways. **County and District Road Maps.**
The base map used in this book was adapted from these.

PERIODICALS

Ames, Susie M. "Federal Policy Toward the Eastern Shore of Virginia in 1861." **The Virginia Magazine of History and Biography,** October 1961, pp. 432-459.
"Chincoteague-Strategic Virginia Refuge for American Waterfowl." Virginia Wildlife, September, 1947.
Pratt, Richard. The Ladies' Home Journal, April 1963, pp. 75-7.
Turman, Nora Miller. Inventory of the Estate of Argoll Yeardley of Northampton County, Virginia, in 1655, ed. by Nora Miller Turman and Mark C. Lewis. Virginia Magazine of History and Biography, October 1962, pp. 410-19.
Turman, Nora Miller. "Hand Loomed American Linen," **The Weaver,** July-August 1941, pp. 28-30.
Maryland Historical Society Magazine, IV and XIV.
The Virginia Genealogist, July 1957 - December 1958. Census Rolls for 1800.

UNPUBLISHED MATERIALS

Anderson, Charles F. "Some Extracts from the Ancient Records of Northampton County, Virginia, from 1632 to 1712," 1856.
Hamilton, Robert. "Lighthouses of the East Coast." A term paper, 1949.
Holloway, Sonja Lewis. "The Chincoteague Naval Air Station," McMaster Essay, 1956.
Krieger, Robert L. "Wallops" (Autobiographical and research material pertaining to John Wallop and NASA on the Eastern Shore).
Lewis, Emory. "Pioneers of Public Education in Accomack County, 1870-1925." McMaster Essay, 1935.
Tarr, Thalia Jones. "Benefactors of Chincoteague," McMaster Essay, 1936.
Turman, Nora Miller. "A Brief History of Education in Accomack County," by Nora Miller Turman, Henry L. Derby, Oliver C. Greenwood, W. Avery Lewis and John W. Waterfield, Jr., 1963. (Typescript and tape recording in the Accomack County School Board Office.)
White, Fairy Mapp. "Turlington Camp Meeting" (mimeographed), 1957.
Wise, Henry Alexander. "A Brief History of Education on the Eastern Shore of Virginia," 1928.

NEWSPAPERS

The Eastern Shore News. Onancock (files)
The Peninsula Enterprise. Accomac (files)
Richards, Albert A., comp. Fifty-fifth Anniversary Edition of **The Peninsula Enterprise,** August 8, 1936.
Sturgis, W. J., M.D. "Beginning and Early Years of the Northampton-Accomack Memorial Hospital," **The Eastern Shore News,** November 26, 1953.

Index

Accomac (Drummondtown before 1883), 65, 82, 166, 199, 208, 213, 218, 228
Accomack Country Club, 235
Accomack County organized 1634, 25, 27, 28, 41, 42
Northampton 1642, 43
Second Accomack 1663, 64, 70, 75
Accomack Courthouse, 133
Accomack County Courthouses (See courthouses)
Accomack News, 257
Accomack Parish (1663-1763), 80, 101, 102, 123, 138, 156
Divided in 1773, 163, 185
Accomack Plantation, 3, 8, 9, 10, 13, 14, 15, 16, 18, 19, 22, 28, 35
Accomack River (Cherrystone Creek), 4, 5, 8, 14, 40, 41
Accomack Territory, 77
Accomack and Northampton with West Virginia, 190
Accomack-Northampton County line, 76, 79-80, 85
Adams, E. E., 225
Howard H., 263, 270, 273
W. J., 225
Addison, John, 143
Age, Recording law, 64
Allen, Edmund, 91, 125
Alworth, Bulbegger, 65
American Revolution, 129-32, 145, 154, 155, 189
Ames, E. Almer, Jr., 263, 272
Susie May, 278
Anderson, Bessie B., 233-4
Naomi, 100
William, 100
Andrews, William, 24, 27, 29, 44, 52
Anglican Church (before 1776, Protestant Episcopal after 1789), 31, 63, 101, 130, 131, 136, 145
Anne, Queen, 92
Architecture:
Big House, Colonnade and Kitchen, 187-88
Big House, Little House, Colonnade and Kitchen, 148-49
Classical Revival, 169
Dormer Window, 90-91
Gambrel Roof, 113, 140-41
Manor House, 258
One Room and Loft, 146
Siamese Twin House, 147
Two Room and Loft, 135-36
Argall, Samuel, 5
Arlington, Earl of, 77
Arlington Plantations, 45, 46, 77, 114-16, 121, 137
Arms and Ammunition, 10, 44, 130, 146, 149, 185
Arbuckle, James, 125
Artists, Traveling, 164
Asbury, Francis, 144
Assateague Island, 72, 104, 106, 171, 172, 183, 184, 194, 223, 247, 259, 260
Assateague Lighthouse, 171, 184
Assawoman Church, 86, 102, 124, 161, 207
Assawoman Creek, 71, 100, 143, 194, 246
Association for the Preservation of Virginia Antiquities, 259
Atlantic Female College, 197
Atlantic Magisterial District, 194, 197
Attorneys, 110, 168
Authors of the Eastern Shore 1940-64, 278-80
Automobiles, 213, 221, 222, 247
Avery, Isaac, 136
Ayres, John H., M.D., 211

INDEX 295

Bacon's Rebellion, 78-9
Bagge, William, 125
Bagwell, Henry, 21, 35
Baker, Daniel, 57
  Elijah, 136, 145
Ballast, 109
Ballots, See Voting
Baltimore, Lord, See Lord Baltimore
Baltimore, Md., 173, 185, 197, 219, 232
Banks on the Eastern Shore, 230
Baptist Church, 136, 145, 169, 197
Barnes, A. Parker, 257
Barracks, 189, 263
Battle of Pungoteague, 162
Battle of the Barges, 132, 164
Baylor Survey, 205
Bayly, Catherine, 164
  Thomas H., 133
  Thomas M., 161, 178
Bay Side Road, 94, 139, 161
Bayview, 180, 193
Bear and the Cub, The (play), 66-7
Beebe Ranch, 261
Bell, F. B., 234
  Thomas, 139
  W. P., 213
Belle Haven, 168, 179, 194, 209, 228, 256
Bennett, Henry R., 202
  Richard, 54, 55
Berkeley, William, 43, 49, 50, 62, 64, 70, 71, 74, 77, 78, 79
Bicycle, 205
Bills of sale, 28
Birdsnest, 203
Bishop of London, 102, 103
Black, William, minister, 102, 103
Blackstone, Thomas H., 230
Boats, 5, 10, 150
Bolton, Francis, minister, 7, 9
Book of Common Prayer, 54, 62, 136
Books, 58, 69, 144, 159, 180
Borum, John T., 257
  Julius W., 256
  Thelma, 257
Boston, 128, 129
Bowden, E. J., 225
Bowdoin, John, 125, 138
  John W., M.D., 211, 233
  Peter, 155, 165
  William, 156

Bowdoin Hungars, 138, 233
Bowman, Edmund, 70, 75, 163
  Sarah, 81
Bowmans Folly, 163, 207
Branding irons, 39, 165, 261
Bridgetown, 173, 199, 203
British soldiers, 118, 125, 131, 132, 161
Broadwater, 223
Broiler industry, 254
Brown, Devereaux, 64
  John, 167
  Tabitha, 88
  Thomas, 75
Browne, Peter F., 185, 186
  Thomas Bayly, 207
Brownsville, 167, 217
Bulkley, Mary, 19
  Richard, 7, 19, 26
  Thomas, 19
Burdett, Alicia, 46, 87
  Thomas, 46, 87
  William, 24, 25, 27, 29, 45
Burgesses, 9, 19, 21, 35, 47, 49, 53, 62, 87, 97, 118, 126, 129
Burials and burying grounds, 9, 22, 31, 36
Burton, William A., 211
Burtons Chapel, 136
Byrd, Ben D., 257
  William II, 114
  William S., 193

Calendar Change (January 1, 1752), 116-17
Calvert, Eleanor, 137
  Leonard, 25, 34
Camp meetings, 162, 208
Canada, 107, 118, 124, 211
Canner, Thomas, 2
Canning factories, 212
Cape Charles (now Cape Charles Air Force Base), 4, 7, 14, 19, 73, 110, 171
Cape Charles (established 1884 near Kings Creek), 196, 197, 199, 202, 207, 214, 219, 225, 227, 230, 236-7, 249, 257, 260
Cape Charles Country Club, 236, 259
Cape Henry, 3, 4, 19, 263
Capeville, 165, 167, 179, 180, 191, 193
Capeville Magisterial District, 196
Cary, R. R., 185

Castor oil, 128, 167-8, 173
Cattle, 23, 24, 26, 28, 39, 40, 45, 46, 61, 69, 85
Cedar Island, 195, 262
Census, Colonial (See beginnings of chapters)
  United States, of 1790, 138; of 1800, 156-9
Chamber of Commerce, 257, 266
Chapman, Phillip, 45
Charles I, King, 16, 17, 19, 20, 25, 36, 43, 49, 51, 92
Charles II, King, 62, 75, 76, 83, 92
Charlton, Ann, 60
  Bridgett, 60
  Elizabeth, 60
  Stephen, 29, 44, 50, 54, 60
Cherrystone Creek (Accomack River), 40, 110, 175, 179-80, 190, 193
Chesapeake and Delaware Canal, 173
Chesapeake Bay Bridge-Tunnel, 263-5
Chesapeake Bay Ferry Commission, 249, 251
Chesconnessex Creek, 110, 189
Children of the American Revolution (CAR), 259
Chincoteague Bay, 71, 179, 194, 225
Chincoteague Baptist Church, 145
Chincoteague Creek (Mosquito Creek), 110, 131
Chincoteague National Wildlife Refuge, 247
Chincoteague Naval Air Station, 244, 246, 251, 252, 263
Chincoteague Ocean Beach, 259-60
Chincoteague Toll Road and Bridge Company, 236
Chincoteague Town and Island, 72, 104, 106, 154, 156, 176, 185, 194, 207, 218, 220, 222, 223, 225, 229, 243, 248, 261
Christ Episcopal Church, 169
Christian, Michael, 108
Church Neck, 60, 79, 174
Churches Colonial (at four places in Northampton), 25, 48, 49, 80, 86
  (at eight places in Accomack), 54, 81, 86, 100, 101, 111, 122-3, 128

Churches after American Revolution (See also individual names and denominations), 136, 255-6
Circuit Court Judges 1831-1964, 272
Civil War, 183-190
Civil Air Patrol, 243-4
Civilian Defense, 241-242
Claiborne, William, 10, 13, 18, 22, 24, 27, 29, 34
Clarence Burton Barns, 261
Clerks of Court 1632-1964, 273-4
Coast Guard (Life Saving Service before 1915), 220, 245, 246, 262
Cobbs Island, 195, 205, 262
Cockburn, George, 162
Cole, John, 98
College of William and Mary, 90, 105, 113
Colleges on the Eastern Shore, 197, 263
Commercial vegetables, 173
Commissioners of Fisheries 1900-1964, 272
Communion Silver, 31, 256
Company land, 7, 8, 10, 16, 44
Confederate Monuments, 216
Congressmen from the Eastern Shore, 175
Constitutions, Virginia: of 1776, 129; of 1830, 165; of 1851, 175, 177; of 1869, 190, 195; of 1902, 212
Conway, Edwin, 84
Copes, Thomas P., 193
Corbin, George, 136
  Sabra, 164
Corbin Hall, 105
Costin, Elizabeth P., 234
Cotton, Ann, 35
  William, minister, 28, 29, 30, 36, 48,
Cotton culture, 158, 160, 166, 173
County Agent, V.P.I. Extension, 255
County Superintendents of Schools 1925-64, 274
Courts, Accomack-Northampton, 1632-1642, 21, 22, 23, 24, 34, 35, 36, 41
  Northampton 1642-1663, 43, 44, 51, 52, 68, 76
  Northampton 1632 (records continuous)

INDEX 297

Accomack 1663 (records continuous), 65, 68, 70, 76
Courthouses (at Town Fields, Eastville, Accomac and Onancock), 66, 79, 82, 84, 99, 111, 136, 145
Coventon, 145
Craddock Academy, 198
Crafts and trades, 122, 136, 167, 168, 169
Cromwell, Oliver, 49, 51, 56
Cropper, Catherine, 165
  John (Revolutionary War officer), 154, 163-5
  Margaret, 164
  Sarah, 164
Cugley, Daniel, 41, 47
  Hannah (See also Hannah Savage), 41
  Margaret, 48
Culpepper, John, 70
Cuba, 107, 179
Currency, Pounds Shillings Pence, 26, 40, 148-50, 106
  Tobacco, 25, 30, 38, 45, 46, 107
  United States Dollars, 149, 151, 156, 158
Custis, Alicia, 87
  Daniel Parke, 114, 115, 116, 121
  Eleanor, 137
  Elizabeth, 87
  Frances, 114
  George Washington Parke, 137
  John I, 50
  John II, 51, 55, 75, 78, 84, 85, 87-8
  John III, 87, 113, 114
  John IV, 114-16
  John Parke, 122, 137
  Margaret, 114
  Martha, 137
  Tabitha, 87
  Thomas, 133
  William, 76
Custis Hungars (Wilsonia Neck), 284
Custis-Lee Mansion, 116, 137

Dalby, John B., 197
  Thomas, 125
Dale, Elizabeth, 8, 9, 21, 39, 40
  Thomas, 5
Daniel, John T., 257
  Marion C., 257
Darby, William, 66-7

Daughters of the American Revolution, 234, 259
Davis, Jefferson, 185
  Levin Nock, 270, 273
Debtors Prison, Accomac, 134, 135, 136
Eastville, 111
Declaration of Independence, 129
Deed of Gift, 56
Deed of Sale, first recorded, 23
Deep Creek, 99, 110
Defense, 43, 44, 45, 77, 86
Delaware, 94, 130, 199, 202
Delegates, Members of the House of, 1900-1964, 273
Delmarva Peninsula, 94, 130, 173
Democratic Party, 218
Denoon, Harry Lee, M.D., 234
Depression of 1929-1941, 236-8
Devices for Punishment, 37
Dilke, Clement, 14
Dix, John A., U. S. Army, 185
Dize, A. F., 241
Doughty, Francis, minister, 61
Douglas, Edward, 44, 61
  George, 118
  Isabella, 61
Downes, E. V., 234
Downing, A. W., 191
E. W. P., 234
Downings Church, 189
Draft Laws, 121, 220, 221, 240
Drew, Edward, 29
Drivers License, 236
Drummond, Richard, 133
Drummonds Mill Farm, 119, 120
Drummondtown (Accomac after 1883), 133, 134, 145, 150, 168, 169, 179
Ducking Stool, 37, 38, 63
Dulany Foods, Inc., 254
Dunmore, Lord, 129
Dutch Residents, 51, 55
Dutch Wars, 51, 55, 68, 73

Eastern Shore Academy, 198
Eastern Shore Herald, 256
Eastern Shore News, The, 257
Eastern Shore of Virginia Historical Society, Inc., 259
Eastern Shore of Virginia Produce Exchange, 209, 211
Eastern Shore Public Library, 255
Eastern Shore Publishing Company, 257

298　　　　　　　　　　　INDEX

Eastern Shore Yacht and Country Club, 259
Eastern Virginian, 196, 256
Eastville (Horns before 1800), 79, 80, 98, 128, 138, 145, 168, 179, 185, 191, 199, 209, 233
Edge Hill, 165, 166
Edmonds, Alfred B., 257
　Franklin Spicer, 257
　John W., 257
　John W., Jr., 257
　John W., III, 257
Education of Orphans, 61, 81
Elections, 176, 178, 193
Elizabeth City, 6, 9, 13, 47
Elizabeth Island, 7
Elkington, 47, 81
Elks, 257
Elliott, William, 136
Ellis, John, 54
Elzey, William, 211
Emmanuel Episcopal Church, 207, 256
Encyclopedia Britannica, 159
End View, 139-43
Epps, Margaret, 8, 11
　William, 8, 9, 11, 13, 16
Evans, Thomas, 133, 136, 154, 177
Exmore, 199, 203, 228, 239, 254
Eyre, Gertrude, 127
　Littleton, 118, 125, 127, 139
　Severn, 127, 193
　Suzanne, 61
　Thomas, 61
Eyre Hall, 127, 139

Farmer and Fisherman, 256
Federal Officials from the Eastern Shore 1900-1964, 272
Fence laws, 73, 96, 202, 228
Ferries and ferry terminals:
　Cape Charles (town), 200, 219, 232, 237, 249, 250, 256
　Cherrystone Creek, 165, 175, 182, 183
　Hungars Creek, 107, 108, 109, 127, 132, 154, 155
　Kings Creek, 94, 101, 107, 163, 165, 175
　Kiptopeke Beach, 237, 250, 264
Ferry House, 138
Ferry keepers, 95
Ferry rates, 94, 108, 109, 237
Filling Stations, 222, 223

Fines, 38
Finney, Louis C., 163, 185
　Spencer D., 180
Finneys Gate School, 214
Fire Departments, Volunteer, 200
Fisher, Benjamin T., 256
　Fenwick, M.D., 145
Fishermans Island, 240
Fishing Point, 46, 48, 85
Fitzhugh, William Bullitt, 256
Flax, 128, 152, 153, 174, 238
Fletcher, Henry, 125
　Spencer, 217
Floyd, John K., 165, 175
　Matthew, 142, 143
　Sarah, 142
Folkes Tavern, 66
Folly Creek (Metompkin Creek), 163, 171, 207, 208, 235, 262
Forests, 25, 72
Forts, 10, 131, 162, 240, 245
Foxcroft, Isaac, 70
Francis Makemie Presbyterian Church, 169, 189
Francis Makemie Monument, 216-17
Franklin City, 227
Franktown, 173, 180, 193
Free enterprise, 21
Free school land, 102, 103, 177, 197, 248
French and Indian War, 118-121
Funerals, See burials

Garden Clubs, 259
Gargatha or Gargaphia, 71, 72, 143, 194
Garrison, George Tankard, 207
Gasoline Refund System, 227
Gazetteer of Virginia, 166
General Court (1662-1852, Quarter Court before 1662), 62
George I, King, 99, 110
George II, King, 110
George III, King, 124, 125
Gilbert, Bartholomew, 1, 2, 91
Gillett, J. W., 193
Glebes, 9, 28, 29, 48, 122, 123, 143, 161
　House of 1635, 29
Gloucester County, England, 102
Godwin, Joseph, 98
　W. P., 234
　Wrendo M., 250
Goffigon, Edward, 191
Gores Neck, 143

INDEX

Grain, 47, 166, 170, 173, 182, 204, 209
Grange Society, 206
Graves, Ann, 35
  Catherine, 35
  John, 35
  Thomas, 16, 19, 21, 27, 35
  Verlinda, 24
Greenbush, 200
Green Spring, 78
Guardians for Orphans, 45, 82
Guilford, 143, 152, 179, 194
Guilford Creek, 102, 110, 144, 189, 253
Guilford Methodist Church, 144
Gulf Stream Nurseries, Inc., 253
Gunter, Benjamin T. (Judge), 272
  Benjamin T., Sr., 211, 214, 273
  Benjamin T., Jr., 270, 273

Hack, George, M.D., 69
Hacks Neck, 69
Hadlock, 139, 143, 179, 215
Hall, Henry, 194
Hallett, John W., 191
Hallwood, 203
Hamilton, John R., M.D., 234
Hamor, Ralph, 16
Hampton, 95, 107, 108, 154, 175
Handy, Robert B., 197
Harmanson, George, 107, 108
  Gertrude, 127
  John, 125, 137
  Matthew, 118
Harmanson-West Camp, Confederate Veterans, 216
Harmar, Charles, 21, 22
Harvey, John, 13, 16, 19, 25, 34, 36
Hawleys Creek (Indiantown Creek), 110
Health departments, 255
Henderson, William Carey, M.D., 234
Herrman, Augustin, 74
Hickman, Milton T., 250
  W. H., 226
Hill, Tabitha, 88
Hills Farm, 89-90, 276
History, Eastern Shore, 216, 218, 234, 259
Hodgkins, Anthony, 53, 65
Hog Island, 131, 172, 183, 193, 198, 199, 223, 262

Holden Creek (Crooked Creek), 101
Holland, G. W., M.D., 234
Home and Garden Tours, 237, 261
Home Demonstration Agent, V.P.I. Extension, 255
Home industries, 153, 159, 160, 182, 212, 238, 246
Hopkins Brothers, 183
Horntown, 143, 145, 177, 179
Horseless farm, First, 239
Horsey, Stephen, 54
Hospital, See Northampton-Accomack Memorial Hospital
Hotels, 204, 212, 228
Houses, Sizes of some, 45, 58, 69, 81, 82, 133
Howard, Phillip, 66, 67
Howe, John, 21, 22, 27, 29, 35, 36
Hudson, Richard, 34
Hungars Church, 49, 60, 79, 101, 107, 112, 113, 123, 189, 256
Hungars Creek, 25, 44, 49, 57
Hungars Port, 107, 108, 110, 138, 155, 163, 165
Hunting Creek, 123, 189, 194, 210, 216
Hutchinson, Robert, 64
Hyslop, Levin J., 211

Ice Houses, 170, 171
Indian guide, 50
  Interpreter, 5, 80
  King, 3, 4, 8
  Traders, 6, 50
  Trading, 8, 40, 43, 51, 57
  War, 52
Indians, 2, 3, 5, 26, 51, 77
Ingleside, 145, 185
Inspection laws, 105
Inventories of Estates, 25, 30, 142, 159
Irish potatoes, 182, 204, 209, 211, 219, 221, 225, 236, 237, 240
Islands Magisterial District (Township), 194

Jail, 57, 67, 136
James I, 9, 18, 92
James II, 83, 84, 92
James, Thomas B., 211
  Thomas H., 269, 274
Jamestown, 2, 3, 4, 5, 8, 13, 17, 18, 21, 25, 31, 44, 47, 51,

INDEX

60, 70, 77, 80, 87
Japanese Surrender, 245
Jaycees, 257
Jenifer, Ann, 71, 82
  Daniel, 70, 71, 86
  Daniel of St. Thomas, 72, 133
  Mary, 71
Jenkins Bridge, 196, 207
Jenkins Bridge Academy, 198
Jester, H. J., 225
  LeRoy, 225
Jobes Island, 143, 157, 158
Johnson, John H., 256
  Lemuel, 256
  Thomas, 53
Johnsontown, 180, 193
John W. Taylor Packing Company, 212
Jones, William, 53
Joynes, G. Goodwyn, 214
  Sallie, 215
Justice, Ralph, 118
Justices (Commissioners before 1662), See courts

Keale Hill, 4
Kegotank, 143
Kellam, Lucius J., 250
  Richard, 57
  S. S., M.D., 234
  William, 70
Keller, 136, 203, 206, 212
Keller Fair, 207, 222, 235, 252
Kendall, William, 70
Kerr, Edward, 236
Kerr Place, 104, 150, 215, 259
Kidd, John, 131, 132
Kings Creek, 7, 8, 10, 14, 28, 44, 48, 66, 95, 165, 175, 236, 259
Kiptopeke Beach, 233, 237, 240
Kiwanis, 257
Kosher turkeys, 245
Krieger, Robert L., 263

Land, bought from Indians in 1614, 5
  Certificates for, 28
  Land Reform Act (Headright policy replaced), 68
  Ownership confirmed after proprietary grant, 76
  Patents by headrights, 28
Land Books, 10, 77
Langley Field Research Center, 246, 251, 263
Latin House, 165
Laws, Revised code of, 62

LeCato, Margaret B., 197
  Thomas L., 211
Lee, Robert E., (CSA), 137
Lee Magisterial District, 195
Lee Mont, 203, 216
Leonard, John, 225
Lewis, Parker, 156
License, Ferry keeper,
  Ordinary keeper, 65
  To leave Accomack, 22, 35
Life Saving Service (Coast Guard after 1915), 198-9
Lighthouses, 171, 172, 183
Lions, 257
Literary Fund, 177, 196
Little Creek, 237, 249
Littleton, Ann, 61, 80
  Edward, 56, 60, 61, 80
  Hester, 56, 61
  Nathaniel, 35, 55, 56, 57, 80
  Nathaniel II, 87
  Sarah, 81
  Southy, 61, 70, 75, 80-82
Livery stables, 212
Livestock, 39, 45, 57, 61, 72, 96, 97, 104, 105, 131, 150, 162, 202, 219
  Laws pertaining to, 72
Lockwood, Henry L., 186, 189
Locust Mount, 173, 179, 195
Locustville, 173, 179
Locustville Academy, 198
Lodge, J. Shenton, 278
Lord Baltimore, 18, 21, 25, 94
Lower Northampton Baptist Church, 136
Lyon, James, M.D., 159

Machipongo Academy, 198
Machipongo Creek, 85, 110, 143
McMaster Old Homes Essay Award, 218
McMath, Albert J., 211
  George N., 257, 263
Maddox, Wyle, 259
Magisterial Districts, Accomack County, 177, 193-95
  Northampton County, 177, 191-93
Magothy Bay, 14, 19, 26, 35, 47, 56, 61, 80, 143, 166
Magothy Bay Church, 86, 102, 169
Magothy Bay Point (Cape Charles), 44
Makemie, Anne, 100
  Elizabeth, 100

INDEX 301

Francis, 100-101, 217
Naomi, 100
Makemie Monument, 216-17
Maplewood Golf Course, 235
Mapp, George R., Jr., 250
  G. Walter, 211, 233, 272, 273
  J. Brooks, 234, 272
  John, 138
  John E., M.D., 197
  John R., 197
  Margaret, 197
  Mildred (Mrs. G. Walter), 234
Mappsville, 194, 212
Margaret Academy, 136, 137, 161, 165, 197, 215
Marriages, 22
Marshall, John, 111
Mary, Queen (Daughter of James II), 83, 84, 85
Maryland, 20, 25, 34, 65, 69, 70, 94, 127, 130, 132, 158, 179, 185, 194, 218
Mason, C. W., 215
Masons, 257
Masters, John, 107, 108
Mattawoman Creek (Now the Gulf, originally Mattawoman. Present Mattawoman was south prong of Hungars. Ferry terminal was on the latter), 8, 34, 44, 50, 107
Matthews, Samuel, 62
Meadville, 185
Mears, James E., 254
  J. T., 225
Messongo, 143, 173, 179, 199, 203
Messongo Creek, 100, 110, 189, 194, 208
Methodists, 162, 168, 169, 208
Metompkin (Accomac, village near Parksley Wayside and Parksley R.R. Station), 82, 98, 136, 179, 194, 199, 203
Metompkin Creek, 99, 110, 131, 194, 195
Metompkin Island, 262
Metompkin Magisterial District, 194
Milliner, Wilber Jackson, Jr., 278
Mills, Mrs. J. S., 234
Mills (grain and lumber), 46, 47, 67, 94, 95, 168, 174, 193,
Ministers, 9, 22, 28, 54, 101, 130, 131

Reports to General Court, 22
Michael, John, 79
Margaret, 114
Middle Road, 123, 143
Military Districts, 44, 190
Militia, 44, 68, 73, 77, 85, 87, 92, 101, 106, 107, 118, 121-2, 130, 154, 161, 163, 165, 185
Mockhorn Island, 191, 248
Modest Town, 169, 179
Monkey Sam (NASA Space animal), 262
Morough, John, schoolmaster, 103
Motor Vehicles, 221
Muddy Creek, 143
Muskrat ranch, 197

Nails, 29, 80
Nandua, 56, 80
Nandua Creek, 110, 189
Nassawadox, 49, 52, 64, 232
Nassawadox Creek, 42, 44, 60, 139, 189, 193
National Advisory Committee for Aeronautics, 246
National Aeronautics and Space Administration, 251-2, 262-3
National Guard, 229
National Recorder, 256
Naturalization, 55
Navigation Acts, 52, 55, 57
Neal, John, 44
Neech, Daniel, 70
Netherlands, 43, 51, 52
New Church, 124, 143, 145, 179, 186, 194, 199, 212
New England, 17, 21, 40
Newfoundland, 18, 21
Newspapers, 173, 256-7
Newstown, 194
New Style Calendar, 116-17
New York, 158, 173, 185, 204, 212
Nock, Nehemiah, 257
Norfolk, 121, 154, 175, 200, 210, 225, 230, 257, 262
Normal Department in Onancock High School, 216
Northampton - Accomack Memorial Hospital, 232, 233, 245, 261
Northampton County (named), 43
Northampton Courthouse Post Office, 128, 138
Northampton Protest, 54, 55

INDEX

Northampton Times, 257
North Carolina, 65, 127
Northern Neck, 65, 75, 127
Northwest Territory, 129
Norwood, Henry, 49, 50, 51, 60
Nottingham, Claude, 213
  Jacob, 193
  John E., 211, 233, 273
  Leonard B., 191
  Luther, 215
  Severn P., 191
  Thomas, J. L., M.D., 191
Nuthall, John, 44

Oak Grove Methodist Church, 136
Oak Hall Farm, 203
Oaths, 13, 18, 23, 27, 53, 98
Occohannock Academy, 198
Occohannock Creek, 55, 75, 84, 110, 123, 183, 189, 195
Occohannock Neck, 205
Office supplies, cost of, 65, 66
Ohio Company, 118, 124
Ohio Country annexed to Canada, 124
Old Courthouse-Restored, 111
Old Plantation Creek, 8, 14, 19, 21, 22, 25, 31, 35, 44, 56, 77, 110
Old Style Calendar, 116
Old Town Neck (Yeardley land), 108, 139, 189
Onancock (Port Scarburgh), 4, 83, 100, 101, 111, 144, 150, 178, 185, 195, 196, 197, 213, 228, 256
Onancock Academy, 198
Onancock Creek, 82, 110, 132
Onancock High School, 197, 208, 229
Onley, 211
Only, 178
Ordinaries, 57, 65, 145
Orphans, care of, 45
Overseers of the Poor, 161

Painter, 168
Parish line, 122-3, 194
Park Hall, 145
Parke, Frances, 114, 115
  Henry, minister, 80
Parker, George, 64
Parks, Mahalinda Kellam, 279
Parksley, 202, 203, 208, 243
Parksley Land Improvement Company, 203

Parksley Three Arts Club, 259
Parliament, 9, 52, 53, 54, 55, 56, 92, 125, 128
Parramore, Thomas, 87, 125
Parramore Island, 131, 195, 199, 269
Parsonage house (glebe) of 1635, 29-30
Patents for land, 14
  Land Reform Act, 68
Peninsula Enterprise, 256
Peninsula Ferry Company, 237
Pennsylvania Railroad, 199, 203, 207, 232, 233, 237
Pettit, Margaret, 164
  William B., 211
Philadelphia, 20, 101
Physicians, 110, 168, 169
Pillory, 36
Piper, Charles, 117
Pirates, 85, 106
Pitts Wharf, 110
Pocomoke, 143, 145
Pocomoke River (Wighco), 100, 110, 194
Pony Penning (Horse penning earlier), 104, 248, 260
Popes Island, 199, 220, 262
Pory, John, 7
Postage, 155, 173, 180
Postmasters in 1856, 179-80
Post Offices, 128, 138, 155, 173, 179-80, 203, 208, 218
Pott, Francis, 56, 61
Poultry Diagnostic Laboratory, 254
Poultry Industry, 245, 254
Powell, Stewart K., 241
Presbyterian Meeting House, 236
Prisons and prisoners, 24, 38, 57
Private enterprise, 18, 92
Proprietary grant of Virginia, 65, 70, 75, 78, 83
Protestant Episcopal Church (named 1783, organized in America 1789), 136, 160
Pungoteague, 65, 66, 82, 161, 162, 163, 168, 179, 195, 197, 199, 203, 228
Pungoteague Academy, 198, 215
Pungoteague Church, 80, 101, 111
Pungoteague Creek, 66, 110, 162, 169, 183, 189, 195
Pungoteague Magisterial District, 195

INDEX

Pungoteague Methodist Church, 199, 207
Punishment, 24, 29, 62, 65

Quaker Meeting House, 144
Quakers, 143, 144
Quarantine laws, 69, 70, 106
Quarter Court (General Court after 1662), 62
Quinby, Thomas B., 211

R and G Shirt Corporation, 255
Railroad, 179, 228
Raleigh, Walter, 1
Reade, John R., 193
Red Bank Baptist Church, 193
Red Cross, 241
Regional Regulatory Laboratory, 254
Republican Party, 218
Rich, Benjamin W., 199
  Nathaniel B., 256
Richmond, 129, 131, 162, 167, 172, 173, 178
Roads, 21, 73, 82, 92, 95, 99, 144, 205, 214, 223, 227, 228, 236, 265
Roberts, Elias, 108
  John H., 211
Robertson, John W., M.D., 234, 270, 279
Robins, Joshua, 139, 142
  Mary, 81
  Obedience, 19, 22, 27, 29, 36, 44, 46, 53
  Sarah, 139, 142
Robinson, Elizabeth, 87
Rogers, James S., 234
Roper, Catherine, 35
  William, 35, 44
Rotary, 257
Rotterdam, 50, 55
Rowles, James C., 257
Rubber Tire Era, 223
Ruritans, 257
Russell, Brooks, 251
  Charles F., 237
Russell Islands, 4, 106, 158
Rydings, Thomas, 70, 76

Sabbath breaking, 97
Salt making, 5, 58, 67, 72, 174
St. George County, Petition for, 124
St. George Episcopal Church, 111, 161, 185, 189
St. George Parish, 123, 138, 156

St. James Episcopal Church, 123, 155, 169, 189, 237
St. Marys, Maryland, 25, 71
Sandford, Samuel (donor of Free School land), 102, 103, 177, 197, 248
Sanford, 197
Saunders, Roger, 22, 24
Savage, Ann, 47
  Hannah, 34
  John, 34, 41, 47, 80, 138
  Littleton, 136
  Mary, 80
  Nathaniel, 125
  Thomas (Indian interpreter), 5, 6, 7, 8, 11, 12, 14, 26, 31-34, 41, 138
Savages Creek (Original Mattawoman, now the Gulf), 41, 44, 49
Savage Estates, 34
Savage land, 8, 34, 41, 47, 80, 138
Savages Neck, 44, 80
Saxis Island (Sykes), 158, 248
Saxis Marsh Wildlife Refuge, 103, 248
Scarburgh, Charles, 82, 90
  Edmund I, 19, 22, 23, 24, 26
  Edmund II, 26, 44, 47, 53, 57, 62, 64, 72
  Hannah, 26
  Mary, 72, 73
  Tabitha, 88
Scarburghs Neck, 73
Schools, Private, in Accomack, 197, 218
  Public, 103, 161, 176, 194, 214, 229, 255
Schools, Private, in Northampton, 197
  Public, 168, 176, 195, 197, 215, 229, 230, 236, 255
Scott, A. Preston, 215
  Thomas M., 256
  William T., 200
Scott Hall, 132, 150, 234
Seafoods, 158, 174, 202, 204, 254, 255
Sea Side Road, 94, 143, 145
Sea View, 180
Secretary's land, 8, 10, 13, 14, 24, 28, 34, 35
Selby, T. P., 225
Senators, state, from the Eastern Shore 1900-1964, 272
Sheriff, Office of, 27, 35, 111

Shichans, Esmy, 34
Ships torpedoed in Virginia Waters 1942-45, 243
Silver, 30, 40, 46, 81, 131, 142
Silversmith, 40
Simpson, Southy, 125
Smith, Charles, 183
  Isaac, 125
  John, 4
  Mary, 71
Smiths Island, 4, 85, 165, 171, 183, 189, 191, 198, 220, 262
Soil Conservation program, 240, 255
Sound Beach, 248
Spanish Settlement in Virginia, 2
Spencer, William, 70
Stamp Act, 125
State Highway Department, 227, 236, 255
State Senators from the Eastern Shore 1900-1964, 272
State Troopers, 230, 255
Steelyards (scales), 58
Stocks, 38
Stone, John, 24, 25, 28
  Verlinda, 24, 35
  William, 24, 25, 27, 28, 29, 35
Stores, 144, 145, 152, 167, 168, 169, 173, 194
Stratton, John, 178
Strawberries, 219
Stringer, John, 62
  William, 70
Sturgis, Sallie Pope, 196
  W. J., M.D., 232, 234
Sunday School, 136, 169
Superintendents of Schools, 175, 195, 197, 214, 215, 230, 274
Surveyors, 10, 47, 65, 71
Sweet potatoes, 173, 177, 209, 110
Sykes Island (Saxis), 143, 158, 194, 208

Table and frame, 30, 46
Tangier Island, 4, 106, 143, 158, 159, 162, 163, 195, 208, 223, 242
Tankard, Edward G., 215
  John, M.D., 139
  John W., 191
Tankards Rest, 139
Tanner, Archibald E., 229
Tasley, 203, 228
Taverns, 98, 136, 169, 203

Taylor, Jane Ames, 234
  John W., 212
  Phillip, 44, 47
Teackle, Thomas, minister, 79, 133
Telegraph service, 186, 190, 208
Telephones, 208, 220, 241
Television, 247
Temperanceville, 100, 179, 194, 207
The Folly, 171, 207
Thomas, John, 195
  Joshua, minister, 158, 162
  Symon, 79
  William E., 211
Tilney, John, 64
Tithables, 64
Toast to Prince of Orange, 83
Tobacco, 8, 26, 27, 57, 121, 128, 150, 160, 174
Tobacco warehouse, 107, 108, 138, 139, 144
Toft, Ann. 70, 132
  Annabella, 71
  Arcadia, 71
  Atalanta, 71
Toleration Act, 211
Tories, 128, 129, 130
Tourists, 237, 261
Trappers, 105
Turkey Pen, 179
Turlington Camp Meeting, 206, 208
Turtles, 174
Tyler, John, 175
United Daughters of the Confederacy (UDC), 216, 234
United States (Federal) Officials from the Eastern Shore 1900-1964, 272
University of Virginia, Eastern Shore Branch, 263
Upshur, Abel Parker, 168, 174-5
  Ann, 174
  Arthur II, 167
  Caroline, 217
  George Parker, 175
  John Andrews, Commander, U.S.N., ret., 271, 275, 279
  Littleton I, 174
  Thomas Teackle, 217-18
Vaucluse, 174, 175
Vestry, 29, 31, 76, 102, 123, 161
Virginia Beach, 263
Virginia Capes, 263
Virginia Division of Forestry, 254

INDEX 305

Virginia Garden Week Tours, 237, 261, 275
Virginia Institute of Marine Science, 255
Virginia Lee, steamer, 230, 231, 232, 250-251
Virginia Ferry Company, 237, 249, 250
V.P.I. Extension Service, 255
Virginia State Police, 255
Virginia Truck Experiment Station, 255
Voting, 35, 97-98, 123, 177, 178, 183, 190, 194, 195, 202, 229

Wachapreague, 110, 136, 173, 195, 212, 255, 256
Wachapreague Creek, 110, 195
Walker, J. C., 234
Walkley, Margaret, 234
Wallop, John, 70, 263
Wallops Island, 104, 106, 143, 156, 194, 199, 246, 251, 262, 263
Wallops Island Post Office, 251
Wallops Neck, 225, 226, 244, 263
Wallops Road, 94, 143, 194
Wallops Station NASA, 251, 262-3
Walter, Jefferson F., 250, 272, 273
War of 1812, 161, 165, 185
Wardtown, 193
Washington, George, 118, 121, 131, 155, 164, 190
  Martha, 122, 137
Waters, William, 62, 66
Watkins, Henry, 9, 10
Watkins Point, 4, 21, 70
Watkinson, Cornelius, 66, 67
Watson, Carrie Whealton, 259
  E. W., 225
  Herman C., 259
Watts Island, 4, 143, 158, 171, 183, 195
Wattsville, 236
Weaver, James C., 195-6, 197, 256
  Sallie Pope, 256
Webster, John, 41
Weights and measures, 39, 58
Wescott, Hezekiah A., 211
  Katherine Roberts, 280
  Nathaniel B., 234
WESR Radio Station, 251
West, John, 17, 34, 64, 86
West Virginia, 190

Whaley, Zedekiah, 132, 234
Wharton Place, 212
Whealton, D. J., 225
  John B., 225, 226, 227
Whipping post, 38
Whispering Pines, 237
Whitall, John, 70
White, Harry, 202
Whitelaw, Ralph Thomas, 280
Whittington, William, 54
Wilcox, John, 6, 9, 10, 12
Wildlife, 103, 174, 203, 206, 247
Wilkins, John, 23, 24, 25, 27, 29, 46, 47, 125
  S. S., 197
William II, King (Prince of Orange), 83, 84
William and Mary, King and Queen, 84, 92, 100
Williams, John T., Jr., 211
  Walter, 53
Williamsburg, 90, 107
Wilson, M. Smith, 234
Winder, John W., 225
  Richard B., 185
Windley, David, 40
  Joan, 40
Wise, Henry A. (Governor), 154, 163, 178
  Henry A. (Grandson of Governor), 228, 261
  Henry A. (school superintendent), 274, 280
  Jennings Cropper, 218
  John, 64
  John, 125, 128
  John E., 152
  John H., 211
Wiseville (Drummonds Mill), 180
Wisharts Point, 227
Women's Clubs, 259
Works Progress Administration (WPA), 238, 240
World War I, 212, 220, 232, 233
World War II, 234, 235, 240-45
Wyatt, Francis, 18, 40

Yeardley, Ann, 51, 55, 58, 60
Yeardley, Argoll, 16, 17, 43, 50, 51, 55, 58-59
Yeardley, Argoll II, 59, 60, 75, 79, 83, 108
Yeardley, Edmund, 59
Yeardley, Elizabeth I, 59
Yeardley, Frances, 41, 51, 59
Yeardley, Frances II, 59

Yeardley, Francis, 58
Yeardley, George, 6, 8, 16, 83
Yeardley, Henry, 59
Yeardley, Ralph, 17
Yeardley, Rose, 59

Yeardley, Temperance, 17
Yeardley land, 8, 16, 24, 41, 127, 138, 139
York (Yorktown), 94, 108, 114, 132, 154, 173
Young, William, 144, 151

www.ingramcontent.com/pod-product-compliance
Lightning Source LLC
Chambersburg PA
CBHW052053230426
43671CB00011B/1887